Second Edition

As Strong as the Mountains

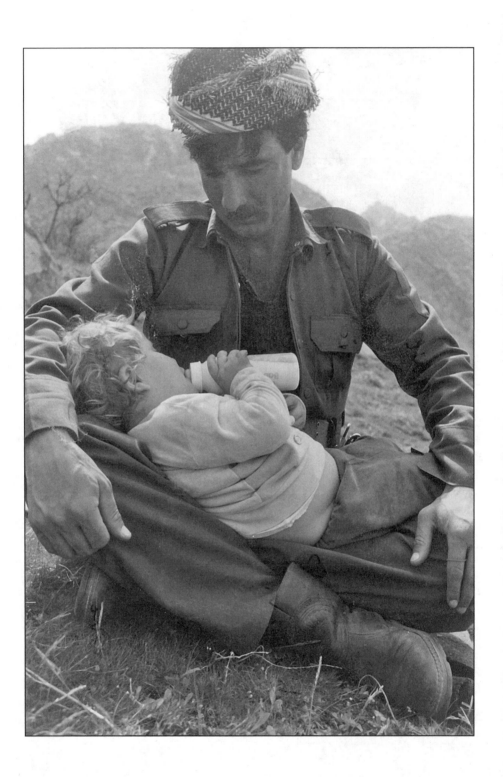

Second Edition

As Strong
as the
Mountains

A Kurdish Cultural Journey

Robert L. Brenneman
North Central University

WAVELAND
PRESS, INC.
Long Grove, Illinois

For information about this book, contact:
Waveland Press, Inc.
4180 IL Route 83, Suite 101
Long Grove, IL 60047-9580
(847) 634-0081
info@waveland.com
www.waveland.com

Cover: Sadik Gulec/Shutterstock.com

10-digit ISBN 1-4786-2930-4
13-digit ISBN 978-1-4786-2930-6

Printed in the United States of America

7   6   5   4   3   2   1

Contents

Acknowledgments   ix

Introduction: Mountain Scenario   1

1   Discovering the Kurds   5
My Journey with the Kurds   7
Understanding Culture   12
Methodology of the Research   12
Difficulties in Doing Research among the Kurds   16

2   History and Ethnic Identity   19
The Suppression of Kurdish History   19
Ancient History until the Ottoman Empire   21
The Islamization of the Kurds   25
Kurdish Identity during the Ottoman Empire   26
The Transition from Empire to Nation-State   28
The Legacy of Atatürk   30
The Role of Turgut Özal   32
The Role of the PKK   32
Developments in Iraq since the Treaty of Sevres   35
The U.S. Betrayal of Mustafa Barzani   37
The First Gulf War and Its Aftermath   39
Internal Factions among the Kurds   41

3   Language and Ethnic Identity   45
     The Development of
       Kurdish in Iraqi Kurdistan   46
     Developments in Turkey   47
     How Kurdish Are Turkish Kurds?   51

4   From Storytelling to Television: 57
     The Decline of Oral Tradition
     Indigenous Knowledge and Oral Tradition   57
     Genres of Oral Tradition   58
     Myths, Legends, and Folktales   59
     Proverbs   62
     Functions of Oral Tradition   67
     Effects of Literacy on the
       Oral Transmission of Culture   70
     Television and Oral Tradition   72

5   Relationships, Roles, and Traditions   75
     Family and Enculturating the Next Generation   76
     Sex and Marriage   80
     Gender Issues   86
     Tribal Structure and Leadership   94

6   Core Values and Religious Rituals   101
     The Importance of Hospitality   103
     The Importance of Honor   105
     Courage   110
     Other Important Values   111
     Shame and Guilt Cultures   116
     Religious Values and Rituals   120

7   Rapid Urbanization and Culture Change   125
Displaced Kurds   126
Imagined Communities in Urban Regions   131
Urbanization and Traditional Values   132
Asabiyya   134
Urbanization and Anomie   134
Lessons from the Kurds   135

8   Update: Mountains, Malls, and War   139
The Cessation of Civil War   139
The Aftermath of the War in Iraq   140
Restoration of the Caliphate   142
The Eschatology of the Islamic State   146
The War and the Kurds   148
IS Are Not the Only Bad Guys   149
Kurdistan and Turkey: Places of Refuge   151
Can IS Be Defeated?   160
Globalization and Urbanization
   among Iraqi Kurds   160
Some Kurds Explore Their Pre-Islamic Roots   163
Kurdistan: Transformed but Not Paradise Yet   164
Changes in Turkey's Attitude
   toward Iraqi Kurdistan   165
The Kurdish Corridor   165
Turkey: Optimism and Concern   167
From Mountains to Malls   170

Bibliography   173
Appendix A: Worldwide Population of the Kurdish People   181
Appendix B: Glossary of Foreign Words   183

Acknowledgments

It is impossible to name everyone who has contributed in the process of seeing this book come to a second edition.

My mother celebrated her 91st birthday last November. Thanks, Mom, for believing in me. It is hard to imagine having a closer brother–sister relationship than I have with my sister, Elaine and her husband, Dr. LeRoy Coleman.

My wife, Sherry, and I just celebrated our 41st anniversary together. How can one say enough about a life partner who has stood by me and trusted in me and kept my feet on the ground for so long?

Our sons, Aaron and Joshua. There are so many memories we share from our time in Turkey, Northern Cyprus, and Iraqi Kurdistan that we can laugh about today even though they may not have seemed so funny then. Aaron's wife, Mariya, from Antakya, Turkey, and their children Rebeka and Lukas are a joy to stay with whenever I am in Istanbul. Joshua and his wife Amber and their children Cole, Ellie, Belle, and another on the way, frequently bring great joy to us and fortunately are not so far away.

Leyla, our daughter who shared in all our family experiences in the Middle East, is still my favorite travel partner.

I have been blessed with many deep friendships and hesitate to mention names for fear of leaving some out. Radwan Naqshibandi, the owner of the first Kurdish restaurant in America, has to be singled out. He has given me many insights into the Kurdish mind-set over the course of our long friendship. It was a joy to stay with his family for several days in Duhok, Iraqi Kurdistan, last February.

Jeni Ogilvie from Waveland Press, who worked with me in editing the first edition, has continued to help make this edition a much better book as well. I can't imagine a better editor to work with.

The administration at North Central University granted me a sabbatical leave for the winter semester of 2015, enabling me to spend over three months in Iraqi Kurdistan and Turkey among refugees. Many friends on the faculty, and past and present students, have greatly enriched my life.

Dr. Sharon Ackerman, professor and human rights lawyer, has labored much on behalf of the Kurds. Thank you for supporting my recent travels in the Middle East, enabling me to help some desperate refugees.

Thanks to all of the Kurdish people I have shared life with in many settings. The Kurds have known much suffering but they are increasingly being seen by the world as so much more than victims. Is the famous Kurdish saying "We have no friends but the mountains" still true, or are the days of Kurds fleeing from brutal oppressors to the mountains finished once and for all? Time will tell; as one proverb says, *Bila Xude yar bi, bila hami dinya neyar bi* (in essence: "If God is your friend, it is OK if the world is your enemy.").

In these difficult days we live in, the Psalmist's words are especially significant: "*From the ends of the earth I call to you. When my heart is overwhelmed, lead me to the rock that is higher than I*" (Psalms 61:2).

About the Author

Robert L. Brenneman (PhD University of Minnesota) lived with his family in the Middle East, particularly among the Kurds 1982–1996. He has continued to travel to the area every year since then, and recently spent three months researching and assisting refugees in Iraqi Kurdistan and Turkey. He has especially focused on the Kurdish battle against Islamic State jihadists and the Kurdish transition from victims to the most effective warriors against ISIS brutality. He teaches at North Central University in Minneapolis, Minnesota.

The shaded area indicates where Kurdish people are the majority (the area is called Kurdistan unofficially by some Kurds).

Introduction
Mountain Scenario

It is a cold winter night high up in the mountains of Kurdistan. The snow is piled high on the straw roof of the two-room stone house. A wood-burning stove sits in the middle of the room surrounded by blankets and thin mattresses. Sitting close to the stove to stay warm is a family of thirteen, ranging from a newborn baby to two very elderly people who occupy the most prominent place in the center of the circle. Four generations are represented around the fire. The oldest male of the family, or the *patriarch*, is the chief storyteller, the source of the village's sacred history. His aging wife sits near him, helping the younger mothers with their small children. A middle-aged man, who is the father of eight children and who recently became a grandfather when his oldest son married and brought his new bride into the home a year ago, reaches his hands toward the stove. His seven other children, four boys and three girls, ranging in age from three to sixteen, mingle around the fire. The older girls are helping to serve tea and *kalaches* (a Kurdish sweet). The boys throw some more wood on the fire as they play with the younger children.

As the wind blows through the cracks in the stone, everyone is very thankful for a warm fire and hot tea. The patriarch looks over his offspring as he drinks his tea and nibbles at his *kalache* with his rotted teeth. His son and his family are a source of great pride for the patriarch. He begins to think of their life together as father and son. The old man has been a good Kurd. He has had ten children, including five boys and two girls who are still alive, and now his oldest son has a grandson. The patriarch has a reputation for honor in the village and in the surrounding areas. Two of his sons live nearby with

1

their families, raising animals and farming as have the generations before them. Two of his sons and their families are living in the closest city, a one-hour walk down the mountain plus a two-hour car ride away. The last of his sons, who was accepted as a refugee in Canada, is the only one of the sons who got a university education, resulting in his getting a job with a humanitarian organization. His daughters married good men, but both of them are now living in cities away from Kurdistan.

The old man has fought for the Kurdish people. He looks at his son, whom he taught to hunt and shepherd, and remembers how he carried him across the mountains as they escaped from the government troops who were destroying villages and killing their kinfolk. Years later, they had to escape again, but this time his son was able to walk and climb the mountains by himself, carrying a weapon in one hand and his firstborn child in the other.

The Patriarch wonders whether his descendants will be able to stay in the village where his ancestors settled ages ago, or if they will have to escape again by fleeing across snowy mountain ranges. The mountains have proven to be the only dependable refuge for the Kurds—to be trustworthy friends and to offer their strength when the savage armies of oppressors have invaded time and time again while the rest of the world seemed not to care. Yet the mountains have

Kurdish family living in the mountains of Kurdistan.

demanded their due, and many a Kurdish child has frozen on those mountains of refuge, unable to survive the march to the valleys on the other side.

Will his descendants live in tents in refugee camps in less than friendly neighboring countries, as he was forced to? Will they give up on life in the mountains and move to the cities outside of Kurdistan, abandoning the traditional life that the Kurds have known for centuries? He still remembers the pain of burying three of his children who did not make it, two dying on the mountains during one of the escapes and the other dying in a refugee tent city, due to the disease-ridden unsanitary conditions. Yet, the patriarch knows he was more fortunate than many others.

At least he had seven children who did survive.

The patriarch wonders about the future of his people. Will the Western nations sell them out again to the dictators who reign over the lands the Kurds call Kurdistan? Will the young people who are migrating to the cities outside of Kurdistan remember their history and heritage, or will they lose it and deny their Kurdishness in order to fit in better with the children of their oppressors? It seems that the Kurds are as far away as ever from any hope of having their own country ruled by their own people. Yet, the patriarch is thankful. The Kurds have outlasted many oppressive regimes over the years and will continue to do so. Kurdistan may not be a place on the maps of the world, but it is a real place in the hearts of the people. And no matter what they face, more Kurds are being born every day.

The patriarch quiets the children. He takes a long sip of tea and begins to tell stories—the stories that he heard from his father, who heard them from his father, who heard them from his father. . . .

Key Terms

I have included a glossary of Kurdish, Turkish, and Arabic words mentioned in this text in appendix A, but it is essential to understand the following words and concepts before reading further.

Kurdistan does not appear on any official political maps. It designates the region located within the four major nation-states of Turkey, Iran, Iraq, and Syria in which the majority of the people are Kurdish. There are millions of Kurds living outside of Kurdistan, however. In fact, Istanbul, Turkey, has more Kurds than any other city in the world, although it is far from the traditional Kurdish homeland.

Turkish Kurdistan, Iranian Kurdistan, Iraqi Kurdistan, and **Syrian Kurdistan** refer to the predominately Kurdish areas within the larger nation-states. However, only in Iraq is Kurdistan a term that is used freely to describe the region where the Kurds are the majority.

Kurdish diaspora is a term used to refer to the almost two million Kurdish people who migrated to other countries from the four major nations where Kurds have traditionally lived. In many instances, that same number of Kurds, willingly or not, has migrated within their respective nation-state outside of the predominately Kurdish areas. Perhaps *in-migration* or *internal diaspora* are better terms to use when referring to these people.

Kurdayati is a term I use to convey a sense of Kurdish ethnic consciousness. After interviewing many people about what this word means, I think it can be summarized as the sense of cultural distinctiveness that makes the Kurds different from their Turkish, Persian, and Arab neighbors. Some writers have used *ethnonationalism* as an English equivalent to *Kurdayati*. In this book, I prefer to use an indigenous Kurdish word to refer to the overall subjective sense of what it means to be a Kurd. I have especially focused on three aspects of *Kurdayati*: a distinct ethnic identity, the maintenance and transmission of Kurdish oral tradition and folklore included in indigenous knowledge, and elements of a rapidly changing Kurdish culture.

Kurdish refers to the language of the Kurds (in addition to being an adjective for things pertaining to the Kurds). Probably language more than any other factor has contributed to the Kurdish sense of distinctiveness. Because of the lack of opportunity to develop a standardized Kurdish language, there are some major dialects and many minor ones (see appendix B). I describe the battle for the Kurds to maintain their language in more detail in chapter three.

Question for Discussion

- The book begins with a mountain scenario as the patriarch, with four generations of his family surrounding him, begins to tell stories that he heard from his father. Do you know of any stories, or some type of oral tradition (like praying before eating a meal), that have been passed down in your family from generation to generation?

Chapter 1

Discovering the Kurds

In 1991, when the armies of Saddam Hussein drove almost two million Kurds to seek refuge in the mountains of Iran and Turkey, continuous television coverage exposed a people about whom millions around the world had previously been ignorant. The Kurds resurfaced in the news in 2003 when Saddam's 1988 chemical weapons attacks against the Kurds (which had received little attention at the time) became part of the justification for the U.S. invasion of Iraq and the subsequent war there. In both cases, the Kurds were suddenly thrust upon the world stage, no longer living, suffering, and dying with little of the world's attention upon them.

The Kurdish people are the largest ethnic group in the world without their own homeland, numbering between 30 and 45 million people divided among Turkey, Iran, Iraq, and Syria. Thus, the Kurds are a transnational people in that, like the Hmong, Berber, Roma, Tuareg, Fulani, and many other ethnic groups, they can be found in large numbers in multiple nation-states. Being without a homeland has had a significant psychological impact upon the Kurds. Kurds say that the Arabs, Turks, and Persians (Iranians) agree on only one thing: under no condition must there ever be an independent Kurdistan administered by Kurds.

Throughout their history, the Kurds have experienced many types of oppression: forced assimilation, suppression and denial of their own ethnic identity, the outlawing of their language and other forms of cultural expression, and outright genocide. "The Kurds have no friends but the mountains" is the most quoted statement by Kurds about their collective experience. It reminds them that time after time, they have been forced to flee to the mountains for refuge, the only "friend" that has proven trustworthy.

The Kurds of Northern Iraq (Iraqi Kurdistan) are, for the most part, the United States' staunch allies; they are eternally grateful to the United States

5

A typical mountain village in Northern Iraq.

for saving them from Saddam Hussein's brutality, which resulted in the massacre of Kurds, the destruction of their of villages, and miserable living conditions for millions who escaped death. The devastation of thousands of villages by Saddam's murderous campaigns no longer blot the landscape to the same degree they once did. Since 1991, the Kurds have rebounded and made incredible strides toward developing a modern region within Iraq. They have established universities, shopping centers, and an increasingly democratic government in the regions that they govern. (See chapter 8 for an account of the situation in Iraqi Kurdistan as of October 2015.) There is a reserved sense of optimism among the people. Although major problems still wait to be addressed, I could not but marvel during a subsequent visit at the changes that have occurred since 1991 when I first visited Iraqi Kurdistan. The Iraqi Kurds' ability to survive and outlast their oppressors helps us to better understand other stateless ethnic groups without a central homeland. This is especially true for those groups facing urbanization and modernization after centuries of being primarily rural societies and relying on oral forms of communication to maintain their ethnic cohesiveness.

Compared with the Kurds of Northern Iraq, the Kurds of Turkey (*Küzey Kürdistan* [Northern Kurdistan] is a phrase the Kurdish nationalists often use) present a far more complicated dilemma. In the eyes of the world, the actors in this drama are not so clearly on the side of either good or evil, and the issue of where their loyalties lie is as complicated as other issues that vex the Middle East.

This book offers specific insights to increase knowledge about the fourth largest ethnic group in the Middle East—a group that is of great strategic importance in Turkey, Iraq, Iran, and Syria. Three of these countries (Iran, Iraq, and Syria) are or have been considered "enemy" countries of the United States, and Turkey's previously strong opposition to the United States' military involvement in Iraq has contributed to turning many Turks into less-certain allies.

My Journey with the Kurds

The Kurds are a remarkable people. They have known great suffering, betrayal, and neglect yet demonstrate a zest for living, incredible hospitality, indomitable courage, and a love for their culture and traditions that has survived through the centuries. Now they are confronted with the challenge of urbanization. I have followed the Kurdish dilemma since the early 1980s, when my family and I began a fourteen-year period of living in Turkey and Northern Iraq. I have also returned to the area numerous times since 1996, the year my family and I left Northern Iraq to move back to the United States.

From 1982 to 1991, I taught English to adults at three different institutions in three different locations. In Istanbul, Turkey, I had several Kurds among my students. Some were totally assimilated into mainstream Turkish culture, while others were more outspoken about their Kurdishness. Still others were especially devoted to Islam. These three dimensions of the Kurdish experience—assimilation, nationalism, and relation to Islam—alerted me to the complexities of what it means to be a Kurd in Turkey.

After our years in Istanbul, I taught in an English-language school located in a very volatile area in the heart of the Kurdish region of Turkey. The director of the school was candid and said I would be carefully monitored by secret police in and out of the classroom. With so many beautiful places in Turkey that are flooded with tourists, he said, there would be suspicion about why I chose to teach in a city that is far removed from the historical tourist sites and beautiful beaches. It was also a tragic time in Iraq as Saddam had launched the *Anfal* operation (*Anfal* is an Arabic word taken from the Qur'an that grants Muslims the right to plunder or spoil their enemies; see chapter 2), and thousands of Kurds were forced to flee to Turkey and were housed in refugee camps in the city where we lived. Fighting between the Turkish government forces and the PKK (*Partiya Karkeren Kurdistan*, "Kurdistan Workers Party") was at its peak, with daily skirmishes resulting in 30–35 thousand deaths. I was strongly discouraged from learning any Kurdish and from discussing Kurdish issues during this time because any interest in the Kurds could lead to my deportation and bring harm to the school.

My final two years were spent at a university in Northern Cyprus, an island-country recognized by no one but Turkey, which has been the scene of ongoing negotiations to reconcile relations between the Turkish and Greek Cypriots. There were students from Kurdish regions, but most of them had been assimilated into the culture of upper-class Turkish life. In addition to these Kurdish students, a fairly large percentage of construction workers and manual laborers who sought work on the island were Kurds. They tended to congregate in their own *kahve* (a place where only men gather to drink tea, play cards, and socialize) and associate with others who originated from the same region.

It was in 1991, as I was finishing my teaching in Northern Cyprus, when I heard about the massive numbers of refugees fleeing from Saddam's armies to neighboring Turkey or Iran. After returning to the States, I was approached by the director of an NGO (nongovernment organization) about going to Northern Iraq to assist in the resettlement of thousands of displaced Kurds. NGO workers interviewed refugees and internally displaced people who were in the process of returning to their homeland under Operation Provide Comfort.[1] The NGOs wanted to learn what would motivate refugees to return to their ancestral villages. Most Kurds were living in refugee camps, in the forced collective villages built by Saddam, or in public buildings like schools, factories, and even prisons at the time. To be able to return to their ancestral villages and become economically self-sufficient, most people stated that they would need shelter, a decent road that would enable them to get to the market and health-care facilities, and a primary school. Some requested either animals (sheep or goats) or seed for planting. Some people never did return, however, either having gotten used to city life or losing the deeds to their original land in the village. In many cases, widows did not want to return to their villages without a husband, most of whom were killed by the Iraqi government.

Although Northern Iraqi cities were not destroyed like the villages, people in the cities still had a strong feeling of devastation and uncertainty. Saddam continued to make threats to return and take back the land, and Turkey could close the border at any time and make life almost impossible for the people, as foodstuffs were in short supply and their availability was dependent on an open Turkish border. As my colleagues and I were assessing the community's needs on behalf of the NGO and determining what our response would be, we were amazed at the friendliness and cheerfulness of the Kurdish people we met.

We first fell in love with the children. With huge smiles and great enthusiasm, they addressed all foreigners, including women, by saying, "Hello mister." A cute girl, probably three years old and barefooted, rushed up to us at full speed from about two blocks away just to say, "Hello mister." People frequently invited us for tea, and although we spoke no Kurdish at that point and most of them did not speak English, they were glad to have us there. Perhaps the presence of foreigners was a sign that the world community would not ignore them as it had in the past. Six months later, my family and I moved into the region, which became our home for the next four years.

Those four years were filled with promise and pain. The returning Kurds, under the guaranteed protection of the United Nations and Operation Provide Comfort, were thrilled to be in their homeland again, and they faced the rebuilding of their destroyed villages with great optimism. Despite the ever-present threat of Saddam's return, the invasion of Turkish troops twice into

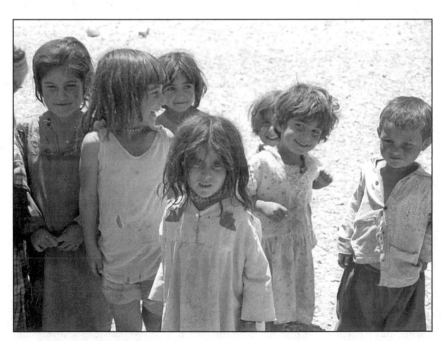

Iraqi Kurdish children.

the region to pursue PKK rebels, and very difficult living conditions, much reconstruction was accomplished. After about one year, the electricity, which came to Northern Iraq through Arab-controlled regions, was cut. So that my family and I could experience what the majority of the people, who could not afford generators, were going through, we lived by candlelight for the most part and slept on the roof at night because of the intense heat inside the house. The electricity had been cut for about a month, when the sounds of hundreds of rifles being fired in typical Kurdish fashion signaled the return of electricity. The celebration ended six hours later when the electricity was cut again; this time for almost two years. The Kurds attributed the temporary restoration of electrical power to Saddam's use of psychological warfare; he wanted to raise their morale so he could demoralize them again.

The most difficult experience was not the threats from Saddam or even enduring the two years without electricity; it was the civil war that broke out between the two major political parties in Northern Iraq, the PUK (Patriotic Union of Kurdistan) and the KDP (Kurdistan Democratic Party). Even the Peshmerga (literally, those who face death), Kurdish freedom fighters who fought courageously against Saddam and who were so revered by all Kurds, aligned with separate parties and fought against each other. When the enemies of the Kurds waged war, it seemed to unite the Kurds and the people remained upbeat and optimistic, but when Kurd began to kill Kurd, we witnessed a major drop in morale. Almost every Kurd who was educated and had the means tried to immigrate legally or illegally. The previous optimism was gone, and the working conditions, although always difficult, became contentious and discouraging. The people became more demanding and less grateful; some even talked about the good old days when Saddam ruled and people had cars, took vacations, and had plenty to eat. Saddam had predicted that within five years the Kurds would want him to return. He knew enough about Kurdish history and Western indifference to make the prediction that the Kurds would fight each other and they would welcome him back to restore order. Fortunately, except for a very brief period, his prediction never materialized.

Conditions in the country remained difficult as the border with Turkey became a major ordeal to cross. If someone working with an NGO were to leave Northern Iraq for a medical emergency, to buy supplies, or for a holiday, the Turks would allow the person to cross their border at that time, but they would not allow him or her to cross again to get back into Kurdistan. As a result, many capable people left and did not return. Nevertheless, our work went forward. We distributed the necessary construction materials for a simple shelter, including cement, sand, poplar trees and mats for the roof, and door and window frames. Our engineers supervised the building of schools and shelters, with the villages providing most of the labor. We built school-houses with 3–6 rooms, depending on the size of the village or village clusters, in most locations. We also oversaw road reconstruction and built some small clinics. During my time there, we built approximately 11,000 shelters, about 25 schools, and several small clinics. We were also able to repair and winterize hundreds of homes, many of which belonged to widows whose husbands were killed during the *Anfal* campaign (see chapter 2).

With my oldest son ready to begin college, we returned to the States in June of 1996. In the time period between 1996 and 2015 I tried to follow the Kurdish situation both through printed sources (newspapers, magazines, journal articles, and books) and by communicating with Kurdish people living in the Western world. I also visited Turkey and Iraq almost every year—visits that ranged in duration from several weeks to four months.

Like other writers and researchers who have spent time in Turkey and have learned its language, I have fallen under its spell and love the land and its people. I count the days until my annual trips and delight in showing students its historic and natural wonders, introducing them to friendly, hospitable people, and letting them experience the culture and the energy of a country that is on the move and undergoing massive changes. While this book focuses on the Kurdish dilemma, there is much more to Turkey than this. I truly hope the people of this wonderful land will be able to find a just solution to being fair and just to all of its citizens, as the United States and virtually every country struggle to do. Note the words of Bernard Lewis, perhaps the leading Western scholar on Islamic history and commentator on the Middle East:

> Of the fifty-seven member states of the Islamic Conference, only one, the Turkish Republic, has operated democratic institutions over a long period of time and, despite difficult and ongoing problems, has made progress in establishing a liberal economy and a free society and political order. (2003, p. 163)

This research, then, is the culmination of several decades of living among, working with, and interest in the Kurds. It is neither an exhaustive history of the Kurds nor a contemporary assessment of their political status. Rather, it is a cultural journey that touches on prehistoric times and continues forward in time to events in the twenty-first century. Kurdish voices, speaking from their ancestral mountains and the *diasporas* (massive migrations) in Western

Europe, the United States, and Canada, resonate in the book. Before describing the methodology used for gathering the data, let's clarify what *culture* is.

Understanding Culture

Hundreds of definitions of culture have been used by anthropologists, with only small nuances of meaning or wording separating one from the other. Anthropologist George Foster's simple definition, "*Culture* is the shorthand term for these rules that guide the way of life of the members of a social group" (1973, p. 11), is concise and easy to grasp. Clifford Geertz (1973) argues that culture is not an experimental science in search of law but rather an interpretive one in search of meaning. No matter how perplexing a culture may appear to an outsider, it "works" for the community, giving its members a sense of cohesion in coping with the complexities of life. There are aspects of Kurdish culture that perplexed me, and I had to keep in mind that my own culture would likely appear as perplexing, illogical, and strange to the Kurdish people as theirs at times did to me. As Peacock says, "Yet out of these exposures to "harsh light" has come an appreciation of what we have termed culture—an enduring way of thinking and of ordering our lives that survives the struggle to survive" (2001, p. 3).

Anthropologists often use an iceberg to clarify the concept of culture. Above the water, one can see the tip of the iceberg, representing the material and visual aspects of the culture. This includes food, clothing, architecture, artifacts, types of transport, people's gestures and mannerisms—readily observable characteristics of a society. Beneath the surface is the rest of the iceberg, representing the core values, worldview, beliefs, and cognitive dimensions that insiders inherently grasp, but outsiders have to intentionally attempt to learn. While the surface or outward aspects of a culture can be readily observed, the underwater dimension requires time, patience, and conscious effort to understand.

Methodology of the Research

The Kurds have most often been portrayed as victims caught up in the drama of Middle Eastern politics. They are a piece of the complex puzzle, an important piece that needs to be put in place when searching for solutions to the problems facing the Middle East. One method to sort out the puzzle is to do *ethnographic* research. *Ethnography* is a description or a picture of a contemporary culture. In order to write a description or create a picture, the researcher must learn as much as possible about the particular culture and grasp its members' way of looking at the world. The *ethnographer* absorbs different aspects of a culture by conducting *fieldwork*—spending a significant amount of time living among the people, participating in their way of life, and conducting interviews. As Peacock says, "Where some want instant answers, anthropologists doubt the validity of any knowledge achieved easily" (2001, p. 76). What makes anthropology such a fascinating discipline is its holistic understanding of culture that includes all aspects of life. Of course to begin to understand a different culture than one's own requires a significant investment of time and effort. Van der Elst argues that culture includes "ideas of every sort: meaning, values, ethics, religion, laws, politics, science, philosophy, art, novels, music, dance, games and all the rules for making and using and performing all of the above" (2003, p. 32). After over 30 years of seeking to understand Kurdish culture I feel like I am barely scratching the surface of what there is to learn. Yet, the journey has been well worth it!

Conducting Fieldwork

Accepting that fieldwork is the heart of ethnography, it is important to establish what it means to conduct fieldwork. Ethnographic fieldwork is primarily based on the two tools of *participant-observation* and *ethnographic interviewing*.

Participant-observation is a type of experiential learning in that it comes through living with the community members, practicing their way of life, and learning their language. For me, participant-observation meant spending nights with refugees in their tent camps, doing *dawet* (Kurdish circle dancing) at weddings and other types of celebrations, and climbing mountains to talk with *re spi*s (village elders) and hearing their stories about their escapes from Saddam's armies. I observed intense poverty as I talked with widows and their children, whose husbands and fathers had been killed by Saddam's regime. These victims were living in bombed-out buildings without heat or electricity. I also saw evidence of the "new rich" in Turkey and Iraq—those Kurds who have prospered from the changes occurring in their respective countries. Participant-observation involves observing the culture and describing in detail what one is seeing, a process that Clifford Geertz (1973) calls *thick description*. It furthermore involves participating in the life of the culture, a kind of *deep hanging out*, to coin Renato Rosaldo's (1989) well-known phrase.

Kurdish women and children in public buildings after their villages were destroyed in the 1988 Anfal operation.

Those two phrases, thick description and deep hanging out, were like a mantra to me, as I spent many hours hanging out with and observing Kurds in as many different situations and locations over a time span of many years.

Participant-observation alone is not enough to ensure an accurate understanding of a community. Interviewing members of the community is essential to ethnographic understanding. There are many types of interviews to use with cultural informants. Although I conducted some *formal interviews*, which I tape-recorded, I primarily conducted *informal interviews* with many people about their specific experiences and the events they had lived through. These interviews were not recorded and I did not write down what my respondents and I discussed until after our conversations were over.

The Kurds in Iraqi Kurdistan were only too happy to share information about their lives with me. During formal interviews, they did not mind being recorded and were not afraid to speak out. I focused my recorded interviews on *re spis* due to the expanse of their life experiences, such as the *Anfal* operation, the multiple destruction of their villages, their escapes to the mountains of Turkey and Iran, and aspects of how they see their culture changing. In Turkey, I informally interviewed a broad spectrum of informants from teenagers to the elderly, from villagers to city dwellers. From May until September of 2005, I conducted over 100 informal, nonrecorded interviews in Turkey. In Iraqi Kurdistan, I recorded 7 interviews, and conducted about 20 informal interviews. In this book I also occasionally draw upon 8 previously conducted formal interviews with Kurds living in the United States and Canada and have conducted many other formal interviews with Kurds in the West for previous research. I illustrate certain points by drawing upon previous encounters with Kurds, beginning in 1982 when I first met them in Turkey.

Handling the Data

Ethnographers often collect hundreds of pages of field notes based on their participant-observation and interviewing. Furthermore, there is another dimension to their research—investigating what others have already learned about the culture. Anthropologist Harry Wolcott (1999) uses three E words that summarize the elements involved in data collection: *examining, experiencing,* and *enquiring. Examining* focuses on what others have written, including not only ethnographic studies, which in the case of the Kurds are surprisingly few (due to so much media focus on the Kurds as the early "heroes" in the battle against the Islamic State, it would not be surprising to see more graduate students focus on the Kurds for various types of research), but also full-length histories, chapters in books dealing with Middle Eastern issues, and especially articles in scholarly journals. *Experiencing* is participant-observation—information written up in field notes utilizing thick description. *Enquiring* is primarily the data collected during both formal and informal interviews. Handling the three elements of ethnographic data also involves *analysis*—the breaking down of the data into underlying themes. Without analysis, field notes are merely random pieces of information that do not tell a consistent story. And, finally, there is *interpretation*, in which ethnographers seek to draw conclusions from what they have learned during the fieldwork. This is best done in conjunction with informants of the host culture to guarantee an accurate interpretation.

An example of wrong interpretation is when I noticed all throughout Turkey that many restaurants, tea houses, and fast-food places used *kursi* (short, four legged stools with no backs) and small tables instead of full sized chairs and bigger tables. Because *kursi* used to be found primarily in the eastern part of Turkey, which is predominately Kurdish, I assumed that Istanbul and other western cities where Kurds have migrated, which are outside of the Kurdish region, were starting to accommodate to Kurdish culture. When I expressed my observations to several informants, they said it was an economic not a cultural reason for using *kursi* and small tables. By using them, the restaurant or tea house can fit more customers into their establishment and increase profits. Furthermore, *kursi* become uncomfortable much faster than full-sized chairs, so customers do not stay as long after they have eaten. By checking with several informants, I was able to correct my inaccurate assumption.

One other element that must also be considered is *representation,* which focuses on how ethnographers present their research to those who do not have firsthand experience. For example, I could present the Kurds according to their cultural ideals, romanticizing their traditional way of life in the mountains, their bravery as they resisted well-armed government troops, their hospitality toward strangers, and the strength of their families and kinship system, which have withstood all efforts to assimilate them into the cultures of their respective nation-states. However, I could also focus on not so positive aspects—honor killing, blood feuds, and more recently, drug running, pimping, and organized crime. Good ethnographers balance *ideal culture* with *real culture,* overly romanticizing neither the entire culture nor certain aspects of it. Conversely, they avoid focusing primarily on negative aspects. It is important to recognize that every culture has both commendable and not so commendable dimensions.

Difficulties in Doing Research among the Kurds

One reason for a lack of research among the Kurds, especially during the time period prior to 2007, is the lack of accessibility to their traditional homelands. It is difficult to get official permission to do ethnographic research in Turkey because the Turkish government feels that singling out a particular group for study stirs up social fragmentation. The government of Turkey does not want individual ethnic groups to assert their own identity in place of the greater identity as a part of Turkey. Large studies of a sociological nature have been conducted in Turkey, but the data are divided usually by region, not by ethnicity. Although most people in Southeast and Eastern Anatolia (the Asian portion of Turkey)[2] are Kurds, there are also Arabs, Turks, Assyrians, and other smaller ethnic groups living there. In western Turkey, which is predominately Turkish, there are millions of Kurdish migrants, but they are not generally identified by ethnicity. Therefore, I cite only a few statistical studies conducted in Turkey that are significant.

Iraqi Kurdistan has also been inaccessible to social scientists until the late twentieth century. Many Kurds told me that until Operation Provide Comfort,

Turkish Kurdish women and their children in a make-shift refugee camp in Northern Iraq.

they had never seen a Westerner. Most studies conducted there, rather than being ethnographic, have been of a historical-political nature, concerned with how the Kurdish dilemma relates to Middle Eastern politics and economics.

One of the difficulties in ethnographic research is not allowing ethnography to become journalism. Journalism tends to focus on the unusual or on a special event or happening. It also tends to focus on newsmakers—important or well-known people and their activities. In contrast, ethnography is more concerned with the ordinary daily life of normal people, unknown beyond their own circle of influence. Furthermore, stories written by journalists often include political commentary or contexts. Although it was often impossible to avoid political issues that affect the lives of Kurds, I limited the amount of political commentary included in this text.

As I conducted my fieldwork, I often found it a challenge to focus my discussions with informants on general aspects of the culture, as most of my informants wanted to discuss the economy and the struggle for making ends meet. Financial stability is certainly an important cultural aspect, but it was a need so foremost in the minds of many Kurds that it inhibited my ability to access other cultural information. Andrew Mango (2004) points out that in heavily Kurdish Siirt, a city in troubled southeastern Turkey, state-sponsored employment rather than Kurdish cultural rights were the people's first concern; the chant "build us a factory" was heard more often than slogans about Kurdish rights.

Questions for Discussion

- Think of a culture or subculture about which you are curious, whether or not you have had the opportunity to spend time among its members. How might you go about doing fieldwork among them? What difficulties might you encounter? What might "deep hanging out" entail?

- Reflect upon the iceberg analogy—visual or material culture can be readily observed, but values, beliefs, worldview, and the cognitive dimension of culture are submerged as most of an iceberg is submerged under the water. In a culture with which you are familiar, which aspects of the culture might be observable immediately? What aspects would take some in-depth fieldwork to uncover?

Notes

[1] Operation Provide Comfort was a joint effort of the United States, Great Britain, France, and Turkey to protect the Kurds and to begin relief efforts among the almost two million people who had fled over the mountains to the borders of Iran and Turkey. At the height of the effort, almost 30,000 troops were involved in the relief effort (Bulloch & Morris, 1992). Eventually NGOs under the United Nations took over the effort, addressing both the immediate relief needs and the reconstruction of the destroyed villages.

[2] Anatolia, Turkish *Anadolu*, refers to the 97 percent of Turkey that is in Asia. About 3 percent of Turkey lies in Europe, including much of Istanbul, although Istanbul also contains millions of people on its Asian side, divided from Europe by the Bosphorus Straits.

Chapter 2
History and Ethnic Identity

Among the important elements of Kurdish history, which spans millennia of time, is the development of a distinct Kurdish ethnic identity. Author Samuel Huntington (1996), best known for his controversial book, *The Clash of Civilizations and the Remaking of World Order,* says, "In coping with identity crisis, what counts for people are blood and belief, faith and family. People rally to those with similar ancestry, religion, language, values, and institutions and distance themselves from those with different ones" (p. 126). Historically, Kurdish identity has been based on religion, for example being a Muslim, or tribal affiliation, such as being a member of the Dosky or the Balandy tribe. The sense of a distinct Kurdish ethnic identity that includes but also extends beyond religion or tribe is relatively new but increasingly strong. This identity shift occurred for the Kurds after World War I, as Turkey changed from being an empire, with a strong foundation in religious identification, to a modern European-style nation-state, and the Kurds were forced to redefine their own sense of ethnic consciousness.

The Suppression of Kurdish History

Kurds realize that they are a very ancient people with long ties to their homelands, but they possess little historical information about their beginnings. When asked whether they know anything about their being possible descendants of the ancient Medes, the inhabitants of Media, Kurds respond: "We have heard something about the Medes, and that they are our ancestors. But we never had a chance to learn about them. The [Arabs or Turks] don't want us to know about our heritage and culture." They are also vaguely aware of being an Aryan people connected with Europe and ethnically and linguistically related to the Persians. The Kurds sense that tracing their origins back to antiquity (*ethnogenesis*) is important, but few have been able to do this kind of research in an academic setting. The situation is beginning to change, especially in Iraqi Kurdistan, where new universities have opened and new departments of Kurdish studies have been added to previously established institutions. Turkey also has begun to change its policies and has allowed departments focusing on Kurdish studies to be opened in universities and allow private language schools that teach Kurdish to operate openly.

Historically, the Kurds have appeared on the world stage as mountain people who were feared because of their fierce raids and fighting ability. A record of their first interaction with Europeans appears in the writings of the Greek author Anabasis who stated that the Greek army, when retreating from Mesopotamia to the Black Sea, had to face a people known as the *Karduchoi* around the year 400 BC. When stripped of its Armenian plural ending, this leaves *Kardu,* most likely the name given to the mountain tribes of the region. The image of mountain warriors is a far cry from earlier portrayals of the Kurds as victims and powerless people. Many early historical accounts pertaining to the Middle East, were written by *hegemons* (those in control), and the Kurds, at least until quite recently when they captured the world's attention in their courageous battle against the Islamic State, were not in a position of hegemony for over 800 years.

Despite the lack of attention to the Kurds' beginnings and their way of life by some, Mehrdad Izady points out:

> A significant body of archaeological evidence points to the Kurdish mountains as the site of the invention of agriculture approximately 12,000 years ago (Braidwood, 1960). From the Kurdish mountains, the revolutionary technology later spread into the neighboring lowlands of Mesopotamia, the hills of western Anatolia, and the plateau of Iran. By about 8,000 years ago, it had further spread into North Africa, Europe, and the Indian subcontinent. As such Kurdistan is the point of origin for many common crops and domesticated animals. (1992, pp. 23–24)

Evidence of the Kurds' high level of skill in growing wheat, barley, lentils, grapes, and other crops is accompanied by findings that some of the earliest domestication of sheep, dogs, and pigs was done by ancestors of the Kurds before the ninth millennium BC near modern Diyarbakir in Turkish Kurdistan.

Ancient History until the Ottoman Empire

The centuries of invasions, warfare, migrations, intermarriage, and ethnic mixing make tracing Kurdish ethnicity from antiquity difficult, but there is a likelihood that Kurdish history dates back to Madai, one of the grandsons of Noah and a son of Japheth (Genesis 10:2). Biblical maps show the ancient Medes inhabiting the regions where the Kurds are still found today. Dutch theologian Ellen Van Wolde (1997) traces the various sons of Japheth to their ancestral places of residence, stating that Madai was the Medes who migrated south of the Caspian Sea and north of the Tigris River. This area has been predominately Kurdish since antiquity and includes the mountains of Ararat in eastern Turkey, where Noah's Ark allegedly rested as the flood waters receded (Genesis 8:4).

From the time of the Neo-Assyrian Empires (1180–609 BC), a large community of exiled Jews existed in Kurdistan. Andrew Bell-Fialkoff (1996), in a book tracing the history of ethnic cleansing, affirms the biblical account of the Jewish exile, stating that 27,290 Israelites mostly of the upper classes were exiled to Gozan and Media in modern Kurdistan in 721 BC (p. 7). Approximately 124 years later, the southern kingdom of Judah was conquered by the Babylonians. Bell-Fialkoff estimates that 10,000 of Judah's leading citizens were exiled to Babylon. These exiled Jews appear to have been very successful in converting nearly all of central Kurdistan to Judaism. It is possible that the familiar biblical story of Daniel in the lion's den dates to this period. The book of Daniel declares that it was King Darius the Mede who, after Daniel was spared from being eaten by lions, made a decree that all of the people should follow the God of Daniel. This might have been a key event in the conversion of that part of Kurdistan to Judaism.

The city of Zakho in Northern Iraq, where my family and I lived for four years, had a Jewish quarter until after the founding of the modern nation of Israel in 1948 when practically the entire Iraqi Jewish community of 125,000 was airlifted to Israel in 1950–1951. Zakho is situated on the banks of the Khabur River, the place mentioned as the location of the exiled Jews in the eighth century BC.

In addition to the Medes embracing Judaism, there was a time when many Medes were Christians. The Kurdish converts to either Judaism or Christianity could have formerly been part of the belief system called Yezidism or Yazidism, one of the cults of the angels.[1] (The Yazidis have appeared in the world news quite frequently as major victims of the Islamic States' onslaught

Ancient fortress city of Amedia.

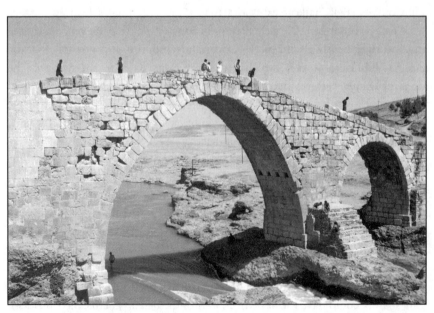

Well-known bridge in Zakho, Iraqi Kurdistan.

in Northern Iraq. See the first footnote at the end of this chapter for a fuller explanation concerning Yazidi identity, core beliefs, and practices.)

Izady (1992) says the native Kurdish religion of the Cult of Angels strongly influenced Zoroastrianism, which introduced the priestly office of the Magi into the region. According to Matthew's Gospel, it is Magi from the east who followed a star to Bethlehem and were the first non-Jews to acknowledge the Christ child (Matthew 2:1–12). Furthermore, according to the New Testament, on the Day of Pentecost when the disciples of Jesus (who were Jews) were "filled with the Holy Spirit and began to speak in other tongues as the Spirit enabled them" (Acts 2:4), one of the languages they spoke was the Median language, making it feasible that these Jews converted the Medes to the Christian faith, beginning approximately 50 days after Jesus was crucified, as they returned to their homeland on the Khabur River. Small communities of Kurdish Christians who resisted conversion to the faith of the Prophet Muhammad in the early days of Islam's rapid spread throughout the Middle East still exist in the area today.

Jwaideh (2006) discusses the origin of the Kurds at a deeper level than others, providing us with an alternate perspective of Kurdish origins. He

Exiled Jews among the Medes, 8th century BC.

points out that the Kurds are far from being a pure Iranian or Indo-European people, as waves of conquerors and their armies have swept across what is now Kurdistan, leaving their racial, cultural, and linguistic mark on the people. The earliest inhabitants of the Zagros mountains, the Guti, the Lullubi, and the Kashshu, were related to the Elamites. It was in the second millennium BC that the Hittites, an Indo-European people, overran Mesopotamia, Anatolia, Armenia, and Kurdistan, which gave the Kurds their Iranian character over a slow and long process. Jwaideh calls this the *Iranization* of the Zagros and Taurus mountain peoples. This was brought about by the appearance of Medes and the Persians and other Iranian peoples into Kurdistan. This perspective does not necessarily contradict biblical narratives of Media being the grandson of Noah and hence the grandfather of the Kurds. It does point out that the Kurds are an ethnic mixture of ancient peoples, including the Medes and Iranian peoples, as well as previous indigenous peoples to the region.

There is as much obscurity about Kurdish origins as there is about most ancient ethnic groups, but the blurry Kurdish origins carry important political ramifications for the Kurds that are evident today—being oppressed and manipulated by other people groups. İsmail Beşikçi is a Turkish professor of sociology who has been imprisoned defending the rights of Kurds in Turkey. He writes:

> The Kurds have lived in Kurdistan for 4,000 years, whereas the Turks started to move from Central Asia through Khorassan into Iran, Kurdistan, Iraq, Syria, and Anatolia in the second half of the eleventh century. . . . They [the Turks] have humiliated and degraded the original owners of these lands. . . . To wipe out the Kurdish nations, its language and its culture is barbaric. . . . Wanting the Kurdish people to be free, wanting them to live in equal conditions with the Turkish people is taken to be propaganda undermining the national pride of the Turks. In fact, demanding equality for the Kurdish people, or the removal of bans on Kurdish language and culture, definitely cannot undermine the national pride of the Turks. (cited in Entessar, 1992, p. 195)

As an example of the repression of Kurdish identity, Turkish nationalists like to claim that there has never been a distinct Kurdish language; rather Kurdish is a mixture of Turkish, Arabic, and Farsi. Furthermore, for a long time in official Turkish publications, Kurds were called "mountain Turks" because they lived in the desolate mountain ranges isolated from other people groups and eventually deviated linguistically and culturally from their Turkish roots. This thinking remained unchallenged until the Gulf War, at which time the repressive attitude of the Turkish government toward the Kurds softened. The Turks blame rising Kurdish ethnic consciousness on outside forces whose aim is to divide Turkey along ethnic lines with the goal of weakening Turkey's power in the region.

The Islamization of the Kurds

Yazidism has been considered the indigenous religion of the Kurds. Assuming that many Kurds who originally practiced Yazidism first converted to Judaism and then later to Christianity, how did so many Kurds become Muslim? Kurds first came into contact with the Arab armies that had recently converted to Islam and conquered Mesopotamia in AD 637 (McDowell, 2000). Before that time, the Kurds had resisted the Arab/Islamic armies, but as they saw the inevitable triumph of these armies, one by one Kurdish tribal chiefs submitted to their adversaries' rule. During both the Umayyad (AD 661–750) and the Abbasid periods (AD 750–1299), as well as later, Kurds rebelled against being ruled by the Arabs but were unable to overcome them. Arab rule generally was not overly oppressive, as demonstrated by the significant percentage of Kurds who never accepted the Islamic religion. Eventually, however, it became economically and socially advantageous for the Kurds to submit to the faith of the Prophet. Conversion to Islam was a slow process, except where Kurds came into direct contact with recently converted Arab Muslims beginning in the seventh century. Even in the thirteenth century, Kurds were warring against Muslim tribes as they maintained their Yazidi identity.

The most famous historical Kurdish figure was Salahadin (d. 1193), who defended Islam against the Crusaders and who fought and then made a truce with Richard the Lion Hearted in 1192. Salahadin is still revered as a relatively benevolent (for that time period at least) Muslim leader who triumphed in battle and won the respect of his enemies while saving Islam from the Crusaders. Although Salahadin's ethnic identity as a Kurd is widely acknowledged by the majority of medieval historians, it is denied or ignored by some Muslim historians.

In the tenth century, Turkish tribes began to migrate from Central Asia and invade the regions where the Kurds dwelt. With the cooperation of non-Turkish populations living in eastern Anatolia, it appears that it was a mixture of Turkish and non-Turkish peoples who emerged to establish and rule what became the Ottoman Empire (1299–1923), which was one of the most powerful political entities ever in existence.[2] Through the 1500s Kurdistan was most noticeable as the battleground between the Persians and Turks. During most of the empire's existence, the Kurds experienced relative freedom, living under tribal confederacies called *emirates* well into the nineteenth century.

Kurdish Identity during the Ottoman Empire

During the Ottoman period, Kurdish literature, music, and other expressions of art and culture flourished until the beginning of the nineteenth century. There was still not a strong sense of Kurdish identity, however, and the consciousness of the *ummah* (Islamic community) was far greater than any specific Kurdish national consciousness. Under the *millet*[3] system, non-Muslim ethnic groups, such as the Armenians and Assyrians (Christian in religion) and Jews, were considered minorities, but they had their own identity and were allowed to have freedom of cultural expression, their own schools, and their own places of worship.

In addition to Islam, tribal affiliation contributed to the people's sense of identity. Kendal, director of the Institut Kurde de Paris, states:

> The concept of "I" hardly exists in the corner of a tribal culture's value system: "we" (the tribe) predominates. Individuals define themselves entirely in terms of their tribe. They are first a member of this or that tribe, then a Muslim, a Yezidi, or a Christian. The sense of being a member of a national group, as Kurds for instance, comes a very poor third. (1993, p. 16)

University of Chicago scholar Hakan Özoğlu argues that to govern the fragmented Kurdish tribes, the Ottoman state tried to mold the tribes into larger units under Kurdish *mir*s (nobles) who were allegedly descended from Arabs, hence giving them religious status as possible descendents of the Prophet Muhammad. The *mir*s, to maintain their power over the tribes, relied on the Ottoman state to back them. Starting with the sixteenth century, the Ottoman Sultans, after conquering the Kurdish regions, allowed the Kurdish emirates to maintain a strong degree of autonomy, not wanting to drive the Kurds into the hands of the neighboring Persian Safavid dynasty. This semi-autonomous existence remained until the early decades of the nineteenth century (Taspinar, 2005). By the nineteenth century, the last Kurdish emirate was fully integrated into the Ottoman system. From these former nobles, rather than the middle classes, most of the eventual Kurdish nationalist leaders, who helped define Kurdish identity in the latter days of the Ottoman Empire and in the early days of the Turkish Republic, were produced.

The Ottoman Empire experienced impressive growth and expansion during 1453–1566. This prosperous period was eventually interrupted by naval defeats, economic stagnation, rebellion in Anatolia, and administrative breakdown. The eighteenth century saw efforts at reform, diminishing centralized authority as provincial autonomy strengthened, and a series of wars with Russia. In the nineteenth century, the empire was forced to deal with ethnic uprisings as many principalities declared their independence. Throughout this period, Western imperial powers were building merchant enterprises near Kurdistan, but it was the Russians whom the Ottomans feared the most. Furthermore, the Christian Armenians, who often felt no loyalty to the Ottoman Empire's Muslim-dominated government, assisted the Russians in their designs for Anatolia. The Ottoman authorities then appealed to the predominately Kurdish population to be ready to lay down their lives to protect their lands and property and defend Islam from the Armenian *kafir*s (infidels).

Moving into the early days of the twentieth century, the Kurds were still part of the Islamic *ummah*, enjoying a somewhat privileged position due to their devotion to Islam, and they continued to be used by the Ottoman rulers to fight against the non-Muslim *millet*s. The Kurds had previously sided with the Ottoman sultans in preserving the empire from outside threats, primarily the Russians. Many Armenians were unashamedly pro-Russian at this time, and no doubt many Kurds, fearing the loss of their lands should the Russians, with Armenian backing, invade their homelands, joined forces with the sultans. Sultan Abdul Hamid II appealed to Muslim solidarity and granted unprecedented power to Sheikh Ubayd Allah, a Kurd, to wage war against the Christian Armenians in the name of Islam. As the Ottoman Empire, by then labeled as the "sick man of Europe," continued to deteriorate, voices for change were frequently heard.

For many years, as Jwaideh (2006) points out, the Committee of Union and Progress (CUP) was working clandestinely toward a more secular, European approach to government, culminating in the Young Turk revolution of 1908. Initially, Turks, Kurds, Arabs, and even the non-Muslim Armenians celebrated the revolution. However, reactionary forces, both externally and internally, worked against the movement. Sensing the weakening of the empire, Bulgaria, with Russian encouragement, declared independence, and two days later, Austria-Hungary announced the annexation of Bosnia and Herzegovina. Internally, forces loyal to the sultan raged against the movement. The Young Turks began to crush opposition movements, shutting down the political clubs and societies and the newspapers of the non-Turkish ethnic groups in a forced program of Turkification. The Kurds began to feel increasingly alienated both for religious and ethnic reasons from the Turkish nationalistic and secular-leaning state.

A leading historian of the Kurds, David McDowell (2000), captures this time very poignantly:

> It is a grim irony that the Kurds participated in the destruction of the Armenian people unaware of the Young Turk plans for themselves. An imperial decree authorized the deportation of Kurds for resettlement in West Anatolia, in locations where they were not to exceed 5 percent of the population. Notables and chiefs were to be settled in towns and cities with all connections with their tribes or followers forbidden. (p. 105)

McDowell (2000) estimates that as many as 700,000 civilians were forcibly removed, with thousands perishing and thousands more settling in non-Kurdish regions in western Anatolia. Other Kurds, fearing a Russian-Armenian backlash, also fled their ancestral homelands. I met many Kurds who were raised in areas far from traditional Kurdish regions and trace their location back to the events surrounding this time period.

In 1917, the Russians made another offensive into Ottoman territory, this time taking more lands in eastern Anatolia. The government forcibly evacuated Kurds from the regions around Diyarbakir and forcibly settled the residents in what is today Iraqi and Syrian Kurdistan as well as in various parts of Turkey that are not predominately Kurdish. Eventually Mustafa Kemal (Atatürk) pushed back the Russian forces and, due to the confusion following the Bolshevik revolution of 1917, the Russian military was paralyzed and began to retreat from the region, allowing the Armenians to get a measure of revenge in slaughtering Muslims as the Armenians fled to their new homeland. This homeland was later to become the Armenian Republic.

The Transition from Empire to Nation-State

Redrawing the Map of Kurdistan

With the collapse of the Ottoman Empire at the end of the First World War, the question became what to do with the former empire's lands, which consisted of many ethnic groups, religions, and loyalties. The Sykes-Picot Agreement attempted to divide the former empire into *zones of influence*. In addition to the Turks, the Russians, Greeks, Italians, French, and British each took administrative control over a piece of the former empire's territory. The

Kurds' lands were divided into regions of Russian and French influence, and they feared an Allied backlash against them for their part in the slaughter of the Armenians. Britain desired Mesopotamia (now southern Iraq) for its rich oil potential. A number of options were considered, which would have given the Kurds some *vilayet*s (provinces) in eastern Turkey under British sway, but the Kurds never took separate control of these provinces. Instead, the invasion of Smyrna by the Greeks and Antalya by the Italians rallied the Kurdish chiefs to unite with the Turks under Atatürk to preserve the Muslim empire against the Christian threat.

The Treaties of Sevres and Lausanne

The background leading to the Treaty of Sevres (1920) must be understood in the context of complexities arising from the Armenian rebellion inside the Ottoman Empire during World War I, the British-led defeat of the empire in World War I, and the Turkish war of independence, which transformed the Islamic empire into a modern nation-state. The treaty, which was negotiated by the Ottoman Empire and the Allies (excluding Russia and the United States), divided some territory among Allied powers (e.g., Britain and France) but also called for Armenia and Kurdistan to be independent states. However, the Kurds still primarily identified themselves according to tribal or religious affiliation and could not produce credible leadership. Furthermore,

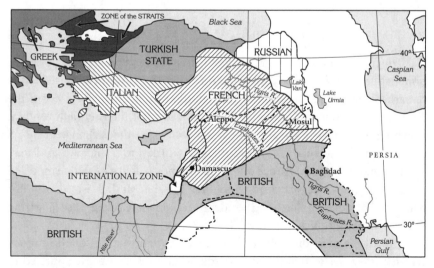

Zones of influence, 1916.

although the treaty was accepted by the Turkish government in Istanbul, it was perceived by the rival nationalist government of Atatürk in Ankara as being forced upon Turkey. This paved the way for Atatürk to quell civil war rumblings inside the country and fight for Islam against outside aggression. With everything in flux, it is not difficult to understand why the Kurds responded to Atatürk's call to join him in the fight. Upon taking control of Turkey, Atatürk rejected the Treaty of Sevres. For the Kurds, the treaty was possibly the best opportunity they ever had to have a homeland, and they mourn their inability to take advantage of that opportunity.

To replace the Treaty of Sevres, a new treaty was negotiated in Lausanne, Switzerland, between Turkey and the Allied powers in 1923. The treaty allowed Turkey to recover territory it lost under the mandates of the Treaty of Sevres, as well as regain full sovereign rights over all its territory. The new treaty did not include a provision for any type of Armenian or Kurdish state. Turkey got much of what it wanted with the exception of oil-rich Mosul (now in Iraq), which came under British control. Although the Lausanne Treaty granted cultural rights, including the right of each nation to use its own language, a separate Kurdish ethnic identity began to be increasingly denied; the Turks called the Kurds "Mountain Turks" in all official sources (Bullock & Morris, 1992). The Kurds were now divided between the nation-states of Turkey, Iraq, Iran, and Syria—a division that remains today. Their Kurdish identity was denied or ignored by others until the end of the 1980s (Yegen, 1996).

The Legacy of Atatürk

The modern nation-state of Turkey, with its general pro-Western orientation, nationalistic ideology, and adaptation to modernity, can be traced to the remarkable legacy of Mustafa Kemal, better known as Atatürk (father of the Turks). He was one of the most influential leaders of the twentieth century. Few times in history has a nation seen so much tumultuous change in such a short period of time as Turkey did under Atatürk. From the jaws of defeat, Atatürk snatched victory, drove out invaders, and created a new state modeled after the nation-states of Europe—a first for the Muslim world. Atatürk believed that success in creating a modern nation-state rested in secularizing Turkish society as quickly as possible.

One of the most difficult challenges facing Atatürk in his quest to modernize Turkey was to figure out what role Islam would have. He appealed to the people's traditional Islamic identity when it was expedient in rallying them against outside forces, but to change a society that had been governed by *sharia* (Islamic law) for centuries to one governed by the Swiss code of law required restructuring. He outlawed veils for women and Islamic headgear for men, changed the written script from Arabic characters to Latin letters, and outlawed Qur'anic schools, as well as the Dervish Sufi religious orders.[4] He even abolished the caliphate, removing the visible symbol of Islamic ascendancy, and established a secular capital in Ankara. Atatürk made Turkish the national language of the country and decreed that all of the *millets*, which were formerly based on religion, would be assimilated into the greater Turkish nation. His legacy of secular nationalism became known as *Kemalism.*

While Atatürk did not shun resorting to brutal force, he caused less bloodshed compared to many other leaders of his day. To this day in Turkey, it is a sacred responsibility to support Atatürk's legacy; his picture is hung in every public building, in every classroom, and appears on every unit of currency. One criticizes Atatürk at great risk, although voices of anti-Kemalism (those against Atatürk's policies)—primarily from Islamists and Kurdish nationalists—are now heard more frequently.

A casual visitor to Turkey can sense the struggle the country has in defining itself as a nation; it seems divided between East and West, Islam and secularism, Asia and Europe. It is beyond the scope of this book to discuss the religious situation in Turkey in any sort of depth, but along with the Kurdish issue, the role of Islam in modern Turkish society is one of the most debated and controversial topics.

The Break between Kemalism and the Kurds

On March 3, 1924, the same day that the caliphate was abolished, a decree banned all Kurdish schools, associations, publications, and religious training schools (called *medrese*). This dual repression against Kurdish ethnic identity and political expressions of Islam helped pave the way for several uprisings by the Kurds against the Kemalist regime. Turkish professor Omer Taspinar (2005) labels the period between 1924 and 1938 the era of the rebellions, and states that out of 18 anti-Ankara uprisings (the recently established capital of Turkey), 17 of them were of Kurdish origin (p. 79).

It has been debated whether the main motivation for Kurdish uprisings was religious, because the Kurds desired a more Islamic way of life, or ethnic, because the Kurds desired free cultural expression of their Kurdishness. The largest rebellion (in 1925) was led by Sheikh Sa'id and concerned the restoration of the caliphate as well as Kurdish rights. It is estimated that 100,000

Kurds were killed, hundreds of villages destroyed, and one million people deported to non-Kurdish areas of Turkey.

Besides the Sheikh Sa'id uprising, there was rebellion in Dersim, now known as Tunceli, an impoverished and wild area in eastern Turkey. Kendal (1993a) says that according to Turkish Communist Party estimates, 1.5 million Kurds were deported or massacred by the time the rebellion was defused. After 1937, major rebellions by the Kurds had all but died out, and the period 1937–1977 was relatively quiet and uneventful after the Kurdish rebellions had been put down by the Turkish government. Yet the alienation that many Kurds felt toward their government for both religious and ethnic reasons remains today.

The Role of Turgut Özal

Turgut Özal (1927–1993) was Turkey's prime minister from 1983 to 1989 and then president from 1989–1991. Initially, no one knew if Prime Minster Özal, one of the founders of Operation Provide Comfort, would be another in the line of Turkish political figures who would maintain the previous policies that denied the existence of a separate Kurdish ethnic identity. His stance was clarified, however, when he announced in 1989 that he himself had Kurdish blood and that his mother was a Kurd.

As Michael Gunter (2010) points out, under Özal's leadership both the village guard system and emergency rule was established, two state security measures hated by the PKK. Also, however, Özal introduced a bill into the Turkish parliament to lift the ban against the Kurdish language except in broadcasts, publications, and education. He also argued for amnesty for guerrillas of PKK and hoped to bring them into the political system, as Abdullah Öcalon, the PKK leader, announced a unilateral cease-fire and toned down his demands for an independent Kurdish state. Within two weeks of Özal's death in April of 1993, 300 people were killed in fighting, and relations between the government and the PKK again soured for many years (Pope & Pope, 2000).

The Role of the PKK

In 1974, the ideological foundations of what would become the PKK were laid out in Ankara. Many of the organizers of the PKK belonged to other Turkish leftist parties but had become increasingly disillusioned by those parties' wavering stand with regard to the Kurdish issue. The support for the PKK in some Kurdish areas was probably due more to the renewed sense of pride in ethnic and cultural heritage that the PKK espoused, rather than to its Marxist-Leninist ideology. The PKK demands radical allegiance of its followers and allows women to engage in guerilla-type warfare alongside the men. Loyalty to family and kin, tribe and tribal leadership, and every other kind of loyalty, had to be secondary—loyalty to the PKK and its leader, Abdullah Öcalon, were primary.

To combat the growing influence of the PKK, the Turkish government hired village guards who were recruited from Kurdish tribal groups opposed to the PKK. Scholar Paul White (2000) cites the U.S. State Department, which estimated that the PKK had a guerrilla force of 15,000 and a part-time militia of 75,000 in 1995. Güllistan Gürbey (cited in Pope & Pope, 2000) estimates that in 1996 the village guards numbered 60,000, although I have seen estimates up to 100,000. Kevin McKiernan (2006), a long-time observer of the Kurdish dilemma who has followed events in Turkey and Iraq since the early 1990s, cites the Human Rights Watch report, stating that 80,000 Kurds signed on as village guards, hence saving their villages from destruction by the army. The village guards were paid by the state to battle the PKK, in addition to tens of thousands of government troops who were sent to the region. It is estimated that 35,000 people lost their lives due to the 15-year conflict between the PKK and the Turkish security forces, but even that sobering number does not accurately reflect the damage to the overall welfare of the Turkish state. People fled their ancestral villages as they saw the situation become hopeless. By 1997, over 3,400 villages had been forcibly evacuated, with most of those residents moving to large cities in Kurdish regions of Turkey or to the major cities in western Turkey. Thousands more make up the diaspora of Kurds in Western Europe.

Try to imagine being a simple farmer or shepherd. A group of PKK guerrillas comes to your village and demands that all of the families give them food, water, and even animals. Those who refuse could be shot or called a traitor to the Kurdish cause, so you give them what they want. Later, government troops come and accuse you of aiding the guerrillas and then destroy your village.

While most Kurds supported movements that focused on basic human rights, such as cultural and linguistic expression, only a small minority supported the PKK. Most Kurds disagreed with their violent methods, including the killing of Kurds who opposed them, and their militant atheism. Most

Turkish Kurds also were against an independent Kurdish state, although a majority wanted to see some type of Kurdish self-rule within Turkey (Olson, 1996). The tension between religious identity and ethnic identity continued among the Kurds. A new chapter in this tension was about to be written.

The Hezbollah Debacle

Hezbollah (literally "party of God"—a name also used by several Middle Eastern radical groups) came to the forefront in southeastern Anatolia as a counterterrorist movement to offset the influence of the PKK. Hezbollah began killing prominent Kurdish leaders in the name of Islamic radicalism, fueling speculation that Hezbollah was controlled by the Turkish government. Turkish author Mim Kemal Öke (2005) states that starting in 1980, the state distributed leaflets emphasizing social unity, citing verses from the Qur'an that discourage ethnic division. Kemal Kirişci and Gareth Winrow (1997), both former professors in political science in Istanbul, claim that between 1990 and 1995, over 1,300 "mystery killings" occurred in which Hezbollah, the state, the village guards, and the PKK could have been involved, each often accusing the others of the crimes. In 1997, a mysterious tract began to appear on the streets of the southeastern town of Batman, which called for resistance against the PKK in the name of Islam. Journalist Kevin McKiernan (2006) writes that Batman is the center of Hezbollah activity and that the Turkish military reportedly armed the Hezbollah for *jihad* (holy war) against the PKK.

Hamit Bozarslan (2004), a leading Turkish scholar of Kurdish origin, agrees that Hezbollah was responsible for the deaths of hundreds of intellectuals, including Islamist intellectuals, before the state disbanded the organization in 2000. At the time of U.S. involvement in the war in Iraq (in the early 2000s), Hezbollah was implicated in the bombings of the British consulate, a British bank, and the largest Jewish synagogue in Istanbul. Hezbollah also evolved into a powerful mafia-like organization, with its hands dirty from drug running, prostitution, and other types of organized crime. Some cynically began to express that the state had created a monster that it could no longer control.

Changes in Öcalon's Strategy and His Capture

With the passing of time, Öcalon made an effort to accommodate traditional Kurdish culture. He toned down his antireligious and separatist rhetoric and looked for ways to end the bloody conflict. Iraqi Kurds cooperated with the Turkish government in driving the PKK out of Northern Iraq, and

Syria, the PKK's strongest ally for years, decreased its support. Öcalon proposed a seven-point plan that called for the end of Turkish military action against the villages, the elimination of village guard corps, a return of displaced Kurdish refugees to their villages, and cultural freedom of self-expression (White, 2000).

Öcalon fled to Syria in 1979 and ran PKK operations from there until Syria, under strong pressure from Turkey, finally expelled him in 1998. Öcalon sought refuge in a number of countries, but most governments, afraid of the political fallout, declined to grant him refuge. Öcalon was captured in 1999 in Kenya by a cooperative effort of the CIA and Greek, Israeli, and Turkish security forces. Currently he is serving a life sentence in an island fortress prison in the Marmara Sea. In Europe, the PKK has been accused of extortion, abductions, drug trafficking, and terrorism and has at times interrupted European life with marches and bombings against Turkish targets. In Turkey, there are occasional demonstrations of support for Öcalon, even while others accuse him of selling out after his renunciation of violence and urging his followers to lay down their arms and support the state.

Recent Developments

From a security perspective, there is hope that, overall, the situation is better than it was in the late 1990s, although the cease-fire between the PKK and the government has terminated. Most of the people of Turkey, including the Kurds, worry most about unemployment and the high cost of living. There have been some recent violent clashes between the guerillas and the security forces, leading some to fear that another terrible chapter of terror and violence will break out again.

Developments in Iraq since the Treaty of Sevres

For the first time in their history, however, the Kurds may have backed the winning horse.
    —Kerim Yildiz, former Executive Director of the
    Kurdish Human Rights Project

The area that is now the modern nation-state of Iraq had been under Ottoman administration for centuries. The dilemma of the Kurds being divided among the nations of Turkey, Iran, Iraq, and Syria can be traced to the developments described below.

The Role of the British in the Development of Iraq

Oil-rich areas in what is today Iraqi Kurdistan became the target of British interests in the 1920s. The British were aware that the Kurds wanted an independent Kurdistan. The oil-rich, predominately Kurdish Mosul region, together with Basra and Baghdad, which contained both Arab and Kurdish subjects, were put together to become a new territory named Iraq, with Emir Faisal as king. In 1930, a new Anglo-Iraqi treaty ended the British mandate and recognized the new Arab kingdom in which the Kurds were not mentioned. Seven years later, Turkey, Persia, and Iraq signed the Saadabad Treaty—the first of a long line of treaties with the aim of suppressing any Kurdish aspirations for independence. The Iraqi Kurds have not experienced absolute denial of their ethnic identity as did the Kurds in Turkey, but they have encountered severe oppression. The Iraqi government's desire to control the oil, uranium, and rich mineral wealth that lay beneath the ground in all areas of Iraq provides additional motivation to oppress the Kurds.

The Role of Mustafa Barzani

Rarely has anyone been accepted as a true representative of the Kurds by the majority of the people, but if there were a modern symbolic figure, it would be Mustafa Barzani. His life is one of intrigue; his struggles on behalf of his people took him to the centers of power in Washington and Moscow as well as to exile in the former Soviet Union and Iran. As is true of his people, Barzani was betrayed in his quest to find friends for the Kurds among Turkey, Iran, Syria, and Western nations. He helped bring rulers to power, and he helped bring them down when they broke their promises to grant the Kurds their freedom.

Among those who opposed the practices of the Iraqi monarchy established by the British was Abdul Karim Qasim who, in 1958, overthrew the monarchy with the help of the entire democratic opposition, including Barzani and the Kurds. After consolidating his power, however, Qasim outlawed the Iraqi Communist Party as well as the KDP (Kurdish Democratic Party), the major Kurdish party. The autonomy that had been promised was rejected, and pressure on the Kurds to assimilate into Arab culture increased. In September 1961, faced with bombing attacks, the Kurds launched a movement to reestablish democracy in Iraq. The Kurdish movement was indigenous to Iraq, however, and it did not attempt to influence Kurds from Turkey or Iran. In 1963, the Baath Party eliminated Qasim but quickly proved that it was even worse than the previous regime and instigated a reign of terror. According to

Gunter (2004), the Kurds were more numerous than the Arabs, but under the Baath Party, hundreds of Kurds were killed, and the city of Kirkuk, the center of the oil industry, experienced *Arabization* (relocating Kurds to Arab regions and replacing them with ethnic Arabs). The Kurds have always considered Kirkuk part of Kurdistan, and hence, after they were forced to flee in the early 1960s, they returned in 1974. After Saddam's Arabization schemes, Kurds fled again, but came back after 1991, a move that has continued to this day.

In 1970, the GOI (Government of Iraq) agreed to grant the Kurds linguistic and cultural rights. This is one of the major reasons the Kurds in Iraq have been able to maintain their language more successfully than the Kurds in Turkey. In 1971, Kurdish was introduced as the language of instruction in certain regions at the primary school level of education, but it was not allowed at the secondary level. This level of autonomy was not to last, however, and by 1974, Kurdish families again began to be deported from Kirkuk. Between March 11 and 15, almost 100,000 Kurds joined the 1.5 million already in the free Kurdistan regions (areas under less Iraqi government control). By the fall of 1974, the number of Kurds seeking safety and refuge in Iran was 145,000—another example of the Kurds fleeing over the mountains for refuge.

The U.S. Betrayal of Mustafa Barzani

We do not trust the Shah. . . . I trust America. America is too great a power to betray the Kurds.

—Mustafa Barzani

In the early 1970s, the Shah of Iran, with the cooperation of Henry Kissinger, former U.S. Secretary of State, called on the CIA to equip the Kurdish resistance with some arms to be able to withstand the GOI forces in Kurdistan. Barzani was quite naive in his relations with the Americans; he did not understand that the main goal of the U.S. was not to help the Kurds but to keep the Iraqi government busy fighting the Kurds rather than the Iranians, so that Iran would be free to counter Soviet influence in the region. The Shah abandoned the Kurds when the GOI made territorial concessions to his country in the Persian Gulf on the condition that Iran would stop supporting the Kurdish resistance. Without supplies, Barzani's Peshmerga forces were cut off and faced a massacre. At least 500 villages were razed in the initial counterattack by the GOI, and 1,400 more were destroyed by 1978. A further 600,000 Kurdish people were placed in collective resettlement villages away from the mountains, where the GOI could more easily control them. The Baath Party–

led government even offered financial awards to Arabs who took Kurdish wives—another attempt to assimilate the Kurds. Ironically, despite these gloomy developments, there was some economic progress with hospitals, schools, and new universities built across Kurdistan.

With one-third of the population of "free Kurdistan" consisting of displaced people, the Kurdish troops either sought refuge in Iran, surrendered to GOI forces, or escaped to their old friends—the mountains. The GOI continued their forced Arabization, and by 1976, 200,000 Kurds had been uprooted from their homes and deported to the Arab regions of the south, scattered around the country in groups of three or four families. Another 30,000 to 40,000 were deported to Kurdish regions further east (Vanly, 1993). This was the first time the Kurds felt betrayed by the United States, but it would not be the last.

The Iran–Iraq War

In 1979, three events occurred that had and continue to have a profound effect on world events. In that fateful year, the Soviet Union invaded Afghanistan, which contributed to the former superpower's eventual demise. Thousands of young men throughout the Muslim world joined in the war against the Soviet imperialists—including Osama bin Laden—and learned how to wage *jihad* against superpowers. After the Soviet Union dissolved, bin Laden turned against another perceived imperialist power—the United States.

Also in 1979, Ruhollah (Ayatollah) Khomeini overthrew the U.S.-supported regime of Mohammad Reza Shah Pahlavi and began a Shi'ite Islamic revolution that put fear in the hearts of the more moderate Sunni Islamic regimes, as well as the Western world. Nineteen seventy-nine was also the year that Saddam Hussein took absolute power in Iraq. Within a year, he attacked Iran with a full military onslaught. No doubt Saddam, who is a Sunni, was afraid of the possibility of Iran stirring up Iraq's Shi'ite population, estimated to be 60 percent of the total population.[5] I will not go into detail about the Iran–Iraq war (1980–1988) beyond pointing out how it further complicated the Kurdish situation. Many Iraqi Kurds who fought in the war were horrified when they were forced to fight against their ethnic kin in Iranian Kurdistan on behalf of a government that had oppressed them for so long. The situation was further complicated by the fact that many Iraqi Kurds fought for the Iranians against their own government. There were also some Iranian Kurds who, feeling betrayed by the Islamic government of Ayatollah Khomeini when it did not keep its promises for greater Kurdish autonomy, fought for the Iraqi government. Other Kurds hid in the mountains for years, risking capture and execution, so they would not be forced to kill their own kin.

Barzani's own clan helped Iran capture a strategic area of Iraq. In retaliation, Saddam's government paraded 8,000 of Barzani's clan through the streets and executed them as traitors.

The U.S. Unofficially Sides with Iraq and the *Anfal* Operation

In 1983, a special envoy of the U.S. government assured Saddam that an Iraqi defeat would be contrary to U.S. interests and that he would receive assistance. Knowing that the world community did not want him to be defeated, Saddam was able to launch the *Anfal* operation. Because the Qur'an grants Muslims the right to plunder or spoil their enemies, especially non-Muslims, Saddam used *Anfal* to justify his genocide of the Kurds, despite the fact that the large majority of Kurds are Muslims. By 1985, Saddam had razed almost 200 villages and then appointed his cousin, Ali Hasan al Majid, as governor over Northern Iraq. Al Majid was known by the Kurds as *Kimya Ali* (Chemical Ali) for his use of chemical weapons against the Kurds. He razed 500 more villages, executed thousands, and used a scorched-earth policy to destroy agriculture.

Human Rights Watch (1995) reported that Saddam launched eight *Anfal* operations, including the most notorious one at Halabja where 5,000 Kurds died in one night from chemical attacks. By the end of the war in 1988, 4,000 villages had been destroyed, 1.5 million had been forcibly resettled, and hundreds of thousands more sought refuge in Turkey or Iran. Estimates of those killed are around 180,000.

Fear of an Iranian victory against Iraq led most Western governments not to condemn the genocide. They also did not want to disrupt the flow of oil, or lose the huge contracts given to companies to rebuild Iraq after peace settlements with Iran. As bad as Saddam was, he was considered less of a threat than the Iranians, and within a year, the U.S. was selling sensitive military equipment to Iraq.

The First Gulf War and Its Aftermath

On August 2, 1990, Saddam sent his forces into Kuwait. Saddam justified his actions by pointing out that traditionally Kuwait was a part of Iraq until the British created new nation-states in the region after World War I. Furthermore, Saddam felt that Kuwait did not pay its share of the cost of the war with Iran—a war he felt he fought on behalf of all Sunni Muslim countries in the region. Over the next several months, U.S. President George H. W. Bush began uniting a coalition that sought as much Muslim support as possible to drive the Iraqis from the oil-rich Kuwait. It appears that former President Bush, while not giving a direct promise of U.S. aid, implied that the U.S. would help the Kurds (and Shi'ites in the south) depose Saddam after his defeat by U.S. forces in Kuwait. Saddam's army was quickly routed by the coalition forces and driven from Kuwait in disarray. The Kurds and Shi'ites then took the opportunity to revolt.

In March of 1991, Ranya, a small but important city, fell into Kurdish hands, and within a few weeks, Saddam was in retreat in both the Kurdish north and the Shia south. In Iraqi Kurdistan, the rebellion was spontaneous rather than coordinated, as masses gathered in each city to denounce Saddam and destroy posters and wall reliefs of their oppressor. They also marched on the mayor's office, the secret police building, the prison, and the military garrison if there was one (Yildiz, 2007). As Kurdish confidence rose, thinking that their long-time enemy was on the verge of defeat, 100,000 of Saddam's finest troops, the Republican Guard, departed from Kuwait to counter the Kurdish attacks. By March 30, Kurds began to flee to the mountains to escape

Saddam Hussein's picture used to be in the star before being shot away in 1991.

the genocide they knew was coming. Eventually 1.8 million Kurds sought refuge in either Turkey or Iran, having climbed the mountains that divided the countries. With 1,000 people per day dying from the cold, British Prime Minister John Major, U.S. President George H. W. Bush, and Turkish Prime Minister Turgut Özal established Operation Provide Comfort. Although thousands of lives were lost before the aid came, the fact that the U.S. and its allies intervened at all made President Bush a hero to the Kurds, and parents began to name their newborns "Bush." Operation Provide Comfort declared a safe haven above the 36th parallel; Saddam was restricted from flying over the region and was not allowed to send troops to the no-fly zone.

To keep the humanitarian aid flowing, which had to pass through Turkey to get to Iraqi Kurdistan, a compromise with the Turks had to be reached. Turkey gave permission to the U.S. to fly sorties over the region from their base at Incirlik, but in return, intelligence about PKK activities had to be reported to the Turkish military. This established a distinction between the *good Kurds* (those in Iraq) and the *bad Kurds* (Turkish), a division that has somewhat decreased with time but still affect relations between the Kurds and the Turkish government (see chapter 8).

Internal Factions among the Kurds

Without a doubt the Kurds have been victims of outside aggression, oppression, and betrayal. Yet, they often have acted in ways that tragically contributed to their demise—primarily by infighting among various factions. The two major political parties in Iraqi Kurdistan, the KDP (Kurdistan Democratic Party) and the PUK (Patriotic Union of Kurdistan), have battled against each other, sustaining a feud that is somewhat based on tribal rivalries.

Saddam, as well as leaders in Turkey and Iran, has played on these differences to further divide the Kurds and keep them from speaking to the world community with one voice. I can vividly remember how the morale of the Kurdish people went from being very optimistic and upbeat to almost totally despairing when civil war broke out between the KDP and PUK in 1994. Before the civil war, despite having suffered so much under Saddam, the Kurds were united and hopeful for their future. After the factional fighting broke out, however, everyone seemed bent on getting out of Kurdistan by any means possible. Fortunately, for many years since 1997, the KDP and PUK have mostly gotten along with each other and are speaking as a united voice for the Kurds in the post-Saddam government of Iraq.

On September 3, 1996, the Military Coordination Center (MCC), a small base for the representative coalition of American, British, French, and Turkish troops, pulled out of Northern Iraq. This created a panic in the region. Fearing that Saddam would be free to return, Kurds who worked for NGOs appealed to the Office of Foreign Disaster Assistance (OFDA) for help. Iraqi law stated that any Iraqi citizen who collaborated with a foreign power would be considered an enemy of Iraq, could be tried as a traitor, and would face capital punishment. A list of 7,000 Kurds who worked with NGOs was compiled and most were eventually evacuated to Guam, while thousands more Kurds were left behind to face Saddam's wrath. Contrary to expectations, Saddam did not launch a move into Northern Iraq, and the U.S. continued to fly sorties over the region. There was one especially low point during this period when Saddam was allowed into the city of Erbil by the KDP to control the region and put down PUK resistance. The PUK then appealed to Iran to counter GOI forces.

In the same year, the U.N. resolution took effect that enabled Iraq to sell off its oil for food and development-related items—13 percent of which was to be designated for Iraqi Kurdistan. While the Oil for Food program was riddled with corruption and perhaps did not benefit the rest of Iraq very much, it played a major role in contributing to Kurdistan's overall prosperity. This state of affairs continued until the buildup for the second Gulf War.

Changes in Northern Iraq

In 2003, Turkey wanted to send 10,000 troops into Northern Iraq, a move that was strongly opposed by the Kurds. The U.S. government sided with the Kurds, and in July, U.S. troops apprehended Turkish commandos in Suleymania, Iraq. The troops had been sent to destabilize the Kurdistan Regional Government (KRG). These events led to a further rupture between the United States and Turkey (Gunter, 2005).

By 2005, the KRG had restored much of what Saddam destroyed by rebuilding well over half of the 4,000 destroyed villages. In Duhok, there was one secondary school in 1992, but by 2002 there were 12 as well as a new university, a technical school, and an institute of fine arts. Between 2002 and my visit in June of 2005, hundreds of housing units were constructed, including homes for the *Anfal* widows.

At sunrise, December 30, 2006, Saddam Hussein was executed by hanging, for crimes against the Iraqi people. Ultimately he was executed for a fraction of the crimes he committed against the Iraqi people and was not hanged

The Citadel in Erbil.

for ordering chemical weapons attacks and genocide against the Kurdish people. No doubt the Kurds will find his death bittersweet—relieved that their enemy is finally vanquished but disappointed he was executed before he had to account for all the sufferings he caused. (See chapter 8 for a fuller treatment of events in Iraq since 2006.)

Questions for Discussion

- This chapter discusses the suppression of Kurdish history resulting in an uncertain *ethnogenesis*. Are you familiar with other ethnic groups whose collective history has been suppressed?

- How much do you know about the origins of your own particular ethnic heritage? Is ethnic origin something that is important to you? Why or why not?

- The author mentions that the morale of the Kurdish people was high when their enemies were outside forces, but when Kurds began fighting against their fellow Kurds, they lost hope. Why would this happen?

Notes

[1] Yazidism has been likened to Zoroastrianism because of its dualism, in this case between God and *Malak Tawus* (the peacock angel). God is somewhat of a passive entity, but Malak Tawus, who is a fallen angel, needs to be placated so no harm comes to the community. Yazidis believe that Malak Tawus will ultimately repent and be restored to divine favor. Sheikh Adi, the patron saint of Yazidism, is said to have attained divinity through transmigration, and is thought to be one with Malak Tawus (Jwaideh, 2006). Izady (1992) says Sheikh Adi is an avatar of the Universal Spirit and a reincarnation of Malak Tawus himself.

The Yazidi have often been accused of being devil worshippers and have suffered much persecution at the hands of Muslims. I have attended many of their feast days, and have been quite impressed with their sense of community and hospitality. Kurdish oppression against the Yazidi who are fellow Kurds seems to have decreased, but those under Arab control still suffer greatly. For a fascinating and much fuller explanation of Yazidi faith, culture, and history see Gerald Russell's *Heirs to Forgotten Kingdoms: Journeys into the Disappearing Religions of the Middle East* (2014).

[2] The Turkish *Kai* tribe is not well-known. The Ottoman Empire was named after its dynastic founder Osman, hence in Turkish *Osmanli.*

[3] During the Ottoman Empire, people were divided by religion into various *millet*s, primarily Muslim, Christian, or Jewish. Later, the religious identity was de-emphasized, and *millet* came to mean primarily a nation.

[4] The Dervish Sufi orders were a unique feature of Ottoman society. In some ways they resembled monasteries in Medieval Christian society, although celibacy has never been a part of Islamic religious life. Caroline Finkel (2007) states that the earliest Ottoman rulers, including Osman's son, Orhan, gave land to establish a dervish lodge. Throughout Anatolia, Dervish Sufi orders provided the people with a mystical type of Islam, based on *dhikr* (literally, remembering or reminding), the repeating of the names of Allah through which adherents hope to be mystically absorbed into the oneness of Allah. Therefore, conventional Sunni Islam, with its orthodox expression of Islam, was often practiced side by side with the more mystical Sufi Islam, particularly the famous Whirling Dervishes. Unlike in some countries, where Sufis were branded heretics and persecuted, they were quite popular in Anatolia. Atatürk, however, saw them as backwards and responsible for keeping the Turkish masses from moving forward into the modern world, hence outlawing them upon coming into power.

[5] Shi'ite (from shi'at Ali, party of Ali) worldwide number between 150 million and 200 million, or 10–13 percent of the world's Muslims (Pew Research Center, 2015). The Sunni–Shi'ite divide was the first major rift in the Islamic world, when in the seventh century, Ali, who was the son-in-law and cousin of the Prophet Muhammad, was killed by Sunni Muslims, and later his sons, Hassan and Hussein, were also martyred. Shi'ites believe that Ali, as a close relative of the Prophet, should have been his successor and caliph of the Muslim community, but Abu Bakir was chosen instead. Ali eventually became the fourth caliph, following Umar and Uthman.

Chapter 3

Language and Ethnic Identity

Kurds point to everything from language to dress and from kinship structure to the way they dance at weddings as symbols of their distinctiveness. Over the years, Kurds have made efforts to preserve their distinctiveness (i.e., their ethnic identity) by resisting assimilation. Therefore, it should not be surprising that whether implicitly or explicitly expressed, much Kurdish indigenous knowledge concerns resistance to their more powerful neighbors' domination. Izady (1992) expresses the struggle for identity well:

> In many respects contemporary Kurdistan demonstrates signs of a retarded national evolution. Its people are bewildered in regards to their collective national identity. In short, they stopped evolving in the early 1920s, while their neighboring nations grew and evolved to create a uniform national ideology, culture, language, national history (true or invented), ethos and political culture. (p. 186)

Traditional Kurdish stories that I describe in chapter 4 often have political overtones and are a form of resistance. In music, lyrics of resistance were often sung. Because language is such an important part of ethnic identity, in a sense, every word of Kurdish spoken is a type of resistance:

> Well, to be a Kurd you have the Kurdish language that you speak, and because our parents are Kurds and we came to life as Kurds, we are proud to be Kurds. We feel that Kurds and Kurdish culture are better than the other cultures around us like Arabic culture, Persian culture, and Turkish culture. Really we are very proud to speak Kurdish, to be a Kurd, to live in Kurdistan in a Kurdish land, which we believe is Heaven on earth. That's

why we should live on our land like Kurds; we have to keep and defend our land. (An Iraqi Kurd living in the West)

People are afraid to speak Kurdish at home. They are afraid and embarrassed that people will think they are uncivilized and ignorant. (A Kurd living in Istanbul)

The above statements represent two different perspectives about language, the core of the identity issue among Kurds. In both Iraqi Kurdistan and Turkey, many developments concerning language need to be highlighted.

The Development of Kurdish in Iraqi Kurdistan

It is ironic that it has been in Iraqi Kurdistan where the greatest development of the Kurdish language has taken place and the overall sense of Kurdish ethnic consciousness is the strongest. While it is in Iraq where the Kurds have been the victims of the most notorious oppression, they have also enjoyed more cultural freedom there than in Turkey, Syria, and Iran.

Although Kurdish formal education was limited under the Baath regime, in the 1970s–1990s, it at least existed, and Kurds could conduct their affairs in their own language, unlike in Turkey, Iran, or Syria. This is not to make light of the Iraqi Kurds' difficult struggle to maintain their language and culture. Kurds were characterized as uncivilized and backward, a stigmatization often experienced by out-groups in other countries, such as by Indians in the United States. Arab civilization was always portrayed as superior, the ideal that other peoples in Iraq should assimilate into. Kurds, therefore, were transported to Arab regions of Iraq where they were expected to assimilate into Arab culture; forced Arabization was a frequent occurrence. Yet, Kurdish was at least taught as a second language in the school system to Kurdish students, and there was a strong literary tradition, especially among Sorani-speaking Kurds.

Since 1991, the Kurds have been more free to use their language, it has become their language of education and business and social interactions. It is quickly becoming the language of reading and writing, something that was not true before 1991. In fact, Kurdish has replaced Arabic as the language of education so thoroughly that some Kurds are afraid that the new generation will find it difficult to live in Iraq due to their increasingly weak grasp of the Arabic language. Others see little problem with this and hope to see English become the lingua franca spoken between various ethnic groups in the country, with Kurdish being the common language spoken among Kurds as Arabic is among Arabs.

When I first visited Northern Iraq in 1991, the Kurds had just begun to return to their homeland after the first Gulf War. They were experiencing their first taste of freedom, including freedom of self-expression. It did not take long, however, for the results of forced Arabization to surface. All official correspondence was carried out in Arabic, the language of the Kurds' oppressors. Although the Kurds wanted to break away from speaking Arabic, Kurds had to overcome several obstacles in order for all of them to speak, read, and write a uniform Kurdish language. Not only was so little Kurdish spoken during Saddam's rule but also each area spoke a different dialect. For example, in the area where our NGO was located, the little Kurdish that had been spoken in the public schools before 1991 was in the Sorani dialect, which was not a widely spoken dialect in the Bahdinan area. Furthermore, the Kurdish language had so many words borrowed from Arabic that people could not communicate without using the mixture of languages. And finally, purifying the language had to take a backseat to rebuilding homes, schools, and basic infrastructures destroyed by Saddam's troops.

Nevertheless, the use of the Kurdish language has made remarkable progress since 1991. Kurdish is taught as the language of instruction in all schools except for a few that cater to Arabic-speaking migrants who move to Kurdistan for better security conditions. There is still a shortage of books and reading materials, especially those written in the Bahdinan dialect, but more are being published. The Kurds have high regard for writers, folklorists, poets, historians, and other people with literary skills, and as basic survival and security becomes less of a preoccupation, literary expression should continue to develop and expand.

An advantage the Kurds have in Iraq is that the level of Kurdish spoken is everywhere on the rise. People speak it in shops, in schools, at social events—in every strata of life—and departments of Kurdish studies at universities in Iraqi Kurdistan flourish. Kurds have an unprecedented chance to develop a literary tradition that will contribute to a strong sense of *Kurdayati* in every sphere, without replacing the oral tradition that has survived through the centuries (see chapter 4). The same cannot be said in the other nation-states where the Kurds reside.

Developments in Turkey

Unlike Iraqi Kurdistan, where Kurdish is universally spoken as the medium of communication, many Turkish Kurds know little if any of their language. Although speaking Kurdish outside of the home is no longer illegal, as it was prior to Özal's administration, people fear that speaking Kurdish can lead to problems with authorities. I regularly noticed that the same employees at a hotel or restaurant who were thrilled to speak Kurdish with me quickly switched to Turkish when their employer approached.

In Diyarbakir, the emotional center and unofficial capital of the Kurdish territory in Turkey, one hears little Kurdish being spoken except among peasants who have recently migrated to the city. The men have to learn Turkish quickly to have any hope of finding work, leaving only the women as the primary Kurdish speakers. In the late 1980s I asked a Kurdish friend of mine in Diyarbakir if his Turkish-speaking teenage sons knew Kurdish. The father had no idea if they had learned any of what should have been their mother tongue, so he asked them. Both sons replied that they knew only a smattering of the language. Kurds are working hard to pressure the government to allow Kurdish language education.

Although Kurds cite many components of culture in defining what it means to be a Kurd and what makes Kurds distinct from their neighbors, language is the most cited distinction among my informants. Kurdish has often been dismissed by Turkish official publications as a hybrid mixture of Arabic, Farsi, and Turkish, but due to their isolation in the mountains, a so-called Kurdish language evolved. Following the denial of a distinct Kurdish language comes the denial of a distinct Kurdish ethnic identity—Kurds are merely nomadic Turks or Arabs who, in their isolation, took on a new identity.

Language Death

> My family was forcibly settled in this region [a non-Kurdish region of Turkey] as a result of one of the Kurdish uprisings. We went to Turkish schools and gradually we just assimilated into Turkish life. I guess I am a Kurd, but I speak no Kurdish and don't really feel like a Kurd. (A Kurd from Turkey)

When the dominance of the majority language is so overwhelming that it becomes too difficult to maintain the use of the mother language and the younger generation feels no need for the old language, language death will occur.

Throughout my fieldwork I met many people who, having moved to Istanbul, Adana, or other large cities, made no effort to keep Kurdish alive; as a consequence, their children do not speak the language. In some cases, the parents may still communicate in Kurdish, but due to the language of school and community being Turkish, the children often do not speak Kurdish. In other cases, total assimilation has occurred where Kurds have had little exposure to their language and cannot even say basic greetings in Kurdish. For some, it threatens their identity as Kurds and is reason for concern; for others, it matters little. One father, who left the Kurdish region in the middle 1970s, told me that not only did he not teach his children Kurdish but also it would be a mistake to because he believed it would contribute to a weakening of the national character of the country. He even hinted that the rise in Kurdish consciousness was an Armenian plot to divide Turkey, something that nationalistic Turks have said all along.

In villages, Kurdish is spoken widely, although those who have gone to school often speak a mixture of Kurdish and Turkish. In one village near Adiyaman, the parents point out with pride that their children are bilingual. In villages, Kurdish is more essential as the vehicle of communication and children are more likely to speak it despite being educated only in Turkish. In the city, however, many children see no advantage to knowing Kurdish and often say they can understand some of it but cannot speak it. The fate of the Kurdish language depends on whether it is spoken at home and on each generation's willingness to preserve it as a component of identity.

In a Kurdish region of Turkey, I took a group of American students to a small village. The group of foreign students attracted quite a crowd in this off-

Kurdish children on a rooftop in southeastern Turkey.

the-beaten-path community. I tried to speak Kurdish with some of the children, but they answered my questions reluctantly. When I switched to Turkish they became enthusiastic and bubbly. The father of one of the children said it was tragic that children are reluctant to speak their own language as if it were something to be despised or ashamed of.

The prevalent attitude that Kurdish is the language of the ignorant, uneducated, uncivilized villager, while Turkish is the language of the educated and civilized urbanite, will be difficult to change. Even in a predominantly Kurdish city, I often heard children call each other *pis Kürt* (filthy or obscene Kurd). Assimilated Kurds who lived in our apartment block always spoke to each other in Turkish and did not like having to speak in Kurdish to maids or handymen who did not know Turkish well.

I met a young woman from a Kurdish city whose fiancé was from Egypt. I asked her if she was Kurdish. She took offense, as if I were assuming that she was wild and uncivilized, and he was surprised that I would ask her such a question, even though her home city was predominately Kurdish. She did say, however, that she had some relatives who *might* be Kurds. She then joked with her fiancé that he had better be careful with her because she was Kurdish and *vahşi* (wild). Sometimes eastern Turkey is described as *Vahşi Doğu* (the Wild East), a takeoff of the Wild West mystique of American cowboy films that Turks love to watch.

Kurdish women speak Turkish to each other even in Bağcilar, an area of Istanbul that is heavily Kurdish. When I asked about this, I was told they are not afraid to speak Kurdish, but rather they are *ashamed* to speak it and wish instead to conform to the language of the city.

Discrimination and Identity

Kurds and Turks are often said to be indistinguishable physically; therefore, Kurds don't experience racism and/or discrimination based on physical appearance. Yet, physically, people are generally classified as being *esmer* (black hair, dark brown or deeply olive skin), *kumral* (lighter brown hair, lighter skin), or *sarişın* (blond hair, fair skin). Due to its relative rarity, *sarişın* is a popular coloring, and many women have dyed their hair blond. Turkish songs are full of lyrics about beautiful *sarişın* women, and pictures of blond Western and Turkish sex symbols are on display everywhere. *Esmer* is often looked on as less beautiful, and very dark people are often called *Arap* (Arab) or *zenci* (black). There is probably a higher percentage of Kurds who are *esmer* than Turks, although there are so many exceptions that appearance alone does not account for most of the discrimination that Kurds say they suffer. In one sense, therefore, the basis for discrimination in Turkey is different than the racism one encounters in the United States.

When Kurds speak of overt discrimination, they refer to a geographic discrimination rather than discrimination based on physical appearance. When people approach an employer about a job, they are asked where they are from. Upon hearing that an applicant is from a Kurdish region, the employer might say the position has been taken or offer the person a lower-paying position within the company. Because a person's birthplace is written on his or her identity card, the person cannot lie about it and say he or she is from another region of the country.

How Kurdish Are Turkish Kurds?

The battle to define what constitutes Kurdish self-expression has been challenging. Former Prime Minister Turgut Özal, who supported the limited right of the use of Kurdish, felt the best solution is for the Kurds to be assimilated into the Turkish mainstream and enjoy the prosperity that comes for all its citizens as the state progresses technologically and economically. Many Kurds have chosen a type of dual citizenship; they consider themselves Turkish when speaking of their general geographical or national identity and Kurdish when desiring to focus on their ethnic distinction. An example of this dual identity is one of Turkey's most famous writers, Yaşar Kemal who recently passed away; he allegedly called himself "the most Kurdish of all the Turks and the most Turkish of all the Kurds." It is not at all unusual to hear Kurds talk about *Türk halkı* (Turkish people) when making a point about the people of Turkey in general and not addressing the Kurdish issue specifically.

What makes up a person's identity is a complex, subjective, seemingly contrary mixture of origin, history, language, worldview, and other components. One Kurd I talked with grew up in a Kurdish region, but after living in Istanbul for 35 years, he no longer speaks or feels Kurdish. I met another man who grew up in Istanbul, but when he was in his thirties he discovered his Kurdish heritage and has become a fervent Kurdish nationalist, despite speaking almost none of the language. I met Kurds so passionate about their Kurdishness that they talked continuously about Kurdish issues, Kurdish heroes, Kurdish rights, and related topics. I met others who said they were Kurdish, but they love Turkey, are proud to be a citizen of it, and deeply resent it when

Turkey's treatment of the Kurds is used as justification to delay Turkey's admission into the European Union. I have heard nationalistic Kurds denounce those who deny or care little about their Kurdishness as *inkarcı* (denier) *or satılmış* (those who have sold out). On the other extreme are Kurds who view the entire rise of Kurdish ethnic consciousness as an evil conspiracy to divide Turkey that has been instigated by outside powers.

Without question, Turkey has made major steps, positive or negative, to assimilate the Kurds into mainstream society. During recent visits, I was surprised to see how many restaurant owners, hotel owners, and sales personnel in the famous *Kapalı Çarşı* (Grand Bazaar, the largest marketplace in the world under one roof), are Kurdish. Turkey can truthfully point out large numbers of Kurds who have prospered—from Ismet Inönü, the second leader of Turkey and Atatürk's successor, to representatives in Parliament, businessmen, writers, entertainers, doctors, and people in every other sector who have successfully made it in Turkey.

Most Turks deeply resent it when Turkey's treatment of the Kurds is compared to the U.S. treatment of African Americans or to the former Apartheid policies in South Africa. The issue is political, not racial, and Kurds are not officially second-class citizens. Many Kurds agree with this assessment and have little sympathy for those who focus on the victimization of their people. I met many Kurds who arrived in Istanbul with nothing and have overcome poverty to become successful. They have much in common with the self-made men or women who are so admired in American culture. Yet, nationalistic Kurds point out that they have often become successful at the cost of denying their identity. They point to people like Leyla Zana, who was sentenced to 15 years in prison after she wore the Kurdish colors on her headband and declared the brotherhood of the Turkish and Kurdish people when she was sworn into the Turkish Parliament. Her declaration of brotherhood while wearing Kurdish colors was offensive to the Turks.

I experienced firsthand this complexity in back-to-back encounters. I had spent several hours with an impassioned Kurdish nationalist who saw reality primarily through the lens of the oppression of his people. He felt that Turkish businessmen are given preference in landing major government contracts and that Kurdish businessmen face more obstacles and red tape. He said, "The government is trying to destroy our language by destroying our villages and assimilating the Kurds into urban society." He himself became successful without selling out or denying his Kurdishness, but many others who made it did so by denying their identity.

Two Kurdish salesmen, formerly from villages in eastern Turkey, now living in Istanbul.

Then, while taking the train to where I was staying, a man sitting across from me began to berate the hypocrisy of the Europeans and Americans who are pushing for Abdullah Öcalon to be given a new trial. In his way of thinking, America pulled out all the stops in killing Osama bin Laden, whom they hold responsible for the death of 3,000 Americans. Why then is Öcalon, whom the man on the train sees as responsible for the death of 35,000 Turkish citizens, deserving of another trial rather than torture and execution? He went on to say that Kurdish human rights are a smoke screen that Europe uses to cover up the real reason they do not want Turkey to be part of the European Union.[1]

How does one speculate about how representative the views of these two men are of their respective communities when their views are polar opposites? Can nationalist Kurds, who see the Turks as an occupying force of colonization and exploitation, live peacefully with those who perceive increasing Kurdish consciousness as a Western plot to weaken and divide Turkey? I hope the majority of Turkey's people do not see the issue in such extreme terms, but there is definitely a strong polarization between many Turks and Kurds. Kurds told me they can be good friends with Turks, but there can be no relationship with *milliyetçi* (nationalist) Turks, whose numbers are growing.

Even Turkish friends of mine who are far from being Turkish nationalists pointed out that there was little focus on Kurdish ethnic identity until the 1970s. Before then, people simply identified themselves as *Mardinliyim* (I am from Mardin) or *Diyarbakırlıyım* (I am from Diyarbakir), both heavily Kurdish areas. Some point out that the rise in Kurdish ethnic awareness is a reaction to hyper-Turkish *milliyetçiliği* (nationalism). Others see it as an indigenous movement that sprang up in Kurdish soil after lying dormant for so long.

Yet, there are encouraging developments. Kurdish cultural institutes have opened in cities where parents can send their children to learn to read and write Kurdish. While most Kurdish writers like Yaşar Kemal write in Turkish, Mehmed Uzun is one who writes in Kurdish—and encourages others to do the same. Satellite television broadcasts Kurdish programs, from Iraqi Kurdistan as well as Europe, in Turkey. A limited amount of Kurdish programming is broadcast on Turkish television, but it will likely increase. Turkey may not see a renaissance in the Kurdish language, like the one in Iraqi Kurdistan, but as Turkish Kurds move into better economic situations, they can concentrate less on survival and focus more on cultural and linguistic development.

Ethnic identity is a complex, somewhat subjective construct that is hard to pinpoint. Harvard anthropologist David Maybury-Lewis (2002) expresses it clearly:

> Ethnicity is like kinship. When people recognize each other as belonging to the same ethnic group, they feel like ethnic kin, vaguely related to each other through common descent, but so far back that no one can trace the precise relationship. The ethnicity of such a group is their ideal of their own distinctiveness from others. It is invariably based on a sense of common history, usually combined with other characteristics, such as sharing the same race, religion, language, or culture. (p. 47)

According to one survey (Pope & Pope, 2000), only 22 percent of the people polled said the solution to the Kurdish problem is the establishment of a separate state. Meanwhile, 50 percent were opposed to creating a separate state. Furthermore, the vast majority of Kurds seem to feel a sense of dual membership. They are citizens of Turkey, a pivotal nation-state that they are proud to be a part of, but they also want to be recognized as Kurds, with their own distinct cultural expression.

Questions for Discussion

- In general, the Kurds in Iraq have suffered more overt oppression than have the Kurds in Turkey. Yet, the Kurds in Iraq have not faced the same degree of ethnic and linguistic suppression that the Kurds in Turkey have faced. Which group do you think has faced greater difficulties? Why?

- Do you think that the Iraqi Kurds or the Turkish Kurds have a brighter future? Why?

- What are the major characteristics discussed in this chapter that distinguish one ethnic group from another? Do you think it is important for ethnic groups to be aware of their distinctiveness, or does it primarily serve to divide people from each other?

Note

[1] Joining the European Union has dominated Turkish politics for years and is a topic of regular conversation among all levels of the population. Having made formal application to be accepted, the European community is divided about whether or not to accept Turkey. Opponents point to the weaknesses of the Turkish economy, its rapidly growing population, the unsolved issue of Cyprus, and its human rights record (for example, the dramatic rise of violence against women under President Erdoğan's rule) as reasons not to accept Turkey. All of these, plus European fears of millions of poor Muslims flooding Europe for work, have made this a controversial issue in Europe.

USA Today (October 18, 2015 edition) says that German President Angela Merkel will offer $3.4 billion to help Turkey settle refugees. She will also push for visa-free travel within the EU for Turkish citizens, and reopen the bid for Turkey for membership in the EU. In the past this visa-free travel to Europe would be like a dream for many Turks. Due to the continual rejection of Turkey's acceptance into the EU as well as Turkey's economic boom while some EU countries' economies struggled, there seemed to be less of a push from Turkey to be included in the EU. However, recent developments in Turkey (November 2015) have made many Turks nervous about their country's future for economic and political reasons, and many Turks and Kurds might migrate in large numbers to Germany if conditions worsen. With the large numbers of Muslim migrants already "flooding" Europe, how will EU countries respond to possible large numbers of Turks and Kurds migrating to their countries in addition to the hundreds of thousands from Syria and other predominately Muslim countries already vying for acceptance?

Chapter 4

From Storytelling to Television

The Decline of Oral Tradition

In oral systems of communication honor was given to those with age, retentive memories, skill in using the proverbs of the tribe, and the power to make forceful presentations before a gathered audience. With the introduction of literacy, recognition and power were given to the young people who did well in schoolwork where reading is all important. Often, however, the young people came back from school not knowing the stories and oral art of their people. They lacked many of the traditional requirements for leadership.

—Herb Klem, *Oral Communication of the Scripture*

Indigenous Knowledge and Oral Tradition

If the Kurds are descendants of the Medes, it is reasonable to classify them as an *indigenous* (native to the area) people of the Middle East. They certainly predated the Turks and the Arabs in the region even if there is some ambiguity about their origins. *Indigenous knowledge,* also called traditional knowledge, is the collective understanding of a particular culture group about how the world works. This understanding encompasses long-standing beliefs, norms, and values that the group possessed before colonization and before being subjected to the state-sponsored educational system. Cultures rooted in oral tradition, versus literary traditions, express and transmit their culture orally through legends, myths, folklore, songs, proverbs, and poetry. The

Kurds are one of many groups that have relied on oral tradition as a means of transmitting their culture and distinguishing themselves from others. As is happening with many culture groups, as the world shrinks and more and more indigenous groups come into contact with literacy-oriented and technologically savvy cultures, oral tradition is being superseded by other forms of communication, which has led to cultural changes.

Various types of oral tradition have been a major venue through which Kurds have transmitted their history, interests, survival techniques, spiritual beliefs, and distinct sense of Kurdish identity to the next generation. In Kurdish culture indigenous knowledge is generally transmitted from generation to generation by the *re spi*.[1] It is the elders who are considered trustworthy by the community because they possess a reservoir of cultural wisdom collected through generations of time. As one Kurdish informant expressed:

> I love the language, my Kurdish language. When you learn [Kurdish] proverbs it gives you wisdom and more understanding about life. The proverbs come from old people who have experience in life. If you comply with these proverbs you will be a good man. You will be a good member of society.

Indigenous people have faced the challenge of maintaining their way of life against the forces of oppression and colonialism. In the days before electricity was extended to Kurdish villages in Iraq, in the evenings people gathered in either a home or a *diwan* (a big room set aside for group meetings with pillows along the wall rather than furniture) to sing traditional songs that have been passed down through the years, discuss and gossip about events that affect the village, and sometimes, during holy seasons, talk about religion. The most important activity they engaged in, however, was storytelling.

Genres of Oral Tradition

There are many genres of oral tradition. Often memorized stories, poems, or songs are considered to be *epics;* that is, they use set phrases or language that is formulaic—language that can be easily memorized. The *narrative* form of expression uses language that is more informal and "everyday." Two well-known epics among the Kurds were performed by *stranbezh* (singers) who traveled from place to place and often charged money for singing their songs. Wadie Jwaideh (2006) points out that *Mame Alan* is the most popular of Kurdish epics and is the closest expression of a true national epic there is. The

Kurdish poet Ahmadi Kahn transformed the epic legend of *Mame Alan* into poetry in the form of the famous *Mem u Zin,* a romantic tale with political overtones. *Poetry* resembles an epic story or song; the rhyming and cadence in poetry often require that the exact wording be used for every recitation of the poem. *Proverbs* and *anecdotes* are brief statements or phrases, shorter than stories, myths, and legends. *Legends* are often perceived as being factual, although they are not verifiable; they are more recent than *myths.* Other differences between legends and myths are that the contexts of legends can be secular or sacred, with human characters taking on the roles of antagonist and protagonist, whereas myths refer to sacred events typically involving nonhuman characters often from a supernatural world. *Folktales* are fictional, always secular, and have human or nonhuman actors. Genres of oral tradition in oral societies may be as diverse as those of written sources in literate societies.

All genres of oral tradition have a "quest for meaning" (Finnegan, 1992) as their unifying factor. The meaning may be in its societal functions, perhaps in its psychological significance, meaning to the culture, or the effect on the audience, but oral tradition is, first and foremost, a way of communicating meaning. I have often seen Kurdish Peshmerga with AK47 rifles, ammunition, and grenade belts over each shoulder weep openly at the recitation of poetry. They do not seem to feel that displaying emotion distracts from their manhood or that shedding tears as they listen to an emotional poem about romantic love or their deep attachment to their homeland—the two most common themes of Kurdish poetry—is an unmanly act. Examples of each genre of oral tradition mentioned above can be found among the Kurds.

Myths, Legends, and Folktales

Ruth Finnegan (1992) defines myths as "prose narratives which, in the society in which they are told, are considered to be truthful accounts of what happened in the remote past" (p. 147). Sometimes the distinctions between myths, legends, and folktales become blurred. For the purposes of this book, I treat them as the same genre "family." What is important is what the Kurds say about their own origins. They know they are an ancient race of people with long roots in the region. Many had at least heard about their alleged ancestors, the Medes, but knew little about specifics. One legend that has stood the test of time is about Kawa the Blacksmith, the Kurdish hero of Mesopotamia.

Kawa is a popular figure among Kurds, and his story is the source of the *Nuroj* (literally, new day) celebration, marking the beginning of spring and the most celebrated Kurdish holiday. The legend says a king by the name of Zahhak was suffering from a strange malady that could only be relieved by eating two human brains each day. So, each day two people had to be killed, but the king's executioner had mercy on the victims and killed only one a day. He then mixed a sheep brain in with the human brain and was able to fool King Zahhak. He then sent the rescued person away to the distant mountains. In the mountains of their exile, the rescued people eventually married, raised crops and animals, and called themselves Kurds. One day, Kawa the Blacksmith decided that the practice had gone on too long, and he rallied the people of the mountains to rebel against the king by attacking him. Kawa lit a bonfire and commanded each family involved in the rebellion to light a bonfire to spread the word about the time of the attack. The custom of lighting fires on each *Nuroj* (March 21) continues today.

A well-known myth is about King Solomon, the famous king also mentioned in the Bible, but in a very different context. King Solomon wanted to add more women to his already large harem. He sent some of his *jinn* (from which we get the word *jinni* or *genie*, spirit beings who may be good or evil)[2] to Europe to bring back the most beautiful blond-haired and blue-eyed beauties they could find. The *jinn*, however, could not resist the beauty of the women and ended up having sex with them. King Solomon proceeded to punish the *jinn* and exiled the women and their offspring to the Zagros Mountains where they became ancestors of the Kurds. Apart from the legendary aspects of the story, there is an air of mystery about why one finds among the Kurds the occasional blond-haired, blue-eyed individual who stands out among the generally black-haired and brown-eyed Kurds. European travelers throughout history have commented on this phenomenon, and Kurds still frequently mention it. Many Kurds, whether or not they believe the King Solomon legend, believe they are Aryans, a European people who became dark because of cohabitation with Arabs and other darker-skinned people who invaded their homelands over the centuries. They will often point to words like *nu* (new) or *sherim* (shame) to show similarities between the Kurdish and English languages to verify their European ancestry. On a more academic level, Kurdish is usually considered to be an Indo-European language, and Kurds are generally classified as an Indo-European ethnic group.

Mehrdad Izady (1992) mentions children's stories in which the characters are bears, foxes, beavers, and other animals that take on human characteristics. One mythical character is named Khidir, who is omniscient and permeates the environments of both land and water. Izady calls Khidir one of the avatars (divine embodiment) of the Universal Spirit who has supernatural powers, rules over nature, and can be called upon for help.

Another popular figure in folktales is Shah Khushin, another avatar of the Spirit. Shah Khushin is conceived when his mother, the virgin Mam Jalala, while bowing to the sun is impregnated by a sun ray that entered her throat when she yawned during the ritual. Mam Jalala's father orders her to be killed for shaming the family by becoming pregnant, but his six sons, when attempting to strike her, are petrified in the air. The voice within her womb declares himself as the new avatar of the Spirit, and in supernatural fashion, he is born after being in his mother's womb for only 21 days. The number 21 is the total of 3 times 7, two of the sacred numbers in Yazidism—the indigenous religion of the Kurds (Izady, 1992).

There were also many stories about *jinn*, those mysterious spirit beings prevalent in folk belief and among folk Muslims. One man recalled what he heard during his childhood:

> We knew a lot of stories about how the *jinn* make people crazy, how they live in certain people, and how they appear to certain people. At night sometimes I was scared to go to the bathroom. I wanted my older brother to go with me.

There is also the widely held belief that every boy and girl, man and woman, have two angels that sit invisibly on their shoulders. The angel on the right whispers in the ear of the person to do *qenci* (good), while the other angel tempts the person with *xirabi* (evil). Stories about the wrath of God, punishment for sin, and terrible consequences for breaking a moral law are recited to keep children from choosing the way of *xirabi*.

Because the Kurds have had little if any formal education about their heritage, details of the stories and tales vary according to region or according to who is telling the story. But the essence of the story is the same everywhere. Stories revolve around themes of bravery, romantic love in the midst of opposition, and highly esteemed values such as honor, generosity, and goodness. Stories like the legend of Kawa the Blacksmith contain a political message that expresses the hope for freedom and their own homeland. Even romantic stories like *Mem u Zin* carry hidden political messages. One Kurdish historian whom I interviewed stated that until the Kurds win their full rights and have their own homeland, the stories will last as a popular kind of resistance against their tyrannical neighbors.

Proverbs

Proverbs have played a major role in transmitting values to subsequent generations. Kurdish proverbs are cited in various sections throughout this book because of the insight they reveal about the Kurdish worldview and ways of thinking.

Don't Ask the Impossible

In 1993, when Kurds began to cross the mountains from Turkey into Iraq to seek refuge from the Turkish armies bent on stamping out the PKK, I learned firsthand the power of proverbs to communicate truth. In the early days of this "reverse flow" of refugees, many international journalists came to Turkey to report on the event. Turkey was embarrassed about this, hoping to keep the world's attention on the Iraqi Kurds rather than on their own problems with their restive Kurds. During this time, our organization was chosen to be UNHCR's (United Nations High Commissioner for Refugees) main implementing partner in building a camp for Kurdish refugees crossing the border from Turkey to Iraq.

Turkish Kurds seeking asylum in Northern Iraq.

The UNHCR hoped to repatriate the refugees back to Turkey, so they gave us permission to set up only a temporary camp—to construct tents, rather than buildings made out of more-permanent materials for housing and schools. The food rations distributed to Kurdish refugees were in accordance with WFP (World Food Program) standards throughout the world. Each family received a ration of flour or rice, cooking oil, tea, and sugar. One day the refugees and the UNHCR personnel got into a heated argument about the rations. The Kurds pointed out that the ration of sugar, which was supposed to be sufficient for a month, lasted only a day or two. The camp's leadership committee explained that Kurdish custom dictates that they serve all guests tea. Individuals spent their time visiting each other, and they went through a month's sugar and tea rations long before the next distribution. The UNHCR personnel said that the rations were the same worldwide for all refugees. The camp leadership still wanted larger rations, further arguing that the winters are cold and hard in their camp so they need more rations than refugees in Africa or Latin America.

The impasse dragged on with both sides getting angrier with no end in sight. Finally, after listening to the rhetoric for a time, I cited a simple Kurdish proverb, "*Ez bejim nera, tu de beji bidoşa.*" The refugee leaders smiled and burst into laughter. The proverb means, in essence, "I told you it was a male, but you told me to milk it anyway." This proverb is said when someone insists on another doing something that is not in his or her power to do. One proverb spoke more truth to the refugee leaders than did two hours of negotiating by the United Nations. The tension in the room was broken, and the refugees found other ways to buy tea and sugar to serve their needs.

Kurds and Partridges

It was the infighting between the PUK and the KDP—resulting in a civil war in 1994–1998—that led to the disillusionment of the people, in contrast to the initial joy in unity that gripped the Kurds when their enemy was Saddam rather than their fellow Kurds. There is an often-cited proverb about the problem of disunity among the Kurds: *Dinya hemi neyare kewi ye kew ji neyare xwe ye.* The rhyming in proverbs like this in Kurdish make them far more profound than the English equivalent does, but in essence, this proverb says, "The world is the enemy of the partridge, but partridges are their own worst enemy." The proverb compares the Kurds to partridges that are constantly surrounded by hunters seeking to kill them. Yet, instead of banding together, partridges fight against each other. As with the partridges, Kurdish infighting weakens their ability to take on their outside enemies. Kurds say that if they could find a way to unite behind one leader, they could turn their oppressors into their servants.

The Value of Working Hard (*Zirek*)

Heta mirine kirine. (Until death, one must work.)

Heta kefa deste resh nebit, tama devi xwesh nabit. (If your hands are not black from work, your mouth will not get full.)

Turkish and Kurdish residents of cities in western Turkey spoke disparagingly about the flood of migrants from the eastern and southeastern Kurdish regions, whom they accused of spoiling their city. The Turks complained that the migrants were ignorant of city ways, were uncultured, and had too many children. They also blamed the increase in crime in the major cities on the unemployed migrants who were robbing hardworking people of their money. The residents then would tell stories of how hard it had been for them when they arrived in a city like Istanbul with no money, sometimes having a weak grasp of Turkish, and having to work very hard to make it to their present status.

Although Turkey is more of an *ascribed status society* (status inherited at birth) than U.S. society is, there is a strong element of the "self-made man" that is admired. Very wealthy people write their biographies and tell of their former poverty. Kurds who have been successful say they are proof that anyone can make it in Turkey if they are willing to work hard.

In Iraqi Kurdistan, the phrase *zirek* is used to describe a hardworking person. Being hardworking is an admirable attribute, although as I illustrate later, it is not necessarily admired that bosses or wealthy people get their hands dirty by doing common labor. It does mean that, within the system of social stratification, getting the subsequent benefits from working hard is admired.

In a humorous manner, the Iraqi Kurds use the word *zirek* when referring to a man who has fathered many children. A man with ten children is *gelek zirek e.* One with only a few is *ne zirek e.* With increasing urbanization and rising costs, the current size of the average Iraqi Kurdish family—six to seven children—will decrease, although not to the low levels found in European or even Turkish society. So often I have heard Turks express concern that while they have *Avrupalaşmış* (become like Europeans) by having one or two children, the Kurds will have ten or twelve, and two or more wives; stories abound about polygyny among the Kurds and their hoards of children. The instance of a man who had four wives and forty-eight children, some of whose names he did not even know, is often told.

Urban Kurds point out that it is understandable why a village family needs many children to help with the animals and farming. Yet, the practice of having many children has continued in the city, especially among the uneducated. One informant's wife referred to various families in her neighborhood by saying, "That family has ten children, that family has twelve, that family has eight."

No Friends but the Mountains

One of the most famous of all proverbs is *Kurdun heval ninin bes ciya* (The Kurds have no friends but the mountains). Kurdish history is full of various times when Kurds have had to flee from their enemies, and the mountains were their only refuge—their only reliable friend and their only source of strength and support. Below is a compilation of some of my informants' statements about the mountains:

> We are a mountain people. These two things, our language and location, make us distinct. I think the Kurds that live in the villages in the mountains far from the big cities are more traditional. They learn more things

The Kurds' best friends: the mountains of Kurdistan.

than we did [a Kurd who was raised in the city]. They know a lot more stories and more history. I think the mountains are doing a big favor to the Kurdish people. There they are able to defend their rights and fight. I think also that nature is helping us. The Kurds need freedom like their mountains, so high that no one can control them. When they fight the government with simple guns and the government has all its technology like tanks, bombs [fighter planes], they didn't have any other way except to go to the mountains. They come at night and fight the government, and before the sun rises they go back to the mountains. And they are good fighters in the mountains. So the mountains are a good protector. That's why Kurds like mountains.

No Place Like Home

Şam şeker, wilat şerintir e. Literally, the proverb means "Damascus is sweet, but one's country is even sweeter." (This proverb was one I had to quote constantly.) These words are a reminder not to assume conditions are better elsewhere or to forget how nice one's own land really is. The reality of this proverb began for me with a rumor that Israel was accepting Kurds who could give definitive proof of Jewish ancestry. (Most of the Jews who had lived in Iraq, including Kurdish Jews, emigrated to Israel in 1950.) People began trying to uncover documents that would prove that their great-grandmother or grandfather was a Jew who was forcibly converted to Islam and absorbed into Kurdish culture. Other Kurds sold their homes and gave thousands of dollars to racketeers to get across the border into Turkey. Then, with false passports, they tried to get on a plane to Western Europe where they could plead asylum. Few got that far and many died on overcrowded boats or were sent back by authorities after having given all of their money away. Thus, I often repeated the proverb to those so desperate to leave Kurdistan. In a sense, my use of the proverb was prophetic because the genocide that people feared would happen after the NGOs left did not occur.

The Kurds in Turkey also have a strong desire to migrate to Western Europe—the "dream place." Many countries in Western Europe have accepted, as refugees, Turkish Kurds who have proof of being persecuted for political or religious reasons. The United States, however, seldom accepts Turkish Kurds as refugees, although thousands of Iraqi Kurds have been accepted into the United States. Because of the friendship between the American government and Turkey, there has seldom been official acknowledgement of Kurdish oppression in Turkey and hence no justifiable reason for the United States to give Turkish Kurds asylum.

The trafficking of Kurds is a big-money racket, and many Kurds paid thousands of dollars to con artists who never came through with official documentation. I met Kurds in Germany who have sought refuge in churches and live in constant fear of deportation. These Kurds worry that the churches will discontinue their help and turn them over to the government. It is difficult for immigration officials to distinguish Kurdish refugees who may have suffered persecution from asylum seekers whose motivation is to obtain better economic conditions. The Kurds discover the reality of living in the West when, after giving up everything to get there, they arrive only to find they are in worse straits than they were in their homeland (see chapter 8 about the recent refugee crisis).

Functions of Oral Tradition

Each type of oral tradition has a purpose and serves a particular function for the members of a society. Oral tradition sometimes takes on a form of competition by which poets and storytellers challenge each other in contests of verbal and intellectual prowess. Competitors gain honor and respect from their audiences as well as their opponents. As a young Kurd, recalling the mountain culture of his grandparents, said, "Sometimes singers would come and they would sing from evening to the next morning. They challenged each other. People who knew a lot of stories were also highly regarded."

Oral tradition also provides a model that teaches the ideal values of a community. These values help sustain the culture and are a mirror into the worldview of the culture members. Honor is a frequently discussed value among Kurds, both when it was demonstrated and when it was not. The following story illustrates sexual honor. A shepherd, while grazing his sheep one day, came across a boy and a girl doing something *sherim* (shameful). Upon seeing the couple, the shepherd immediately took his long dagger and killed them both with one stab. The villagers regarded him as a man concerned with the honor of the village, and even the parents of the boy and girl were more ashamed of their children than angry at the shepherd. (Today, according to the laws, the shepherd could be punished for this action.) In addition to sexual purity, other commonly held values were taught by means of informal education—primarily through the family. Not to cheat, lie, or steal was emphasized, as were positive values such as respecting the elderly and demonstrating hospitality and generosity. Stories about those who were hospitable and were subsequently rewarded and about those who weren't and were punished were plentiful.

There were also many stories about romance, including *Mem u Zin*. The majority of Kurds I interviewed were familiar with this well-known story about two young people who fall in love against the wishes of their families. Zin's father wanted her to marry the King of Yemen, but she loved Mem and could think of no other. An evil man named Bakir was bent on separating the lovers. He told a lie that Mem was harassing Zin with the intention of making Zin's brother angry. Zin burned Mem's house down and forced a separation between Mem and Zin. Mem then was killed and Zin died of grief at his grave. There is a Kurdish folk belief that if two lovers are not able to be married despite being in love, they will be married in the next life, so Mem and Zin are presumed married in paradise. The story has an alternate ending—that a thorn bush grows out of Bakir's blood, and its roots separate the two lovers even in death. Written by Ehmede Kahn in the seventeenth century, the story has been popularized as a song usually sung at weddings. Shivan, the most famous Kurdish singer, has also recorded a version of the tale. Scholars of orality (the degree to which a culture is entirely orally based as opposed to literacy based) point out that it is a Western concept that stories remain unchanged, whereas in oral tradition, stories can be dynamic, and changes in the narration do not detract from a story's value. Any particular Kurdish oral tradition may be told in different ways with different outcomes without diminishing the power of the story.

Romantic themes permeate Kurdish folklore even though, on the surface at least, the sexes are segregated and affection is seldom displayed publicly. Yet, there are deeper meanings to much of the folklore that go beyond romance. A folklorist alerted me to the political subtext in *Mem u Zin*: "Even our romantic stories such as *Mem u Zin* contain an element of resistance in hidden messages," he said. The two lovers stand for the Kurdish people, whom their enemies are constantly attempting to divide and subjugate. One day, however, they will be free—as Mem and Zin are free in paradise, to love each other. An excerpt from the love story *Mem u Zin* displays a message of resistance:

> I leave it to God's wisdom
> The Kurds in this world's state
> Why are they deprived of their rights?
> Why are they all doomed?
> See, from the Arabs to the Georgians
> Everything is Kurds, and, as with a citadel,
> The Turks and Persians besiege them
> From four sides at once,
> And they both make the Kurdish people
> Into a target of Fate's arrow. (Khani, translated in Nezan, 1996, p. 10)

Other stories that revolve around resistance focus on the courage demonstrated by people who fought for Kurdish freedom, including the Peshmerga who took grave risks when they opposed the forces of the Iraqi government. An Iraqi Kurd who was accepted as a refugee in the United States in 1997 recalled:

> After we took our dinner, my father or a neighbor told us stories about life, about fighting, about Kurdish history.... They told us how the Arabs, Turks, and Persians were against our people and how they destroyed our villages. Like my father said, three times they destroyed my house in the village for no reason but we are Kurds.

Another Iraqi Kurd said:

> What I learned from my family was that my parents had a lot of desire for the Kurds to be free. What my father was trying to tell me was how brave the Kurds were fighting for Barzani. My father did not fear death and neither did Barzani.

Another stated:

> My father used to fight against the Iraqi government for more than 25 years. My mother delivered me in the camp, which was a little hole in the mountain because of the Iraqi fighter planes which used to napalm the entire area.

Among a people who have seen their homes and villages destroyed and had to flee across the mountains to the lands of their enemies at least three times—1975, 1988, and 1991 (see chapter 8 for information on flight in the mountains to evade Islamic State militants)—it is not surprising that the stories so often focus on fighting and bravery in battle. One can imagine spending evenings around the fire or heater, drinking small glasses of tea, while a father, grandfather, or someone from another village tells stories of bravery and courage displayed against those destroying their villages. As tragic as the stories are, they do point to the bravery and heroism of the people, and Iraqi Kurds pass these stories down with pride to their children.

Elements or parts of well-known stories can be used metaphorically to create meaning in other contexts. When parents want to instill strength in their children, they merely point to the mountains and tell their children to be strong as the mountains are strong. Familiar with stories of brave Kurds fighting their oppressors in the mountains, the children know exactly what their parents mean.

The situation is more complex in Turkey where there is not the same legacy of fighting against a common enemy. As a Kurdish informant living in Turkey told me:

In our area of Turkey, even though the people are Kurdish, we were well off and never rebelled against the government. We were proud to be part of Turkey. I guess that is why we never had many stories of bravery in fighting like the Kurds in Iraq have.

The rebellions discussed in chapter 2 occurred too long ago to have eyewitnesses today. The more recent rebellions by the PKK are too sensitive to discuss openly. Perhaps in places where people know each other very well, they can discuss the brave PKK guerillas, but not with the same spirit as Iraqi Kurds discuss the Peshmerga. In Turkey, feelings are more divisive; many Kurds disapprove of the PKK's atheism and brutality against those who do not support them. Furthermore, thousands of Kurds were hired by the government to fight against the PKK guerillas. I believe that one reason why *Kurdayati* is generally much stronger among Iraqi Kurds than Turkish Kurds is due to the heroic stories of courage that Iraqi Kurds have been able to pass down to their children—stories that are more rare among Turkish Kurds.

Effects of Literacy on the Oral Transmission of Culture

There is hardly an oral culture or predominately oral culture left in the world today that is not somehow aware of the vast complex of powers forever inaccessible without literacy. This awareness is agony for persons rooted in primary orality, who want literacy passionately, but who also know very well that moving to the exciting world of literacy means leaving behind much that is exciting and deeply loved in the earlier oral world. We have to die to continue living.

—Walter Ong, *Orality and Literacy*

In certain cultures, not only is oral tradition essential for transmitting, instilling, and sustaining shared beliefs, attitudes, values, and history, but it is also vital to the culture's foundation and to its members' ability to make sense of the world. Walter Ong (with John Hartley 2012) writes that oral tradition helps people store, organize, and communicate what they feel is important to impart to others. Ong, a leading authority on *orality*, estimates that of the thousands of languages that ever existed, only 106 have ever produced literature. Of the current 3,000 languages that exist today, perhaps 78 have a literature.

Many cultures throughout history have had to make the adjustment from oral to written forms of transmitting stories—translating genres that have for centuries been passed down orally into a written form appropriate for societies that have rising rates of literacy. According to David Ben-Amos (1997, p. 809), when this "translation takes place, themes shift from longer to shorter folklore forms, from epics to ballads, from tales to proverbs and jests, and from rituals to children's verses and games."

Unfortunately, oral tradition has not been given its due by current younger generations. After being exposed to reading and writing, young people often prefer or are taught to disregard their culture's oral tradition. Ladislaus Semali (1999) writes about his contemporary African educational experience in which he was taught to respect the beliefs, stories, and myths of non-African peoples, but not the folklore, history, and viability of African beliefs. Similar rejection of indigenous peoples' knowledge by state-administered educational institutions is without a doubt the experience of many stateless ethnic groups, including the Kurds. Many Kurds say that, in school, they studied history but never learned anything about their own history or identity; they studied literature without ever reading any of their own writers' works; and no mention was ever made about Kurdish cultural heritage. Instead, if Kurdish children living in Turkey could not speak Turkish in the primary grades, they could be beaten. Many Kurds shared with me the emotional and physical pain they experienced when teachers beat them for the "crime" of speaking the language they learned from their parents.

David Maybury-Lewis calls the destruction of a people's way of life *ethnocide*. The Kurds have experienced a great deal of ethnocide. In Turkey, they have been called "mountain Turks" who do not have their own language but speak a mixture of Turkish, Arabic, and Farsi. In villages or towns that are totally Kurdish, many children begin school without speaking any Turkish and, therefore, at times are beaten by their teachers for not knowing Turkish. The children are not allowed to speak Kurdish in school. There are no official government-sanctioned holidays to celebrate their heritage or to commemorate key historical events. Even Salahadin, the savior of the Islamic world during the Crusades, is seldom acknowledged as a Kurd. One Iraqi Kurd told me:

> As a kid I was proud of Salahadin because he was a Kurd. The history teacher hated the Kurds so much that he told us to erase from our books that Salahadin was a Kurd and write in that he was an Arab.

The Kurds often asked me about America's own indigenous people, the Indians, and found parallels with their own experience. Both have been stigmatized as being inferior. They have been forced to speak another's language and to attend schools so that they become assimilated into the dominant culture. These measures parse out individuals from their families and villages;

they weaken tribal unity and create divisions. Some Kurds speculate that there is an ethnic connection between themselves and the indigenous peoples who migrated to the Americas millennia ago. They even point out designs on their drawings and handcrafts that resemble American Indian art.

For societies like the Kurds, who have valued oral tradition as a feature of sound leadership and relied on it as a way to keep their culture alive, the transition to new leadership can be difficult. Today's potential leaders, who are being educated in formal institutions that are oblivious to the merits of traditional wisdom, can easily forget the value of indigenous knowledge. Herb Klem (1982) writes about the upheaval in Nigerian society that occurs when young people become literate and no longer respect the knowledge of the tribal elders (or the tribal elders themselves) as they did previously. The disruption to previous social structures can lead to conflict within the tribe. Imagine the changes that occur when a tribal elder, who was previously known as the one who possessed the wisdom of the tribe, is no longer looked up to because he cannot read.

While many of the current generation of Kurdish leaders learned much of their knowledge about the Kurds from oral sources, today's Kurds desperately want their young people to be able to read and write, even if the status of the *re spi* decreases as a result.

Television and Oral Tradition

The importance of Kurdish oral tradition has greatly declined due to the forces of urbanization, modernity, the availability of technology, and increasing rates of literacy. Numerous informants pointed out that, more than any other factor, it was the advent of television that led to the devaluing of oral genres of communication. Evenings that formerly were devoted to storytelling, music, poetry, and drama are now spent watching television—whether in groups at a *kahve* (tea house) or in individual homes. In one picturesque mountain village in Iraqi Kurdistan, a village that at one time consisted of 25 households (*mal*), only three families are left. Each of the households has hooked up a small generator. A *re spi* living in this transformed village recalled some of the stories from his childhood, but he said he no longer passes them on to his grandchildren. Instead, every evening is spent in front of the television. As another elderly *re spi* said:

> Before, we gathered together every night. Sometimes a plate of nuts was
> in the middle [of the room]. Some would tell stories, some would sing,

some would do drama, others told about battles. Since television, how-ever, all of that is finished. Now we discuss what we saw on television, and discuss world problems.

Another informant described times before television:

> You know each village has a leader. He is called *muhtar*[3] or *agah*.[4] So they used to come together at night. They talk, they listen to each other, they tell stories, they tell about situations in the village, in the other villages in the region. They talk about different things. That's part of *Kurdayati*. And sometimes singers would come and they would sing from evening to the next morning. They challenged each other.

In order not to over idealize the earlier way of life described in the scenario at the beginning of this book, it must be said that few people talk about the old days without also talking about the crippling poverty and the constant fighting either among tribes or against the central government. Life was hard, conditions were often bleak, and illiteracy and ignorance about the outside world were widespread. At the same time, it is a shame to see a way of life that sustained the people for centuries become lost due to an invention that robotizes people into being passive viewers rather than cultural participants. Instead of passing down stories of brave Peshmerga fighting to save their people, the new Kurdish heroes of the future may be young musicians and entertainers who have never lived through the sufferings of the past, and who know more about Western pop culture than about their own heritage.

Village elders in Iraqi Kurdistan.

As the Kurds continued to become urbanized and are exposed to increased levels of state- sponsored education, their oral tradition will be transcribed into more literary genres. One informant told me that young Kurds naturally want to be like other young people, and they embrace some of the trappings of the universal pop culture. But he also said that there is much to remind young people of who they are, and they will always value their heritage as Kurds.

Questions for Discussion

- Proverbs are a window into the soul of Kurds and are reflective of their core values and their way of seeing the world. In your culture, do proverbs carry similar importance? Which proverbs do you know that give insight into the values that your society feels is important?

- In addition to proverbs, which other genres of oral tradition are you familiar with?

- The author states that television seems to have been the death of much of the rich tradition in Kurdish oral communication. Has the advent of television led to major changes in your own culture? Cite some examples.

Notes

[1] *Re spi* literally means "white beard" or a village elder. In Iraqi Kurdistan, *re spi*s were generally chosen by the community, and a village could have one or several elders who are respected for their wisdom and their ability to mediate between conflicting members and solve conflicts.

[2] *Jinn,* from which we get the word "genie," play a large role in folk Islamic belief. They are rather mischievous creatures, who are generally feared for their malevolent actions, but they can be good as well, unlike demons in Christianity who are always regarded as evil.

[3] *Muhtars* are elected village heads in both Iraqi Kurdistan and throughout all regions of Turkey. They are more official than *re spi*s are, as they represent the village to the larger government and vice-versa.

[4] *Agahs* (or *ağah* in Turkey) are tribal leaders. In some cases, an *agah* and *re spi* could be the same person. Generally, however, *agah*s were powerful tribal leaders over many villages, although, at the present time, they generally do not have as much power as before. Some *agah*s are loved, while others are hated, depending on their conduct and whether they are motivated by concern and justice for those under them, or by profit and greed.

Chapter 5

Relationships, Roles, and Traditions

A Kurdish friend called me from Michigan about an immigration problem. Another Kurd happened to be at my home when I received the call, so I asked him to talk with the Kurd from Michigan to see if he could answer his questions. Before discussing the matter, however, in normal Kurdish fashion they first discussed which part of Kurdistan they were from, named the head of their *lineage* (a group of people who are related by birth and who trace their descent to a common ancestor), and listed other prominent relatives with whom there might be a mutual acquaintance. Within a couple of minutes, the two men discovered that they are *affinal* (related through marriage) relatives.

Kurdish *kinship* (social relationships linking people through genealogical lines) structure is complicated and not easy to fit into standard anthropological terminology. One problem is that Kurdish kinship terms—words used to identify how people are related to each other—change from place to place. Lale Yalcin-Heckmann's (1991) list of terms used by the people in Hakkâri in southeast Turkey may not be the same as in other parts of Turkey or Iraqi Kurdistan. The sheer number of relations also makes it more complicated to find common terminology. One well-educated leader had 1,000–3,000 kin, most of whom he had never met.

It is often hard for Westerners to grasp that most social interaction among people like the Kurds is based on kin relationships rather than on common interests. By establishing a friendship with one Kurd, a door is opened to meeting a large network of relatives in many places, including his or her relatives in the diaspora. All social and business transactions can read-

75

ily take place within that network of relations. This kind of connectedness has advantages and disadvantages. It can make life easier if one deals with people who are related to each other. But, if there is a falling out with one of the kin, the network of friends can quickly become a network of enemies and can result in *xwin dari* (blood feuds).

The degree of endogamy is weakening with time and especially with urbanization. Bride-price, in which the male arranges to give an agreed on amount of money, gold, or other valuables to the bride's family, seems to be the norm now, which takes the dowry outside of the lineage (Fargues, 1996).

Blood feuds are common in most tribal communities. In a blood feud, all the male relatives of a person who has been gravely dishonored, physically harmed, or murdered are duty-bound to take revenge on the perpetrator or his or her family if the perpetrator cannot be found. Blood feuds often last for generations. Jwaideh (2006) points out that tribal chiefs try to settle disputes before they become major blood feuds. This often involves blood money given by the offender to the aggrieved party. The *xwin* (blood, or in this context—blood money) was often a horse and/or a girl as a bride to a member of the aggrieved family, hoping to unite families and decrease the risks of a bloody war of revenge. As tribalism decreases, and tribal law is replaced by more formal government systems of law, the number, duration, and severity of blood feuds are decreasing.

Family and Enculturating the Next Generation

Xwin nabit av. (Blood doesn't become water.)

—Kurdish proverb

Enculturation is the process of passing down the beliefs, values, and knowledge deemed necessary for people to function as members of a culture. This process primarily tasks place in childhood. Kurdish families are judged by the values they instill in their children and how those values are played out. One Kurdish man in Istanbul said that he was taught to sit up straight and keep his legs together, something that I noticed he did throughout an hour-long conversation we had. While I shifted positions often, crossed and uncrossed my legs, and alternated between sitting up and slouching, he seldom moved throughout the hour. He said learning to sit respectfully is not a Kurdish value necessarily, but it is seen as evidence of proper upbringing. He said he would never sit casually or smoke in the presence of his father, even though he might chain smoke anywhere else.

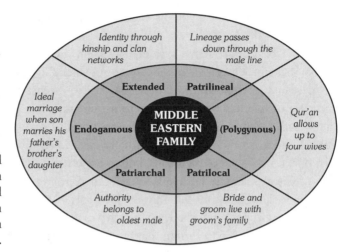

Traditional Middle Eastern patriarchal family system (adapted from Musk, 1995).

As in most other Middle Eastern societies, Kurdish families tend to be *patriarchal* (authority is in the hands of the oldest surviving male), *patrilineal* (inheritance is passed down through the father's line), and *patrilocal* (the recently married bride and groom live with or near the family of the groom). French anthropologist Phillipe Fargues (1996) says among village Arabs that it is quite possible for a woman to meet no one but blood relatives her entire life. She most often would marry the son of her paternal uncle or perhaps even the uncle himself. He calls this "obligatory incest" passed down on society by strict Bedouin nomadic mores. Without a doubt traditional Kurdish culture was steeped in this practice as well.

In rural areas, the head of the family is usually the oldest male—often a father who is living with his son's family—and family members defer to him. (However, due to the large number of men who have been killed, female heads of families are not unusual.) Even those who have been abroad and earned graduate degrees from American or European universities consult their father or grandfather before marrying or making a major career change. The family and kinship (and often tribal) ties are all-important with strong emotional ties between family members. In Iraqi Kurdistan, an acquaintance of mine introduced me to his friend, a man in his late twenties, who took me around the city in his new BMW. The driver of the car is the son of an *agah* and is in love with the daughter of the *agah* of another tribe. Despite the social status and financial standing of the young man's family, the father of the daughter will not allow her to marry a nonrelative from another tribe. Neither the boy nor the girl is ready to disobey the girl's father by eloping and risking his wrath.

This type of patriarchal system may seem archaic and discriminatory against the female members of the family, but when the patriarch is a just and loving man, the women of the family enjoy a strong sense of security. When I told a Kurdish family how close I am to my daughter and how we constantly "hang out" together, a woman commented that the same ties are normal in Kurdish families; although fathers usually pass down their livelihood to at least one, if not more, of their sons, fathers are often closer to their daughters than their sons. Because husbands are seldom affirming of their wives, mothers often look to their sons for emotional support.

When a girl dresses immodestly or behaves in a manner that is considered shameful, it is regarded as a sign that her father is bad or is deceased. Once, I mentioned to an informant that some friends of our family, who have daughters the same age as my daughter, are divorced. He said it is too bad because the girls will "go bad." He assumes that without a father in the home, the girls will look for fatherly influence from the wrong sources and end up doing something shameful (usually meaning having sex before marriage).

A more common problem in the Middle East is fathers who drive their daughters away with overly strict discipline without a corresponding degree of love and affection. The Turkish news showed a father and his brother bodily dragging his daughter down one of the busiest streets in Istanbul because he did not want her going to bars. This was done in front of hundreds of bystanders and ended up on the news. Soon afterwards, large numbers of protestors held up signs demanding an end to that type of parental control.

Parents who move to Istanbul from a village have to cope with raising children in a diametrically different environment. It is not difficult to imagine the family struggles going on behind closed doors between village-raised parents and their urban-raised sons and daughters who are exposed to a looser moral atmosphere or environment.

I had a chance to spend a couple of nights in a village in Turkey with a family, and then visit the daughter after she returned to her university situated about 10 hours away from the village. She has a very close relationship with her father, which seems to result in a sense of independence seldom demonstrated by young women in conservative families. She is uninhibited around males, drives a car and a tractor at breakneck speed, plays soccer with guys, and generally acts more like a suburban American girl than a Muslim girl from a conservative village. When I visited her at the university, she took

Street scene in Bağcılar, Istanbul

me to hang-outs where the students danced, drank, and smoked *nargile* (a Turkish water pipe). Her lack of inhibition surprised me and made me suggest to a Turkish friend that it is her close relationship with her father that gives her this type of confidence. My friend, who is in his mid-fifties, sat her down and told her to be careful to not disgrace her father in any way. He warned her about men who put drugs in girls' drinks and then sleep with them. The girl responded that sometimes she feels her father gives her too much freedom and wishes he were a bit stricter. She is aware of the dangers of men lacing women's drinks with drugs, because it has happened to girls she knows. She attributes many of the problems girls experience to their feelings of not being loved by their fathers. The fathers may be overly rigid and unaffectionate or too lax, not setting guidelines for acceptable behavior.

Kurdish parents and grandparents transmit important moral values to their offspring, as do families throughout the world. In addition to imparting values concerning right and wrong, parents have found it necessary to instill *Kurdayati* in their children, due to the suppression of Kurdish ethnic identity, history, and cultural expression by government authorities. Overall, it appears

Elderly Kurdish woman in Iraqi Kurdistan.

that generally Kurdish families have done a commendable job in passing down both their moral values and *Kurdayati* to their children in traditional rural contexts. Several people said that in addition to fathers and grandfathers, their mothers and grandmothers played a key role in passing down *Kurdayati* in the family, especially in families where the males had been killed or were away fighting.

Sex and Marriage

Sex is discussed somewhat openly, especially among Turkish Kurds, but not as much among Iraqis. Girls still marry young, but not as young as they did 20–30 years ago, and brides are expected to be virgins (especially in the villages). Adultery committed by a woman can result in her being killed by her husband or a male relative; the killing is justified in the eyes of villagers. Male adultery is generally not regarded seriously. Homosexuality may occur among unmarried adolescents if it is discreet. Especially in Turkey, open prostitution has increased due to an influx of women from the former Soviet Union who ply their trade even in small, remote villages. Often older brothers, uncles, and even fathers introduce their sons to the world of paid sex because of the belief that a man is not a man and will even become sick if he does not have sex regularly.

While not generally demonstrated openly, some affection occurs between husband and wife, although most of the social needs of both men and women are met by people (generally relatives) of the same sex. In Kurdish villages, marriage is generally more about economics and children than romance, and it often occurs among kin.

First-Cousin Marriage

At a Kurdish wedding I attended in a Midwestern city in the United States, around 300 to 400 Kurds gathered for the occasion, including many from out of town. Except that the wedding took place on an American university campus, everything about it was traditionally Kurdish, which made it feel like being at a wedding in Iraqi Kurdistan. The women wore colorful *dawet*[1] dresses, each

Dancing (*dawet*) at a Kurdish wedding celebration.

one more brilliant than the other. The music was the traditional wedding music, and because of the extreme heat, most of the men did not wear *jileki Kurdi*. From 7:00 PM until nearly midnight the circle dancing did not stop. The dancing progressed from simple steps that everyone could do to more complex movements that demanded more skill and experience. With the exception of a few of the children who spoke only English, Kurdistan had truly been transported to the Midwest. All of these Kurdish traditions were heartily appreciated and accepted in the host country. One practice, however, had it been known, would not have gone over so well there: the bride and groom were first cousins.

According to King (2000, p. 285), "In Kurdish culture, a FBS/D (father's brother's son or daughter) is the preferred marriage partner." Traditionally, first-cousin marriage was considered ideal, not only among the Kurds but also among many Middle Eastern peoples; ideally a son would marry his father's brother's daughter (FBD). A potential bride or groom is first supposed to be given the opportunity to marry the FBS/D before marrying anyone else. In other words, the FBS/D has first right of refusal. I also learned that first-cousin marriages have never been the only norm and that some people marry even outside of their tribe (*exogamy*), but their families generally know each other well. Parents assume that if the family is good, the boy or girl will be good as well. In the Middle East, marriage unites family and kinship networks to a degree that Westerners cannot easily grasp. It is not considered important for the bride and groom to know each other well before marrying.

I talked to an Iraqi Kurdish *re spi* about first-cousin marriage in his village. He said that some Iraqi Kurds marry cousins, but many marry outside their tribe. He said that he did not marry a cousin and neither did his father or grandfather. He also mentioned that sometimes a daughter will marry into another family for financial reasons, especially when her family has been forced to borrow money and cannot pay it back. The family of a young girl might offer her to a relatively well-off older man to get a debt paid.

Paul Sterling and Emine Onaran Incirlioğlu (1996), in a book focusing on transition among Turkish families, point out that *akraba eviliği* (literally, marriage among relatives, but generally meaning specifically first-cousin marriage) is becoming increasingly discouraged in the media because of fears that it leads to *sakat* (physically disabled) children. Ayşe Güneş-Ayata (1996) cites data from a survey conducted in 1992 that show *akraba evliliği* accounted for approximately 14 percent of urban marriages and 21.5 percent of rural marriages—averaging 17.75 percent compared to 29 percent in the 1970s. While discussing life in Bağcılar with a local informant, I happened to mention some statistics that report an unusually high number of children with disabilities in the area. My informant, without a moment's hesitation, attributed it to first-cousin marriage. Many Kurds acknowledge that the chances of producing physically disabled children increase when close relatives marry each other. Among Kurds in Turkey, and even more so in Iraqi Kurdistan where tribes and traditional kinship structures are stronger, the custom of marrying first cousins is more common. Mate selection, while closely monitored by the family, leaves room for choice by the boy or girl. If their social and economic levels are extremely different, however, strong family reactions may cause the couple to elope.

Another custom is Kurds arranging more than one marriage between families. Two sisters from one family might marry two brothers from another, which ensures both family and economic benefits. This custom occurs more frequently among more traditional families in village contexts. In the city the rules are different; although arranged marriages certainly still occur, there is generally a greater freedom of choice. In the city marriage may be based less on establishing economic ties and more on compatibility. Even so, families are still deeply involved, and the couple may not know each other well. Long courtships are discouraged, and the young couple gets to know each other in the presence of family members.

Romance is a popular topic in Turkish/Kurdish music, films, and television. Movies are often about class differences that keep couples who love each other apart, generally leading to the death of one or both of the lovers. Some youth are throwing off former societal restraints and are choosing to live together outside of marriage, and others are sexually promiscuous.

If a man wants to marry a girl but her family does not approve, he may commit *ravadin* (bride-napping). If the family becomes angry, fighting could break out between the families, resulting in a *xwin dari*. One of the responsibilities of the *agah* or *re spi* is to intervene and try to reach reconciliation among the families. Often *ravadin* is consensual on the girl's part, but the family may not allow her to marry the man, perhaps because of conceived class or status differences. This can lead to feuding if the couple has had sex and the family fears that the girl has been permanently "ruined." This type of situation can be a "Romeo and Juliet" scenario, but if the *agah* or a respected relative intervenes, often bloodshed is avoided. In some cases, rather than being victims of a violent act, the couple is practically excommunicated from the family and it may take many years if ever before the couple is accepted back into the family circle. As mentioned previously, sometimes blood money can be given to the aggrieved family to compensate for the loss of honor.

Polygyny

In many rural cultures, village morality strongly encourages monogamous, multichild, divorceless marriages. Giving birth to and raising many children provides security for parents in their old age, but women do not want their husbands to take on a second wife in order to father more children (Critchfield, 1981). While Islam does allow for a man to take up to four wives if they are treated equally, polygyny (having multiple wives) is seldom practiced. Those who do practice it say it is often for economic reasons. More wives mean more children, which mean more potential laborers. A contributing factor to polygyny is when the first wife is barren, a nightmare that virtually every traditional Kurdish woman dreads. In such cases, either divorce occurs or a second wife is taken.

Because the Qur'an allows multiple wives, Muslim governments can forbid the practice only for secular reasons. Polygyny is discouraged but not illegal in Iraq; it is illegal in Turkey. There, a second wife may have to be disguised as a daughter or another relative, especially if there is a significant age difference. In some remote villages away from government interference, polygyny can be practiced more openly.

An Iraqi Kurdish friend was quite open about having two wives. In fact, when I saw him again after eight years, he told me he took a third wife when his financial situation improved enough to enable him to treat all of them well. He has plenty of children, including many sons who work alongside him. He tried to convince me that I should take a second wife, preferably a Kurdish one. When I asked him why, he asked me what I eat for breakfast. I said that I like to take bread and dip it into *tahini* (a paste made from sesame seeds). "Doesn't it taste good sometimes to dip bread into yogurt instead of *tahini*?" When I agreed, he said, "See, that is why you need more than one wife." To him, this simple illustration was all he needed to justify the practice of polygyny.

Kurds Marrying Kurds

One reason Kurds have been able to maintain *Kurdayati* is because of their strong preference to marry only other Kurds. A Kurdish informant from Istanbul said, "I may have girlfriends in many parts of the world. But when it comes to marriage, she has to be a Kurd." That is not to say that Kurds never marry Arabs or Turks. Saddam Hussein used to give monetary rewards to Arabs who married Kurds in order to faster assimilate the Iraqi Kurdish population. An Iraqi Kurdish informant said, "Our enemies have always tried to get us to marry non-Kurds, and wanted us to marry Turks or Arabs. Kurds should only marry Kurds so we stay strong."

Many Kurds in Turkey, having grown up in non-Kurdish regions, have taken Turkish brides. In a few cases, I have heard of the non-Kurd in the relationship learning Kurdish and raising the children to be bilingual. More often, however, the Kurdish language and culture are sacrificed, and the children grow up speaking only Turkish or Arabic. Among the Iraqi Kurds, marriage between Kurds seems to be more strictly adhered to than in Turkey, although marrying foreigners is not looked down upon and is preferred to marrying Arabs. I know many Kurds living in the United States who have gone back to Kurdistan to marry a Kurdish bride—often a relative—and have had to wait for years for a visa to bring her to the U.S.

In Turkey, men like to say that marrying a woman from a Western country is the best of both worlds. It gives them access to the West, a foreign passport, and prestige in the community. A sexual element is also involved. All types of imported films, including pornography, are readily available to Turkish men, thus increasing the fantasy and allure of the Western female. I know of cases in which Turkish men have gone to Europe and the United States on a temporary tourist visa and have quickly met women willing to marry them. They then marry, but one wonders about the motivation of these men—did they marry for love or to acquire the right to stay in a Western country? It is understandable that men who come from countries where arranged marriages are the norm and where the bride and groom often hardly know each other would not find it disingenuous or distasteful to marry a woman shortly after meeting her.

Certainly, the drive to live in the West is strong and motivates some marriages. In one extreme case, newspapers reported that a Turkish man in his early twenties married an eighty-year-old British woman to gain British citizenship. For the most part, however, the casual Western attitude about divorce discourages Kurds from quick marriages to women from their newly adopted countries. Iraqi Kurds consider divorce to be shameful and evidence of human failure that should be avoided at all costs. In Kurdish society, marriage is a family event—in essence two family networks become united to a degree that is rare in Western society. Consequently divorce has broad ramifications; it brings disgrace to the family.

Dawet

> Dawet is a sign of us preserving our culture. Even our young kids [Kurdish children who have lived their whole lives in the United States] have learned it. Dawet will continue on as long as there are Kurds in world.
> (An Iraqi Kurdish informant living in Minnesota)

As mentioned in chapter 1, my first visit to Iraqi Kurdistan was in the winter of 1991, soon after the first Gulf War. The friendliness and hospitality of the people overwhelmed me. The highlight of that visit was attending my first Kurdish wedding. Here were people who had recently experienced destruction, had escaped to the mountains with Iraqi war planes pounding at them, had lived in freezing weather for weeks without provisions, had their villages destroyed, and had just buried thousands of their dead. Despite these hardships, the community celebrated with the young couple, and they joyfully taught me how to do *dawet*. During a wedding, it seems that troubles are forgotten and the celebration goes on.

Among the many wedding customs, the most prominent is the *dawet*. Men and women interlock fingers and, using various steps and arm movements, dance in a circle for long periods of time. The songs, performed by a singer and a couple of musicians, last a long time. When one song finally ends and another begins, sometimes the particular *dawet* changes. Weddings used to last three days, but now they are often reduced to one full day and night because of the expense involved. Hundreds of people usually attend, but the cost to the family is somewhat offset because guests give various denominations of bills either to the couple or to one of the parents during the celebration. People also tip the musicians to defray some of the costs.

Dawet is not only performed at weddings but also at other times of celebration. Masoud Barzani's appointment as the Serok (leader or president) of Kurdistan was celebrated with several days of dawet and was broadcast on Kurdish television each day. During a series of concerts given by Shivan Perwar, a Kurdish singer and national hero, groups broke out into dawet, and Shivan himself joined in. In villages with mud brick homes and no electricity, I have seen dawet, complete with women wearing the same sparkling Kurdish dresses that their counterparts in the city wear. In St. Paul, Minnesota, upon Jalal Talabani's promotion to president of Iraq, an office he held during 2005–2014, there was dawet as the Kurds living in the Twin Cities celebrated. The exact rhythm and patterns may vary according to region, but the institution of dawet appears not to change, and it is one custom that urbanization has not eliminated.

Gender Issues

Male and female "live" in distinct universes. To some extent, in most Muslim countries the great "outside," the public world, is the domain of men. Even within the home, rooms which the "outside" world might infiltrate are carefully managed so that women will only be found in them when no strange males are visiting. If a woman needs to pass through the "outside" world on some errand or visit, she does so by making herself inconspicuous: she veils herself in varying degrees of anonymity. The woman's world is the dark "indoors," the private world. . . . Men, for their part, are blessed with social and political authority, plus the freedom to move at will in the world. Along with such privileges, they have the duty of supporting their families completely. Women's primary responsibilities are the maintenance of the home and the bringing up of the children. In the home, the woman largely rules as queen and a Muslim male is in some senses a guest of his wife. (Musk, 1995, pp. 23, 25–26)

The above extract summarizes the distinctions between men and women in conservative Islamic society. Andrew Mango (2004) cites a study that claims that in Ümraniye, a working-class neighborhood in Istanbul where most residents are recent arrivals from villages, 44 percent of the women need permission from a male to leave their homes in the daytime. In the evenings, the figure rises to 96 percent (p. 118). This study illustrates that village practices are not totally abandoned upon arrival in the more Westernized major cities. Although most Westerners would consider these practices as evidence of weakness in Muslim women,

> Mernissi states that, contrary to western culture's belief in women's bio-logical inferiority, in Islam "the whole system is based on the assumption that women are powerful and dangerous beings. All sexual institutions (polygamy, repudiation, sexual segregation, etc.) can be perceived as a strategy for containing their power." (cited in King, 2000, p. 228)

The women, walking along the *meydan*[2] in predominately Kurdish neighbor-hoods in a variety of dress from full Islamic garb to the latest Western fash-ions, most likely had to receive permission from their husband or father before going out. It is also likely that the people they walk about with are rela-tives rather than friends or casual acquaintances.

Women's Attire

Women's attire in Islamic societies has often been discussed, especially the *hijab* (head covering). *Hijab, abbiya* (a black robe that covers the hair, arms, and legs and extends to the feet), *burka* (a garment that fully covers the body and the face), and related items of women's dress prompt different reac-tions from people. Some Western female converts to Islam have praised the merits of wearing *hijab,* saying that when they wear theirs, they no longer feel like mere sex objects as they did before they became Muslims. Other women, especially those from within the Muslim world, have written that Islamic attire is a symbol of the servitude and male domination over women.

In Iraqi Kurdistan, urban Kurdish women generally wear a *dişdaşa* around the house and in the immediate neighborhood of their home. It is a loose-fitting, one-piece garment that covers the body from the shoulder to the top of the feet. It is generally made from simple cloth, but sometimes fancier ones are made from more expensive materials. Women find them comfort-able to wear in the extreme heat of summer. Kurdish women entertain guests in their *dişdaşa* and may or may not slip on a *hijab* when men come into the home. When a woman goes to market, she generally wraps an *abbiya* over the *dişdaşa.* On occasion one sees a woman wearing a *burka,* although it is rarely worn among Iraqi Kurdish women.

In gender-segregated Northern Iraq, I had few chances to interview women, but I stayed a few days with a family in which the wife is a trained civil engineer, who stays at home with three small children. She informed me

Woman wearing an *abbiya*.

that *abbiya*s are worn by married women and/or women who are approaching the age of 20. Many single women do not wear the *abbiya*, but may wear the *hijab* or no covering at all. The engineer said there are exceptions, and some women choose to begin the practice of going to market in *abbiya* at a much younger age while others never do. It is only when women are forced by men to wear the *abbiya* that it causes resentment, which this woman says occurs in about 5 percent of the cases.

In the 1970s, women throughout many regions of the Muslim world took off the veil, adapted Western practices with regard to apparel, and began to work outside of the home, thus departing from traditional child-rearing and household roles. Many of these women since have reverted to more traditional roles, saying that "liberation" left them vulnerable to being exploited as sexual objects, spiritually empty, and socially isolated.

Paradoxically, Kurds boast about Suleymania, a city in Iraqi Kurdistan that has always been more liberal with regard to women's roles and more modern in its outlook. Many Kurds say with pride that Suleymania is *wek Avrupa* (like Europe), not only because of its modern appearance but also because of the freedom of its women to work and dress like Europeans. At the universities in Iraqi Kurdistan, the wide range of acceptable apparel worn by women is quite a departure from tradition.

According to Diane King (2000), the female Kurds living in villages in Northern Iraq are in a more dangerous sexual situation than are the women in the cities because the village women come into more contact with men in the course of a normal day. In the village, women/girls are more visible. They carry firewood; milk sheep, goats, and cows; work in the fields; and help raise their younger siblings. Therefore, men are more likely to regularly see the same girl, increasing the chances of infatuation leading to temptation. In the city, women/girls can be secluded more easily and be kept at home in the presence of a relative who can always vouch for their honor; they are seldom seen alone. Again some of these constraints are loosening with time. Village women wear *dişdaşa*, not *abbiya*, even when way from the house. Women in towns and even in cities may be more segregated and dress in more restrictive attire than their village counterparts.

In Turkey, women are incredibly diverse in role and apparel. In general, people agree that *Doğulular* (those from eastern Turkey) are more conservative and traditional than those in western Turkey. But overall, there is variation in how women in Turkey dress. The Alevi Kurds[3] (and Turks as well) often pride themselves that their women seldom wear *hijab* or other types of conservative Islamic dress, and they see women that do wear conservative dress as exploited and oppressed. As one example of the opposite of conservative, I saw a girl of about eighteen get on the minibus I was riding in a Kurdish neighborhood in Turkey. She had long blond hair that protruded through the back of a baseball hat, and she wore tight-fitting blue jeans and a multicolored T-shirt. She could easily have passed as a freshman at an American university; no one would have guessed that she was a Kurd from the Middle East. I was warned about my assumption that, based on apparel, those who are conservatively dressed are sexually conservative, while those who dress like this girl are not. Those dressed in Islamic attire may be more sexually "dangerous" than those dressed like a Western girl. Many men in Turkey seldom hide their glances as they observe women and will often comment about a woman's body or make sexual innuendos; the Kurdish men in Iraq seem somewhat embarrassed when they see a woman wearing Western clothing that reveals either too much skin or the shape of her body, and generally look away.

There is little focus on male clothing, although it should be modest according to the Qur'an.

Gender Differences

Much has been written concerning the complex world of Middle Eastern women that includes their attire, their relationships within the family, and their sexuality. The differences in attitudes toward men and women may start at birth. For example, celebrations mark the birth of a boy in contrast to the almost mournful atmosphere that is present at the birth of a girl. Baby boys are nursed for much longer periods than are girls, leading one to speculate that boys experience a closer relationship with their mothers in their early years than girls do. These practices have prompted Middle East specialists to speculate that in male–female relations women are subordinate to men. From my observations, while boys and girls are treated differently, Kurds truly delight in their daughters.

An Iraqi Kurdish man who migrated to the United States in the late 1970s as a teenager with his uncle's family did not see his mother for eighteen years until he returned to Northern Iraq when the border was reopened. When it came time to return to the United States, this well-educated and successful businessman, dressed in American fashion, expressed more open emotion at the border between Iraq and Turkey than I have ever witnessed. He and his mother beat their chests, moaned very loudly, and hugged and wept, before their final goodbye. He told me how incredible it was to hug his mother again after an eighteen-year void of maternal contact.

Kurdish families take great care in preserving the honor and reputation of their daughters, as the following story illustrates. My daughter was eight when we arrived in Iraqi Kurdistan. For at least two years she played with her girl-friends on the street, kicked balls in empty lots, and played hide and seek in the neighborhood. Then almost overnight her friends began to disappear. We learned that when girls reach the age of 10 or 12 and begin to develop, they are kept inside the house by their parents to be protected. Many would marry within a few years, and the simple play of childhood was over. While my daughter would not even think of marrying for another 10 to 15 years, our Kurdish neighbors were preparing their daughters for the big step in the not-so-distant future.

In Iraqi Kurdistan, when an unrelated guest is not present, the family members (male and female, adults and children) eat together either on the floor or around a table. When guests come to a home, the men eat separately from the women, even among families that are not strictly traditional. Men eat first and the women eat either afterward or in another room. Children eat with the women unless an older male adolescent asks to be included with the men. Sometimes the woman serves the food and tea, while in some families, I never saw the woman again for the rest of the evening after the initial greetings, and the men brought out the food and tea. Traditionally, each person sits on the floor in a circle. Large platters of food are placed in the middle of the circle and people serve themselves from the platters.

In Turkey, even in villages, women sit with the men, although in some families, men and women prefer to eat separately when there are guests. Tea and often Turkish coffee and cold drinks are served to every guest by the newest bride in the family (where patrilocal residence patterns are the norm). If a bride is unavailable, an unmarried son serves the beverages. In some places, women are neither segregated from the men nor totally integrated; rather, the men sit on one side and the women on the other side of the room. Conversation is conducted with others of the same gender, but it often involves both groups when the discussion is about something of interest to both men and women.

Female Roles

It appears that political liberation of Northern Iraq from the iron rule of Saddam Hussein does not automatically mean Western-style liberation for women, as some Westerners thought it would. Traditional roles are still performed by the majority of women, even though some drive, manage shops, and work in government. According to Jwaideh (2006), most writers agree that Kurdish women enjoy far more freedom than Arab women. They are not as secluded, mingle more freely with men, and dress less conservatively. They even dance together at weddings, something that some religious leaders in Iraqi Kurdistan have been concerned about. Jwaideh points out that a Kurdish woman is definitely the queen of the house, and even chiefs are under the thumb of their wives.

Kurds who return to Kurdistan after spending years in Western countries do not want to see Kurdish women emulate Western women or see the level of social mixing and casual attitudes toward sexuality that they have witnessed abroad. They fear that loose family ties, divorce, and perceived shameful manifestations of freedom of expression prevalent in Western society are seeping into Kurdish culture. Nevertheless, the women of the diaspora, having experienced the freedom to choose whether or not to work and how many children to have, will likely struggle to embrace the traditional idea that a woman's primary role is to bring as many children into the world as Allah wills.

Shul e jinek e xilas nebit. (A woman's work is never finished.)

Kurdish men often acknowledge the strength of Kurdish women and their importance as the ones who have held the family and society together. I saw hundreds of women in Iraqi Kurdistan, when there was no kerosene for cooking and heating, go into the woods and cut firewood; they would walk down the road, carrying loads far bigger than themselves and weighing more than their own body weight. I would have our driver pull over to pick up these women. They would throw their load into the back of the pickup truck and climb in there as well, since it was shameful to ride in the cab with strange

Hardworking woman in Iraqi Kurdistan.

men. I never figured out how they managed to balance wood once we dropped them off and helped them reload the heavy bundle onto their backs. My driver would simply say, *jinek e Kurdun zirekin* (Kurdish women are industrious).

Once these women returned home, they had to prepare dinner for their large families (typically six or more children and often elderly persons or the relatives of another family member). Further, they had to prepare the food over a fire that could cook only one thing at a time, serve tea throughout the evening, and give attention to the children. Women were also expected to meet the sexual needs of their husband after the children were finally asleep and—God willing—bear yet another child.

One of the roles that women perform in traditional Kurdish culture is bread maker. In Middle Eastern culture, it is almost as if the bread (*nan*) has a life of its own and needs to be treated with respect. Foreigners have been rebuked by Kurdish children for allowing bread to fall on the ground. Even in cities, leftover bread is usually hung on an outside door in a plastic bag for the poor, rather than discarded. A meal without bread is almost unconceivable to Middle Easterners. When Chinese restaurants first came to Istanbul, the owners quickly learned they had to serve bread along with the exotic foods the Turks were trying for the first time so the customers would feel full. Fortunately, as expensive as some foods become, the price of bread remains cheap.

In the village, bread making is a skill—almost a holy task—that is passed down from mother to daughter. Bread making is a rite of passage for a new bride and a way to gain respect within her husband's family. In southeastern Turkey, I watched my friend's wife and two relatives make *nan*. The wife previously had rolled out a large amount of dough and placed it in a large container. One woman took the dough from the large container, rounded it off, and handed it to my friend's wife who skillfully placed it on a flat round board. She rolled it out with a long stick into an almost perfect circle and flattened it to just the right thickness. Then she passed the dough with her sticks to her mother-in-law who, with her own sticks, transferred the dough to a rounded metal surface where it baked above hot coals for a couple of minutes on each side. After it is baked, each round of *nan* is stacked, one on top of the other, making a stack several feet high.

Baked *nan* is hard and brittle, like a giant cracker. Before it is eaten, it is sprinkled with water and covered with a cloth until it softens. During a meal, one tears off a piece of *nan* and uses it to dip in or scoop up both soup and solid food like rice, onions, tomatoes, and meat or chicken. The Kurds do not eat with their hands in the sense of dipping their fingers directly into rice or sauce, but by breaking off *nan*, they can dip into the food without appearing to be "uncivilized."

In Northern Iraq, I spent some time with a family with eight children. The oldest unmarried daughter was a very pretty, intelligent girl who hoped to win a place in one of the recently opened universities in Kurdistan. She had to study and, at the same time, watch seven siblings, settle their disputes, keep them entertained, help her mother cook, take care of guests, and make sure everyone had plenty to drink. From her appearance, she could have been an outgoing, energetic freshman at an American university. Yet, I worried about her future: would she continue the Kurdish tradition of having as many children as *Xude* (God) wills and raise her children in the same way? Or would she work, marry later, and focus on a career? Which one would be a better option? It was ethnocentric of me to assume that marrying later and having fewer children was the better option for her.

While the majority of girls still marry young, more girls are beginning to go beyond primary school and are attending middle and high schools in towns large enough to offer advanced education. It is likely these changes will affect the marriage age, the number of children per family, and changes in the roles that women assume.

Women and the Transmission of *Kurdayati*

Kurdish women often pass down *Kurdayati;* it is mothers who tell the stories about the bravery of the Peshmerga and instill pride in being a Kurd.

These mothers had to be strong when their husbands were killed or away for long periods of time fighting or working. Generally, however, mothers transmit *Kurdayati* to their children more by their display of courage in suffering than they do through their knowledge of Kurdish folklore.

Unlike most other Middle Eastern peoples, however, Kurdish women have often served as Peshmerga. The nightly world news has often shown female Peshmerga fighting bravely against Islamic State warriors. It appears to be widely believed that if a man in battle is killed by a woman he will not be allowed into Paradise, adding an interesting dimension to the battle against the Islamic State fighters. Women also have played a prominent fighting role in the PKK's struggle against the Turkish military, both in the past and recently in the battle for the city of Kobani in Syrian Kurdistan.

Tribal Structure and Leadership

The Kurds are similar to the Highland Scots in that they have a clan history, with more than 800 tribes in Kurdistan.

—Kermin Yildiz

Dutch anthropologist Martin van Bruinessen (1992) is one of the world's leading authorities on Kurdish tribal structure. He describes the Kurdish tribe as "a socio-political and generally also territorial (and therefore economic) unit based on descent and kinship, real or putative, with a characteristic internal structure. It is naturally divided into smaller units: clans, lineages, etc." (p. 51). Jwaideh classifies the Kurds according to two major categories: the tribal and the nontribal. Traditionally, the tribal have been more nomadic and rural and were the ruling class; the nontribal are more settled and urban. Jwaideh and van Bruinessen use the words *ashirat, taifa,* and *tira* to fit anthropological terminology of tribe, clan, and lineage, but these words may change from dialect to dialect. Furthermore, as van Bruinessen points out, the terminology does not always apply well to all Kurdish societies.

In Kurdish, the word *eşiret (ashirat)* translates as "tribe" or "clan." but the boundaries of what constitutes a tribe are not uniform. My informants said that tribalism in Turkey is pretty much nonexistent except in a few places among very traditional Kurds. Yet, occasionally the daily newspapers print a picture of an *agah* posing with his son or daughter who has recently celebrated his or her marriage with an extravagant wedding, costing tens of thousands of dollars. In two examples, two *agahs*, both from impoverished areas of Turkey, gave the brides (in one case his own daughter, in the other his new daughter-in-law) over 15 kilos of gold in addition to the thousands of dollars they spent on music, food, and hotel accommodations for three days of celebration. This display of lavish giving in the midst of great poverty is the image that come to mind when *agah*s and *eşiret*s are mentioned. In general, however, urbanization, modernity, changing sociopolitical conditions, and more government involvement in the region have all contributed to the tribes' decline in most parts of Turkey. Few regret the demise of the tribes, and many compare the tribal system to feudalism—an antiquated system that needs to be totally abolished.

In Iraqi Kurdistan the situation is different. While the tribes there are not as strong as they once were, they still play a role. People introduce themselves by their tribal name as well as their family name.

> There are a considerable number of clans, tribes, and tribal confederations in Kurdistan today, each with its own defined territory. Many of these tribes have been in existence—with the same names—*for several thousand years*. The modern Zibari tribe, for example, is mentioned as the Saubaru/Sibaru by Sumerian and Akkadian sources. Variations of the tribal names . . . appear in the Greco-Roman, Aramaic, Middle Persian, and Armenian records. (Izady, 1992, p. 74; italics mine)

One informant said the tribes were essential in Kurdistan, the preserver of what is good, "Because the tribes are the soul of *Kurdayati*. They have everything concerning the soul of *Kurdayati* in their mind and in their blood." His opinion, however, is in the minority. The kind of *agah* who governs the tribe is one determining factor in whether or not the tribes are looked on favorably. To me, tribalism is viewed, at least by those in urban areas, as the "good old days" are viewed in the United States. The old ways can be missed, but that does not mean people want them restored.

> There are hundreds of tribes in the Middle East in my region. We have a big family but we don't believe in tribes. Because if the government is fair and treats everyone equally there shouldn't be any tribes because tribes always create problems. One tribe will kill a person and then hatred will grow when they take revenge. So it has always been like that in the Middle East, so I don't believe in tribes. They are hundreds of years old. (An Iraqi Kurdish informant)

Iraqi Kurds who have returned to Kurdistan after living abroad say that the *agah*s continue to carry special privilege and that the law applies less to them. Even in Turkey, where tribalism is supposedly nonexistent, politicians court powerful *agah*-type figures who can influence those under their domain to cast their votes for one particular party over another; some form of the tribes, with the privileges of power for the elites, has remained, even if the institution has been weakened.

Village Leaders and their Roles

Some *agah*s have authority over tribes consisting of thousands of people in hundreds of villages. Others, however, are less powerful and may be in charge of only one village. One informant said it this way:

> We have two kinds of *agah*, two kinds of tribes. In some tribes the *agah* is respectable and he looks after the people like his own children. But in other tribes, the people see him as an evil man and they are like slaves to him. We have some of them that if a member of the tribe comes to meet the *agah*, he is not allowed to walk to meet him and shake his hand. He has to crawl in front of him and he cannot get close to him.

Some of the *agah*s were seen as *jash* (or traitors, Kurds who worked for the Iraqi government against their own people). Others were praised for secretly helping the Kurds while only *appearing* to be loyal to the government.

In comparison with *agah*s, *re spi*s are more highly regarded, but in some cases the same person could be both an *agah* and a *re spi*. One difference is that *re spi*s are chosen by the people in an election and have to maintain their position by being voted on again and again. One older man explained how one can become a *re spi*:

> Often being a *re spi* is passed down from family with a respected family giving the son of the family the honor like a succession of kings. The son gets respect because of the father, and he gets a chance to be the new *re spi* when his father dies. Of course people must be willing to go to him and he must have a good reputation.

The *re spi*, then, has the right to pass down his authority to his son, but only if the people choose him to lead. *Re spi*s who became *jash* were for the most part voted out of office after 1991 when the Kurds were no longer under the GOI.

Responsibilities of Village Leaders

Whether *re spi*, *agah*, or *muhtar* (official head of village appointed by the government), the village leader's responsibilities revolve around a number of important tasks. One of these tasks is to be the representative of the village to the local government. People share with the leader their needs and concerns; he in turn represents them before the government and carries the government's answers back to the people. Especially when Iraq was under Baath control, this had to be a daunting task filled with much peril.

Another responsibility of a village leader is to be a go-between or mediator between families. The leader's duty is to find a just solution in such cases, as land disputes. The leader often mediates between families when a boy and a girl want to marry. He calls the families together to discuss the situation. Negotiations often involve sensitive issues such as the amount of the bride-price, including the amount of gold the man must bring into the marriage— the only real financial security the bride has in the marriage. There may also be discussions about living arrangements, which are generally patrilocal in the beginning of the marriage unless an independent household is established.

The greatest challenge the leader faces is that of managing conflict. Various types of problems occur that need wise advice and counsel between people, families, villages, and tribes. Those who are good at conflict resolution and demonstrate admirable leadership are looked upon favorably, even by the rapidly urbanizing Kurdish population. Probably the greatest conflict-management challenges occur when a girl is *ravandin* (bride-napped) by a young man who wants to marry her but her parents do not approve. In these instances, sometimes the young people go to the *agah* or *re spi* and plead asylum. They may even stay for months with him because the angry family members will not attack an elder's home. The *agah*, not wanting to be in a position of animosity with either family, sometimes arranges for the couple to escape. Often this includes moving the couple from Iraqi Kurdistan to a network of Kurds in Turkey or Syria (although now-a-days, Syria is not much an option). If reconciliation cannot be achieved, a blood feud (*xwin dari*) can

Village elders.

result, which could last for years or even generations. With modernization, however, these practices are decreasing.

I talked with a *re spi* whose son and his family had just returned to Kurdistan from Dallas where they had been living since 1997. The *re spi* is probably in his early 70s and lives in a nice house in the city. He said that he never had to deal with *xwin dari* because most of the village consisted of close relatives. He was a frequent mediator, especially when there was division over issues like marriage. Another *re spi* said he also never had to deal with *xwin dari* during his reign, although he knew of many cases of it. When it happened, often it was blamed on the *re spi*'s lack of skill in keeping the peace.

A *re spi* who is trusted and respected in Iraq is still consulted even after people move to the city or abroad. Some *re spis* who have migrated to the United States are consulted by telephone if there are problems in the village and the new leader has not yet gained the respect of the village families.

Köy Heyeti (Village Committee) in Turkey

In Turkey, each village has a *muhtar* who is elected by the village and paid a salary. Elected with him are *köy heyeti* (a group of three or four men who form a committee) who assist the *muhtar* in the governing of the village but are not salaried. Many of the responsibilities of the *muhtar* and *köy heyeti* are similar to the work of *re spis* in Iraqi Kurdistan. Along with the responsibility, trust has to be earned. They represent the village to the government of the region, and they help settle disputes and act as peacemakers. For example, a woman who continuously commits *zina* (adultery) might be warned by the committee, and they might write a decision against her and submit it to the government, which could result in her being banished from the village.

Were *muhtars* transmitters of indigenous knowledge in Turkey? This was often more of a shared task among all of the elders and not only the responsibility of the *muhtar* or members of the *köy heyeti*. People gathered in the evenings in someone's home or in a special room in the village and shared stories, gossiped, sang, and discussed events and problems that the people faced. Some evenings resembled an informal talent show as people sang, danced, or recited poetry for the audience. Respected, trustworthy *muhtars* seemed to have had a great influence on the people of their village, while others were not so highly regarded.

Are these traditional elders still respected as much as before? After speaking with a number of people on this topic, I conclude the answer is no. A *re spi* with a long track record of trustworthiness and skill in reconciliation may still be consulted, but much of his work has been replaced by more formal institutions of government. Those *re spis*, *agahs*, or *muhtars* who are respected for their integrity, honesty, and wisdom are respected because of who they are more than because of their office. One of my Iraqi Kurdish informants, while reminiscing about his father, a *re spi*, stated,

> My father was a great man and everyone wanted to come to his house and have a conference [with him]. My father was a great leader. He knew lots about Kurdish history and folklore.

Questions for Discussion

- Compare and contrast some of the strengths and weaknesses of the Kurdish family and kinship system, including first-cousin marriage, polygyny, and the clear boundaries between the domains of men and women, with family life in your culture.

- Divorce is not as accepted or prevalent in the Middle East as it is in the United States. Consider the issue of divorce from each perspective. Which do you feel is more preferable and why?

- Compare the traditional role of Kurdish women with the role of women in your culture. Do women's lives generally improve with Westernization?

- Are there similarities between the roles of your community leaders or local government officials and Kurdish *agahs*?

Notes

[1] *Dawet* literally means "invite," but in Iraqi Kurdistan it usually means the circle dancing performed at weddings and other festive occasions. At weddings, people dance in a circle for hours at a time, with each of the women in colorful costume/dress and men in Western or Kurdish clothes.

[2] The *meydan* is like a public square in Turkish cities where traffic is limited and people can walk freely up and down the streets without worrying about cars. The streets are full of shops, tea gardens, and indoor and outdoor restaurants. In large cities, major neighborhoods like Bağcılar have their own *meydan*.

[3] Alevi Kurds are Kurds who follow Ali, but call themselves Alevi rather than Shi'ites. Alevis are rather unorthodox in religious practice because they do not perform the major practices of Islam, such as ritual prayer in mosques, the fast of Ramadan, or the pilgrimage to Mecca. They have their own prayer houses (*cemevi*), but most tend to be more secular in their outlook, and they tend to be politically to the left. Often their religious identity as Alevi, rather than their ethnic identity, is primary. It is puzzling to ask someone if he or she is a Kurd, and he or she replies, "I am Alevi." There are millions of Alevi Turks as well. Alevis have suffered much discrimination and, at times, death at the hand of their Sunni neighbors. Generally the Sunni and Alevi communities do not socialize except among the more secularized youth.

Chapter 6

Core Values and Religious Rituals

> *Values are locally unquestioned standards about relative importance or desirability, and how people should therefore act. . . . Values tell you what to submit to and what to resist, how to treat your friends and fight your enemies, how to live right, how to die well.*
>
> —Dirk van der Elst, *Culture as Given, Culture as Choice*

Values are universal. We know no society that has ever existed without rules governing behavior. Every society has a written or unwritten code of behavior that is reflective of what that society holds to be proper standards of right and wrong.

Despite the animosity that Kurds often express toward Arabs, there is no doubt that due to both religious and cultural factors, the Kurds have been greatly influenced by Islamic values. As values are first learned at home, it is important to point out that there is a lack of literature about the Muslim family in the early days after Islam's domination of the Middle East. French Anthropologist Thierry Bianquis (1996) questions whether this lack is due to family life being considered too intimate, a "secret garden" or simply regarded as too trivial to justify being put into writing. Thus the world of women was the home, far removed from public life, with communication being oral with few written records of daily family life. If there is a dearth of literature about the Arab family for the first nine centuries of Islam, it is not surprising that we know little about Kurdish family structure either. Family life, core values, religious rituals and other topics discussed in this chapter are an eclectic mixture of Kurdish, Arabic, Turkish, Islamic, nomadic, village, Western, and even mountain values. Where one leaves off and another begins is not only difficult but also unnecessary to define. For example, the freedom that Kurds love could be attributed to their being mountain people, because mountain people everywhere—not only the Kurds—tend to be independent. As Izady states:

> Their history and culture are so intertwined with the mountains that the ethnic identity of Kurd on the plain becomes a contradiction in terms. Kurds themselves have a saying: "Level the mount, and in that the Kurds will be no more." . . . To a Kurd the mountain is no less than the embodiment of the deity: mountain is his mother, his refuge, his protector, his home, his farm, his market, his mate, and his only friend. This intimate man-mountain relationship shapes the physical, cultural, and psychological landscape of Kurdistan more than any other factor (1992, p. 188).

We might ask if the above statement could be made about other mountain peoples wherever they are found or is it unique to Kurds. Or consider the strong Kurdish focus on preservation of female chastity, which has been attributed to Islam positively by some of my informants, and negatively by others. Some, however, said it predates the Islamization of the Kurds and is an indigenous Kurdish value.

Children playing football (soccer) at the base of the mountain.

Denise Sweetnam (2004) lists seven core values she has observed in her years spent among the Kurds. These are: generosity, hospitality, honor, shame, loyalty, unity and community, and patience. I have combined generosity and hospitality into one as well as honor and shame. While acknowledging the importance of loyalty among Kurdish values, I think the value the Kurds place on courage, which can include loyalty, is one I have observed more. Sweetnam being a woman, no doubt spent most of her time among women, whereas, I have spent most of my time among men. Normally that might explain why I have listed courage as a core value, which might be regarded as a strongly male value. However, the Kurds are quite proud of the bravery of their women, most recently demonstrated on major news networks in the battle against Islamic State.

Within the Kurdish family (mal)structure, which we will soon examine, the following three core values stand out as especially significant.

The Importance of Hospitality

A story is told about a rich man who wanted to help a poor neighbor without hurting his neighbor's dignity. The poor man had only one lamb and no other possessions besides his little cottage. When the rich man arrived at the poor man's cottage, the poor man immediately prepared a feast for him. After eating, the rich man then offered to buy the lamb for a price that would enable the poor man to buy many more sheep. This would help him to overcome his poverty at a time when wealth was measured by the number of animals a person possessed. The poor man had butchered his only lamb to provide the feast for the rich man—an act of hospitality in accordance with standards of Kurdish hospitality.

While the Kurds are not alone among Eastern peoples in valuing hospitality, they do see it as a sacred responsibility. *Mehvan mehvanet Xude ne* (Every guest is a guest of God) is a proverb that is reflective of the importance given to hospitality. Stories abound among the Kurds about those who refused to extend hospitality, much to their regret when the person turned out to be an angel, prophet, or king. Other stories are told about a poor family that offered sacrificial hospitality to someone whom they assumed was a common person, only to find out that the stranger was an angel or king, and the family was rewarded handsomely. One *re spi* told how three rooms were set aside for guests in his village in eastern Turkey. Each guest was seen as the guest of God and people were allowed to stay without questions being asked about why they were there or how long they would stay. *Mêvanê yekî, mêvanê gundekî* (Someone's guest is the guest of the entire village) was a sentiment prevalent in most villages.

Violating the norms of hospitality can quickly lead to social ostracism. I heard of a case that involved a Western university teacher who spoke Turkish very well and was highly respected by the Turkish/Kurdish community. The teacher promised his children that the afternoon was going to be for family time and he would not let anything rob them of their time together. A prominent guest unexpectedly arrived at their home in the middle of a heavy rainstorm and expected to be welcomed with Middle Eastern hospitality, which always gives a guest priority. The teacher, however, did not invite the person inside after explaining about his promise to the children. The teacher assumed the visitor understood. The incident resulted in the teacher never regaining his former standing in the community. In the teacher's value system, a promise is a promise even if it is made to children. In the Middle Eastern mind-set, welcoming a stranger is a more important value and children should be expected to defer to guests.

Kurds often express the importance of hospitality—*Male min e, male te ye* (My home is your home) is a saying that reflects how village hosts treat their guests—but they also say that in the city the same levels of hospitality and generosity—obligation to treat all guests as if they were guests of God—are impossible to fulfill. In the village, when guests come, a man can leave his work and entertain the guests. In the city, a guest might come when the man is away at work, and his boss will not grant him leave. Because it is considered shameful for a woman to have a male visitor in the home without the husband being present, hospitality is not offered. I have seen both men and women demonstrate great stress and express how much shame they feel when the traditional standards of hospitality cannot be applied. Both the economic conditions and the time constraints of urban living seem to be taking a toll on Kurds, yet because generosity and hospitality are still valued as ideals, a degree of shame still exists when they are not adhered to as before. As urbanization continues, however, traditional standards of hospitality and generosity will be less entrenched in the minds of Kurds, and no doubt feelings of shame will diminish.

One thing has not changed, even if offered more discriminately. Whenever I eat a meal with Kurds, they always serve far more food than I can possibly consume at one meal. Platters of food that could easily feed 10 people are laid out for only one guest. They give little thought to cooking according to what can be reasonably consumed. The anxiety of not having enough for an unexpected guest, coupled with the highly esteemed value of generosity, motivates

Kurds to prepare more than could ever be eaten. In addition to the quantity of the food, the quality also must be at the highest level. Many times I have been served meat—expensive to buy and therefore not found on every table—by a poor family and have wondered when the family would taste it again. *Deste merda, demane derda.* (The hand of the generous is the remedy for problems.)

Besides being generous with food, the Kurds are generous with gifts, which I have been a recipient of many times. Once, I gave a Kurdish man a sample of some very simple American Indian handcrafts. The man was fascinated by anything pertaining to America's natives, and he was quite thrilled with the gift. He overly reciprocated by giving me several types of Kurdish handcrafts, which he could have sold for a fair amount of money. No matter how much I insisted that one or two pieces were more than enough, he would not allow me to leave until I took them all.

Pressure to be generous can become a burden. Kurds in the West find it stressful and financially taxing to purchase the expected generous gifts for family and friends in their homeland. Instead of eagerly looking forward to their visits home, they face them with anxiety. No matter what they bring or how much they send home from their often meager paychecks, the assumption is that they could have done more. Kurds have often told me how difficult it is to explain to those they leave behind that going to the United States or Europe did not automatically make them rich with endless amounts of money to send home.

The Importance of Honor

During our years in Iraqi Kurdistan, we heard often about an alleged bounty that Saddam Hussein had put on the heads of international personnel working for NGOs. The figure was said to be as high as $10,000—a large sum when teachers were receiving about $3 a month and most people were unemployed. Yet, during our years in Iraqi Kurdistan, I can recall only one expatriate having been killed. Another died in mysterious circumstances, and rumors were that his death was more about revenge than the prospect of a reward from Saddam. There was an overall distrust that Saddam would pay the money even if an employee of an NGO were killed. There is another reason that better explains why attempts were not made on the lives of internationals. Because we came to help them and came in peace as friends of the Kurds, we were considered as guests and it would be dishonorable to kill someone who came as a guest. Considering the lawlessness of the region, the total availability of every type of weapon, and the terrible economic conditions, it is a remarkable testimony to Kurdish honor that they treated us with dignity and respect. "Even Saddam said he trusted the Kurds with his life because of their honor" (a Kurdish male informant who witnessed the murder of many of his close relatives by Saddam's regime).

The above example reflects ideal Kurdish culture, but the following personifies the real and is perhaps reflective of a rapidly changing value system. "Forget the old concept of honor. The only thing that matters now is money. How it is acquired does not matter" (a middle-aged informant). While we were living in southeastern Turkey, an unmarried American couple happened to move in next door to us. The landlord of our building came to me and said that the couple's cohabitation was upsetting to him, that it was contrary to Islam, and that it was an affront to his moral values as a Muslim. He wanted me to talk to them about finding another place unless they got married quickly. I talked with the couple about the landlord's concerns (I was the mediator because the landlord spoke no English and the couple knew no Turkish), and I suggested they look for a different place. A couple of days later I asked the couple how their apartment hunting was proceeding. They said it was not necessary to move. They offered the landlord an additional $50 rent a month, and he said he was glad to have them as tenants. The latter story reflects what some Kurds have confessed has become an increasing reality: Kurdish traditional values are being overshadowed by the pursuit of material wealth.

Karama(t)

I had an insightful interview with a Kurd who lived abroad for a number of years and has since returned to Iraqi Kurdistan. He said that in the Middle East, if honor is lost, it causes the loss of karama(t) (dignity). When a Muslim feels that the Qur'an or the Prophet have been dishonored in any way, a violent reaction is almost certain to follow. This was demonstrated when allegations of the defilement of the Qur'an by American troops in Iraq was reported by U.S. media. A rumor said that American troops used the Qur'an for toilet paper. Afterwards, it was reported that the story was never substantiated, but by then the damage had already been done. Numerous deaths of civilians in various countries were alleged to be the result of the troops' behavior, although there was never official confirmation of the story. The rage demonstrated throughout the Muslim world over the caricatures negatively portraying the Prophet Muhammad, which were published in a Danish newspaper in 2005, illustrates reaction to the loss of karama(t) in a graphic way. More recently (2015) was the killing of 12 French citizens by extremist Islamic terrorists in Paris at the offices of Charlie Hebdo, an oft sacrilegious, satirical newspaper. After this incident many Muslim leaders denounced the violence, but tense relations between those advocating the right of free speech versus those who feel it is blasphemous to portray the Prophet of Islam in such a manner will most likely continue.

In addition to violations of religious sensibilities, any perceived violation of a man's household, especially involving the women of the household, can also lead to serious and often violent repercussions. The *karama(t)* and *nāmūs* or *sharaf* (honor) of the Kurdish family rests heavily on the honor of the women of the family. Kurdish women avoid any kind of behavior that could be viewed as improper. A woman will not be seen with a man other than her husband or a close male relative and will not go out alone without someone to vouch for her character. A well-known Middle Eastern adage says, "When a man and a woman are alone, Satan is the third person present."

A *re spi* told me a story that dates back to when the British controlled Iraq after the First World War. One day an English soldier could not resist the beauty of the daughter of a prominent Kurdish man, and he kissed the girl. So the *agah* of the Amediya area, named Shaban, became very angry about this. He said the British crossed a line that should not have been crossed, and he attacked the British forces. The English retreated into the Amediya valley where the Kurds attacked again and defeated the British forces even as far as Bamami. Then the English planes attacked, and the Kurds had to withdraw temporarily, but they eventually attacked the British ground forces again and forced them to leave for good.

Abuse of Women

> Before when the bride and groom spent their first night together, they put a sheet down. If there was not blood on the sheets after consummating the marriage, the girl could be killed. (A male informant in his 50s reflecting on the old days compared with today)

The concept of honor killing, killing a female because she committed sexual or marital offenses, naturally repels many who see it as the ultimate demonstration of male domination over women. For example, the idea of a woman being raped, thereby disgracing her family, and then being killed in order for the family to restore its honor, is condemned in the West as a violation of a woman's basic human rights. If a man and a woman engage in consensual sex, but are not married, the man is seldom punished; this unequal treatment is seen as another demonstration of male dominance. Author Christiane Bird (2005) spoke to numerous Kurds and asked her informants about honor killing. She found that many Kurds do not want to discuss this because of fear that it will cast a negative image on their culture. Nevertheless, she cites a figure of 4,000 honor killings since 1991, a figure she received from Kurdish activists in Iraqi Kurdistan that is impossible to verify. Some murders may not be motivated by a desire to preserve honor, but they are disguised as honor killings so the perpetrator receives a lighter sentence. Conversely, an honor killing could be made to look like an accident to disguise the real intent. Nevertheless, the practice continues throughout the Muslim world (and in some non-Muslim cultures), although many claim that it has nothing to do with Islam but rather was a practice in many cultures before the coming of the Prophet. In both Turkey and Iraq, honor killing previously was dismissed as a lesser crime than other types of murder. Since 2003, honor killing in Iraqi Kurdistan is no longer regarded as different from other types of murder in regard to punishment, but there is no evidence whether this is applied in practice.

In Turkey, when the topic of honor killing comes up, it is considered to happen in the east, hence implying it happens among the Kurds, not among the civilized Turks who are more sexually tolerant. Bird cites experts who estimate 200 honor killings in an average year in Turkey, but, again, it is impossible to know how accurate these statistics are. Parents frequently use minors to do the dirty work of killing a sister or cousin who has violated the sexual mores, assuming the minor would receive a lesser sentence. In 2005, Turkey passed a bill that makes the penalties much stiffer for honor killing as well as for harassment. Previously, if a man killed his wife or a relative killed a daughter who was guilty of *zina* (adultery), it was regarded as a crime of passion and often the perpetrator received a light sentence. With the new legislation, killing a wife even for adultery is no longer justifiable.

When I met up with a friend I had not seen in five years, he said he was divorced from his wife, whom I also knew. After much small talk in a park, he bared his soul to me, telling me that his wife had been unfaithful. He broke down and began to weep deeply while his whole body shook. He said he could tell no one about why they divorced because he would have been marked as less than a man who could not sexually satisfy his wife. He told me how he saw his wife and her lover together and beat up both of them in a fit of anger. The police came, clubbed him, and threw him in jail. The police, however, after hearing the reason for my friend's anger, apologized and said if they had known why he was beating the couple they would not have interfered.

Mango (2004) cites a Canadian sociologist who claims that between 50 and 67 percent of Turkish women are assaulted by males in the household.

Those who spend time in Turkey and develop relationships of trust will most likely see evidence of spousal abuse, especially beating. Sexual abuse is more hidden and secretive, and is usually only revealed to someone who has a close relationship with the one abused. Women fear being perceived as the culprit rather than the victim in sexual abuse cases, and most suffer in silence and shame. This does not imply there is more sexual abuse in Turkey or in other Middle Eastern countries or than in the United States, because there is no way of knowing. It is definitely less discussed, however.

The city of Batman in southeastern Turkey has received much notoriety because of suicide rates among female residents. Batman is a relatively new city filled with men and their wives who have migrated from the villages, attracted by the opportunities afforded by the oil industry and other related industries. Batman's newness makes it a place where the patriarchal structure of the village dominates the mores of the people. However, at the same time, the social networks that people relied on for support when they lived in their village are not present in Batman. Instead, in Batman, poverty, the inability to speak Turkish, and a lack of education cut off many women from even simple diversions like television, because Turkish at the time was the language of the media. (Kurdish media has increased since then.) In addition, Kurdish Hez-bollah, the Islamist group that formed as an alternative to the PKK and is not related to the Hezbollah group based in Lebanon, contributes to the despair many women feel by using religion to justify the mistreatment of women. Reports of women who hang themselves or throw themselves off buildings appear in the papers. The Kurdish treatment of women remains paradoxical: it is a point of pride that their treatment of women is more advanced than the treatment women receive in other Middle Eastern nations, yet the greatest abuse of women, in Turkey at least, occurs in Kurdish regions.

Kurdish nationalists like to say that most of the negative practices, be it honor killing, *purdah* (gender segregation), or extreme male domination of women are the results of Kurds having lived under Arabs, Turks, and Persians for so long. They point out that throughout Kurdish history women have played an important role and had more freedom than other women in the region. They say that when the Kurds get out from under the control of their hegemons, their women will be in even a better situation. Yet, in Turkey, it is the Kurds who are perceived as the ones who are most likely to arrange forced marriages, practice polygyny, conduct honor killings, judge a woman by the number of children she can produce, and have a higher rate of suicide among women than Turks.

Courage

I am still willing to fight and sacrifice my life for the family of Barzani, who have led us Kurds to the victory we celebrate today. (Ahmed Hajee Mirkhan Baarky, a Peshmerga)

Traditionally Kurdish men were judged by the level of courage displayed in warfare. While courage is still considered a virtue admired primarily in men, female Peshmerga have fought as bravely as the best of men.

Among the PKK, women have fought as guerillas alongside the men. The PKK among the Kurds in Turkey, however, do not have the respect that the Peshmerga have among the Iraqi Kurds. Admiration for the PKK is seldom expressed openly, although there have been more open displays of support for the guerillas, especially at funeral ceremonies. Turkish soldiers who are killed in the war against the PKK are called *şehit* (martyr), an adoption of the Qur'anic title for those killed in defending Islam. The PKK also label their warriors as *şehit*. Generally—whether due to fear of the Turkish government or because of disagreement with the ideology and methodology of the PKK—there is far less popular support for PKK warriors than there is for the Peshmerga among Iraqi Kurds.

Earlier I cited the courage demonstrated by the Iraqi Kurds who fought with Mustafa Barzani. The stories are part of the folklore of the people and are transmitted to the next generation with pride. But will stories of Peshmerga courage continue to be passed down if the Iraqi Kurds achieve a measure of peace and no longer have to fight against their enemies? Military service is required for all men in both Turkey and Iraq; it is in the Turkish military that many young men leave the Kurdish regions to perform their military service in other parts of Turkey. For many, after serving for 18 months in modern cities like Istanbul, returning to their traditional village is no longer appealing. Furthermore, many Kurds develop a stronger national identity in the military and feel a greater sense of being part of the Turkish nation—something that remains with them after completing their *askerlik* (required military service).

In the military, Kurds distinguish themselves by feats of daring and combat skills. Many Kurds, whatever their motivation, demonstrate loyalty to the Turkish state by their efforts to squash the PKK rebellion or by patrolling regions where the PKK operate. Because the military is a politically sensitive topic, I refrained from asking Kurds about their military experiences. I wanted to be careful not to appear to be a journalist rather than an ethnographer. Kurds did tell me of the inner turmoil they felt when they heard Turkish government classify their people as terrorists, even though the Kurdish majority does not support the PKK. The few who discussed the PKK topic said the PKK has to be resisted, but at the same time, for there to be any hope of a solution to the problem, the Turkish government needs to address the conditions that created the PKK.

Other Important Values

Respect for Others but Not for Each Other

In Iraqi Kurdistan, our NGO's team of Kurdish engineers worked incredibly hard, driving an hour each way to get to our warehouse, after which they often had to drive several more hours to get to remote villages in the mountains to supervise the construction of shelters and schools. The temperature was often over 100 degrees, sometimes over 120, and none of the vehicles had air-conditioning. Furthermore, none of these engineers received a salary of more than $100 a month. I began to hear increasing allegations of cheating in the distribution of construction materials, with each group of engineers accusing the other. Cheating consisted of ordering more cement, poplar trees (used for roofs), and other construction materials than needed and then selling the excess materials in the market. The returning refugees who were being resettled then accused the engineers of not giving them their proper share of the allotment. We decided to downsize our program considerably, and I had the painful task of firing some very good engineers who had become my friends. I told the engineers that I could not deal with their constant accusations of cheating.

Many years later when I visited Kurdistan again, I met with some of the engineers I had fired. They treated me with the utmost respect, showed me generous hospitality, and set up several of the interviews with the *re spi* for my research. Yet, there was a barrier between us, which I tried to overcome by telling them that I still felt sorry about what happened and how it was handled. I said I could not understand why there had been so much infighting and backstabbing. I learned that the engineers in one city resented that we had hired so many engineers from another city an hour away, instead of hiring their relatives and friends who lived in the city where our headquarters was located. The geographical problem (turf wars) was interspersed with tribal and kinship rivalries that I was also unaware of at the time. The engineers pointed out that it is part of their culture to slander each other and put down anyone who seems to be moving ahead. They said I should not have taken the accusations of the refugees seriously. I confessed my own mistakes in the matter and asked their forgiveness. None of the engineers admitted to cheating, although one privately said that probably everyone felt justified to some degree in playing with some numbers to sell cement and other construction materials in the market because of the low wages. In that sense, I was "vindicated." The incident points to the types of misunderstandings caused by cultural differences. Although the Kurds often demonstrate a lack of respect for each other, for them, the behavior does not have the same negative connotations as it might in other cultures.

The Kurds are not alone in this tendency to show more respect for outsiders and less respect for one another. It is a characteristic found in many cultures, particularly those that have been under domination by others. Attitudes of disrespect by the oppressors pass down to the oppressed who then disrespect their ethnic kin and take on characteristics of the oppressor.

Truthfulness

> As soon as we Turks meet someone, the first thing that comes to our minds is, "How can I con this person?" That is why Turkey does not develop despite having the most natural resources in the world. (A middle-aged informant)

While outside forces are often blamed for Turkey's failure to reach its enormous potential, despite having an abundance of natural resources and almost perfect climate, some blame the problem on the mentality reflected in the quote above. During my years in the Middle East, no virtue seemed more respected and less practiced than truthfulness. Those who can be trusted to tell the truth are said to be very rare. When the people of Turkey want to emphasize that someone is a good person, they often say *yalan yok* (literally, there are no lies). In Turkish, the truthful man is called a *sözü geçen adam* (a man whose word comes to pass).

One young Kurdish man who is involved in tourism expressed frustration with how people constantly scheme and try to deceive tourists. However, it does not end with hustling tourists; it is extended to everyone. Consequently, knowing who can be trusted becomes increasingly difficult as people have been deceived so often. This young man, who is paid a paltry salary to sell souvenirs to tourists, blames the lack of truthfulness on economic factors, which have come into play after moving from the village to the city where familiar social structures do not exist, but serious financial demands do. Trying to survive without a support system leads people to become deceptive—to get as much as they can, even dishonestly. Probably due to the lack of truth telling that seems prevalent in the city, when Kurds want to convince someone they are telling the truth, they often lace conversations with references to the name of God, as do Turks and Arabs as well. Kurds say phrases like *bi Xude* (by God), or *bi Allah,* or *liser Qur'an* (on the Qur'an), or *liser hisar Qur'an* (on a thousand Qur'ans), or just *Qur'an.* They might also say *Wa Allah* or *vallahi* (I swear to God).

Foreigners, in contrast, especially those from the West, are considered to be truthful. *Ejnebi direw nakin* (Foreigners don't lie), even if they are thought to be immoral in other areas. King (2000) confirms my observations that there is little trust in society. Women especially feel they have no one to talk to and often tell things to a Westerner (often about sexual abuse) that they would tell no one else. I have been admonished to trust no one in the Middle East. There seems to be little agreement about why this degree of mistrust and lack of truthfulness are so prevalent.

Friendship

One Iraqi Kurd explained the Kurdish proverb, "There is bread and salt between me and you," like this:

> When they eat a meal with someone and they share bread together, there is bread and salt between them. They are friends but more like brothers. If the friendship is perceived to have been betrayed or one does not protect the other one, the man is said to be *be nan u qwe* [without bread and salt].

Friendship is taken very seriously by the Kurds, and loyalty to a friend is assumed. Friendship means commitment through good times and bad and can get awkward when financial issues are involved. One of the difficulties in Kurdish society, especially in Iraq, is grasping the complex network of acquaintances based on kinship or tribal connections. These networks are so pervasive that it is assumed that the rest of the world operates the same way. When conditions became desperate in Northern Iraq, Kurds assumed I could arrange for them to get a visa from the United States—even directly from then-President Bill Clinton. Although it was never said, I felt like my Kurdish friends perceived me as being uninterested in saving the lives of their families and giving them a chance for a better life in America.

When scholarships were to be offered to especially deserving Iraqi Kurds to do graduate studies at Harvard University, a lawyer, who was a friend of one of my NGO's former employees, sent in his application forms, including references from U.N. officials, but he was not accepted. He felt that his connection to me (through his friend) should be enough for me to recommend him to Harvard, even if I had only just met him. I could not seem to convince him that even if I had known him longer, I did not have the power or connections at Harvard to get him into the program.

The concept of close friendship is known as *girivyati*. Among the Yazidis, if one becomes a *giriv* it signifies a kinship as close as a blood relationship. As an example of *girivyati*, before puberty, a family will ask a man they respect to allow their child to be circumcised on the respected one's lap. This binds the family to the man in a manner that may last generations. Sweetnam (2004) points out something that my informants did not: the *giriv* relationship is so symbolic of kinship that families connected by *girivyati* cannot marry each other. *Girivyati* can be between a Yazidi and a Muslim Kurd, or even an Arab; it transcends religious and ethnic orientation. It is not a practice that is universal among the Kurds, however, and it is not practiced everywhere even among Yazidis.

A key feature of *girivyati* is the commitment to loyalty. When someone in the *giriv*'s "family" has any type of need, it is assumed that the *giriv* will address the need. For example, if someone has an enemy or someone kills a member of the *giriv*'s "family," it is expected, without question, that the *giriv* will seek revenge. Even if the dead person acted wrongly, it is still expected for the *giriv* to help or take revenge on his behalf. It is a call to unconditional friendship and loyalty, a relationship that should be as close as any relationship between blood brothers. It does appear, however, that the institution is weakening and now the *giriv* can refuse to assist the "family" or seek revenge on their behalf if the cause is not justified in the *giriv*'s mind.

Attitudes toward Work

Heta kefa deste resh nebit, tama devi xwesh nabit. (If you don't work until your hands become black, your mouth will not get full.) I previously quoted this proverb, and I illustrate it further with a couple of stories. One day a large truck carrying building materials pulled into the warehouse of our NGO and needed to be unloaded. That day, the laborers who would normally do the unloading were working somewhere else. I was the director of the organization and no matter how much I would have liked to get my hands dirty and do some hard labor, the engineers around me would not let me. This time, however, I insisted and began to unload the truck myself. Eventually the engineers pitched in until the job was finished. I could tell they did not like having to do the work of a laborer. After all, they were college graduates, were from prominent families, and were not supposed to get their hands dirty. I heard the engineers discussing whether or not the laborers would still respect them when they heard about what the engineers did. This attitude is contrary to the proverb above that glorifies having one's hands black from hard work. The Kurds admire hard work and often use the phrase *Ew galek zirek e* (He is very hard-working). Yet the stratification of society regulates what kind of work should be conducted by different types of people. In contrast to the early 1990s, when almost all Kurds were unemployed, now it is South Asians and people from other nations that do much of the manual labor and staffing of fast-food restaurants.

In Turkey, I had a similar experience while I was staying in a Kurdish village with a family that was in the process of fixing up a second-floor apartment with money they had been saving for several years from harvesting pistachios. I happened to visit them in the middle of the work. The contractor said he could not delay his work a day because of a backlog of customers, so my host reluctantly informed me that he would have to help with the work on the last day of my visit. I told him I would be glad to help as well. He was rather embarrassed by this, but I insisted, and I spent a full day sanding the concrete walls to prepare them for painting. The family interrupted me every few minutes to get me to stop. Then visitors came by to watch an American sandpaper a Kurdish home, which was regarded as a major event.

I have tried to explain to my Kurdish friends that there is not as rigid a stratification of levels of work in the United States as there is in the Middle East—that many educated people like to work with their hands, repair their own houses, or voluntarily build homes for the needy. Nurses who are used to a level of prestige in Western cultures are not given the same level of status in the Middle East because nursing is considered degrading work. Doing what Kurds consider to be degrading or low-status work to help my host family was a service that made me feel useful. Convincing them that this type of work did not bruise my ego, but instead brought me pleasure, proved to be quite challenging; they interpret acts of service differently than Americans do.

Tourism and Entrepreneurialism

Thousands of youth from the Kurdish regions of Turkey flood the tourist-rich areas near the Aegean and Mediterranean seas as well as Istanbul in search of work during the peak tourist season. There they are exposed to a lifestyle that makes it hard to go back to the plainness and simplicity of the village. Kurds in restaurants and hotels tell me why such large numbers of them are hired. First, they are willing to work for less money than most Turks. Second, they have an aptitude for learning languages quickly and well—a topic that merits further research. Third, they have the ability to warm up to people quickly. Kurds are proud of being *canı yakın* (literally "close to soul," or very personable and outgoing), and they often compare themselves to foreigners or Turks by saying that Kurds are more *canı yakın*.[1]

Kurds are successful entrepreneurs. A Kurdish village, one of several Kurdish villages in a predominantly Turkish region, was going through a terrible draught, causing farming and animal husbandry to suffer. Most of the men had migrated either to larger cities or to Europe, leaving their families behind while continuing to send monetary support. The people who remained in the village complained about the lack of government assistance, but they also pointed with pride to three Internet cafes and a small library they had established on their own by selling handicrafts or setting up other types of small businesses.

The Kurds in Iraqi Kurdistan are also remarkably resourceful. They find ways to obtain the latest technology as quickly as it arrives on the market in the West. Almost everyone carries a cell phone, many if not most families have a satellite dish, and Internet cafes are springing up everywhere. Smuggling across borders is so pervasive that one can find spices, clothing, and electronics from anywhere in the world sold in one-person shops. Kurdish shopkeepers smile shyly and say something like, "*Millete Kurd zirek in*" (The Kurdish people are industrious).

Shame and Guilt Cultures

When I taught English to adults in Turkey from 1982 to 1991, discussions about cultural differences between Western and Turkish society were of foremost interest to my students. At tea houses and restaurants, in remote villages, in refugee camps, and at work places in urban settings, comparing and contrasting American culture with Kurdish, Turkish, and/or Islamic culture always struck a chord of interest. The West is perceived by Muslims, including the Kurds, as a place of attraction and repulsion and of liberty and vice. On one hand, it is a place that offers unlimited financial opportunity and the freedom to live without societal constraints; on the other, it is a place of degeneration and moral decay.

I often compare what anthropologists call guilt-focused cultures, in which guilt is primarily a matter between the person and his or her conscience, with shame cultures, in which falling short of society's expectations leads to feelings of shame. In Western culture, people make moral choices based on their individualized sense of right and wrong in accordance with their own conscience and values. That is not to deny there are social constraints, but freedom to choose one's religious and moral path, as long as the choice does not harm someone else, is seen as almost a divine right. One person may feel intense guilt about a certain practice, while another person may not feel guilt at all. Middle Eastern Muslim culture, by contrast, is primarily shame focused: a sense of right and wrong comes from society, perhaps more than the individual's conscience. Shame is more pronounced than guilt; individuals' consciences take a back seat to the sense of shame they feel when violating societal norms.

Many Kurds do not understand or are repulsed by Western practices they hear about or see on television. For example, they wonder why people in the West are allowed to live together without being married; why young people are not restricted from premarital sexual activity; and perhaps most difficult for them to understand, how people can be openly homosexual.

It is generally concluded in these discussions that in the West, *günah* (sinful practice) is more open, whereas in the Middle East, practices that violate traditional norms, especially of a sexual nature, also occur but are conducted more secretly so as not to bring shame on the family and the community. I have often heard Kurds discuss the hypocrisy of many of their fellow Muslims who come from very strict, oil-rich Islamic countries, such as Saudi Arabia, where every type of vice is forbidden. When they visit Istanbul or European cities and are away from the constraints of their own societies, they do the very things that are forbidden, including hiring male and female prostitutes, gambling, and drinking alcohol.

After discussing shame and guilt aspects of Muslim and Western cultures, I often asked my Middle Eastern students to list the ideals of their society and contrast them with the realities of everyday life. Then I would contrast American ideals with the realities the students saw on television. We concluded that both Islamic and Western society suffer from failure to live up to the ideals of their religion and society. Each individual and culture contains an element of the divine and carries the stamp of its Creator, while also reflecting the disjointed state of humankind, manifested in behavior that leads to both guilt and shame.

Signs of Moral Laxity

A leading Turkish newspaper reported a survey conducted among 3,500 primary and middle school students. According to this survey, which did not reflect region or ethnicity, almost 20 percent of the students have had sex at least once. Out of this 20 percent, 25 percent had their first sexual experience at the age of 13 or younger. Do these statistics reflect a present reality that would make "sexual honor" as known before obsolete in the days ahead? One can only hope that irresponsible sexual activity does not become rampant.

Diane King (2000), who worked as an anthropologist in Northern Iraq, was able to inquire about changing sexual mores, including prostitution. She cites an increasing acceptance of prostitution to some degree, although it must take place discreetly. Jwaideh (2006) points out that there is no word for prostitution in Kurdish, probably because traditionally it has been so rare. Arabic and Turkish words for prostitution are used by the Kurds today. Even young boys are known to offer themselves to the thousands of Turkish truckers who wait for days for their turn to cross the border to transport petrol. In the past, women had been killed for engaging in prostitution—including those who had no other means of survival, such as Anfal widows. In places like Zakho, a border town, some sex for pay is overlooked by authorities. King cites a woman who says, "After the uprising, the new Kurdish government killed many 'bad women' (accused prostitutes and/or adulterers) in Kurdistan, but now they just don't care so they do nothing about this problem" (p. 252).

In the past, women and men were both ostracized and sometimes severely punished for adultery, but friends have told me that men openly take mistresses in Iraqi Kurdistan with little social disapproval. In Turkey, sexual standards in general are less stringent than in Iraq, especially among men. I was told that men with attractive wives may rent them out at times, although how widely this is practiced is impossible to know.

I have some friends who recently got married. The new bride came from a family that hosted frequent visitors. After the couple set up their own household, they wanted to continue the practice of having guests and invite the husband's friends over for tea and discussion. They have had to discontinue the practice, however, as they heard rumors that their neighbors assumed that the men were giving the newly married husband money to sleep with his pretty, artificially blonde wife.

In the city, one payoff for having many children is the sad practice of fathers who, driven by economic need, marry off their daughters to older men for a substantial bride-price. Equally tragic, and contrary to traditional Kurdish values, are the fathers who loan out their daughters as prostitutes. In traditional Kurdish culture, the entire family took responsibility for protecting the reputation and chastity of the daughters. The differences in new and traditional values are significant. In one city of under 100,000 people, a shop owner claimed that friends of his in the police department told him that there are at least 600 homes in his city where fathers use their wives or daughters as prostitutes in their own homes.

Russian Women and the Changing Moral Climate

There has traditionally been a lax attitude toward prostitution in Turkey, and most large cities have an area that is under government control where men can pay to have sex. Since the breakup of the Soviet Union, Turkey has been flooded with thousands of women from the former Soviet countries and Eastern Europe—including Russia, Ukraine, Armenia, Georgia, Moldova, Azerbaijan, and Romania—who come to Turkey to work as prostitutes. The number and brazenness of these women has, by some standards, gotten out of hand. In some cities, my travel companion and I had difficulty finding a hotel that did not allow prostitutes to ply their trade and bother us throughout the night. There are stories of fathers and sons who fall in love with and fight over the same woman, men who spend all of their money on prostitutes while their families go hungry, and families that break up. In one city, I sat with five men, two of whom admitted to abandoning their wives and taking up with Russian women. In light of the fact that social mores make it unacceptable for Turkish women to express a need for sex or to express pleasure from the act, Turkish men will sleep with the same prostitute over and over, as the less inhibited Russian women express sexual satisfaction more openly, thus fulfilling the ego needs of the men. In many cases, the men eventually fall in love with the prostitutes.

During a day spent with some men who buy and sell fish as a livelihood, we drove a long way over some crumbling roads to reach a remote place near a large lake where they purchase fish from fishermen, after haggling about the price. The building next to the lake is a brothel, normally full of Russian women, but was temporarily shut down due to unsanitary conditions. I asked the men how people found the place, so far away from the major highway and reachable by bad roads that are nearly impassible by car. They replied that no matter how far or remote the place, if there are women the people will come. On the way back to the city, my companions pointed out all of the establishments— one every couple of kilometers—where men could pay for Russian prostitutes. The illicit money from prostitution, primarily using women from the former Soviet states, was estimated at $3.6 billion. Like prostitution, illegal drug use in Turkey is also on the rise. Kurds are very much involved in both drug running and the pimping of Russian girls, which leaves us with the impression that they have ventured a long way from the traditional occupations of shepherding and farming. Many Kurds whom I interviewed blamed the growth of prostitution and other types of social decay on urbanization. It appears, however, that the number of women coming from the former Soviet countries has decreased recently due to better economic conditions in their own countries.

Religious Values and Rituals

Orthodox Islamic Practice

Turkey, a religiously conservative country struggling to maintain a balance between being a modern, secular state patterned after European countries without losing its Islamic heritage, has adopted its own brand of Islam. Mango (2004) cites the following statistics based on a survey conducted in 1999 by a social studies foundation. This survey found that 92 percent kept the Ramadan fast to some degree, 46 percent conducted the five daily required prayers, 62 percent attended Friday mosque services, 68 percent sacrificed sheep during *kurban bayramı* (a festival that marks the beginning of the hajj to Mecca), 7 percent had performed the hajj, and 71 percent intend to someday. However, only 21 percent want sharia (Islamic law) enforced, and most people seem ignorant of what sharia contains (pp. 132–133). If Atatürk could return to his country today, he would be shocked that some people still observe Islamic rituals after he tried so hard to secularize the country. He would be relieved, however, to know that most Turks want their own brand of privatized Islam, not the Iranian or Saudi Arabian type that governs every aspect—religious and secular life.

In a village high in the mountains of eastern Turkey, during the long months of winter when the village is under snow, the men gather in one of the *re spi*'s homes and discuss Islam and other topics until the late hours of the day. One of the well-known men in the village, who formerly was a heavy drinker and womanizer and was said to have connections to the Mafia, evidently had a type of conversion experience in which he became a passionate Muslim who wants to discuss the Qur'an and nothing else. He has even urged the hotel owners who cater to tourists in the area to shut down their bars because drinking alcohol is forbidden in Islam. He also urges them not to give rooms to couples who are not married and to forbid other non-Islamic practices.

Another informant, while reminiscing about his life in the village before moving to a large city, said that for eleven months a year the evening village discussions concerned worldly events. During the month of Ramadan, however, the Qur'an and religion played a dominant role in the discussions. He somewhat wryly made the comment that for eleven months a year the people lived for the devil, and for one month they lived for Allah.

Low and High Religion

Low religion (often called folk religion) is the level of belief that primarily focuses on the manipulation of spiritual forces in order to help those who feel powerless to cope with life's difficulties. Low religion is down-to-earth and deals with temporal concerns or difficulties in life such as barrenness, financial needs, and protection from evil forces. High religion, in contrast, is primarily concerned with the major ethical and philosophical questions of life, including questions of origins, the purpose of existence, and the afterlife.

Kurds cross religious boundaries when life forces work against them. An Eastern Orthodox priest whom I have known for many years says that Kurdish Muslim women frequently ask him to make them amulets with verses from the Injil (New Testament) inside. They then ask a Muslim *hoca* (folk religious practitioner) to do the same with Qur'anic verses. Theological issues that divide Christians and Muslims do not matter to these women. They have concerns that are more pragmatic: protection for them and their families from evil spiritual powers and curses, such as barrenness, the illness of a child, or a husband's desire for a second wife.

Something resembling the hand of Fatima, the daughter of the Prophet Muhammad, is often displayed in homes and places of business as an amulet to ward off evil. Another symbolic ward is the presence of blue beads, *nazar boncuğu*, which people pin on their babies' clothing to protect them from the evil eye of jealousy. Muslim parents fear that if someone with a jealous eye observes others praising a newborn baby or young child, the jealous observer will put a curse on the child. This fear is especially present with regard to male babies, because boys are more desired than girls. This leads some families to dress the infant in an unattractive way, or to dress a boy as a girl. Sometimes parents deliberately dirty a boy's face to make him less attractive and thus less likely to draw the evil eye of jealousy. Almost every child in Turkey has a blue bead pinned on his or her clothing until the child begins to walk. Furthermore, many adults carry the beads on a key chain or attach them to their car. Parents further protect their babies by continually repeating the word *Maşallah* (May God protect) whenever their babies are praised or fussed over. Jwaideh (2006) cites the practice of Kurds standing vigil over newborn babies, particularly boys. The fear of an evil spirit attacking the baby is ever present, especially if envy by a childless older woman is directed against the baby. Sometimes a piece of cloth blessed by a sheikh is used as an amulet to protect against curses.

Jwaideh (2006) highlights the importance of *sheikhs*. Often the leaders of Kurdish rebellions were *sheikhs* like Sheikh Sa'id in the 1925 rebellion in Turkey. *Sheikhs* carried both religious and political power, and especially charismatic *sheikhs* could become quite powerful. Jwaideh cites the biblical verse

"No Prophet has honor in his own country" to show that *sheikh*s were generally outsiders rather than members of the tribe or from the location where they ruled. As a *sheikh* built a reputation for good works and piety, he might establish ties of marriage with the head of a village or a tribal chief. As he became more powerful, he might try to have his children marry people of higher rank, thus cementing the family lines and increasing his influence.

Jwaideh says that the Kurdish character is religiously tolerant but can be driven to fanaticism if incited by a *sheikh*, especially if a perceived miraculous event is involved. There are stories about *sheikh*s who had bullets pass through their bodies without harming them but killing people who were behind them. There were *sheikh*s who could understand another language even if they had not learned it. Because many of these *sheikh*s traced their ancestry back to the Prophet Muhammad, they were regarded as miracle workers with a lot of *baraka* (spiritual power). However, if the charisma was no longer in evidence, the *sheikh*'s power could be reduced quickly.

The contrast between high and low religions was permanently imprinted on my mind during a visit to a well-known mosque in Istanbul. At the Friday noon prayer, there were probably 1,000 men in attendance, performing the ritual Muslim prayer—an example of high religion.[2] But at the shrine of a long-deceased Muslim saint located next to the mosque, most of the visitors were women. In the shrine, the women drank holy water, touched the Prophet's footprints, and made vows to other objects of veneration—especially at the tomb of the saint who is said to help people in distress—an example of low religion. This does not mean that men never practice low religion or that women never practice high religion. Women may experience high religion in groups where women study the Qur'an together, generally with a female teacher. Women and men perform their *salat* (ritualistic prayers) with the women praying behind the men. In some Sufi (Islamic mysticism) groups, there is more mixing of the genders and many of the great Sufi "saints" have been female. Among the Alevis there is generally more female participation in religious rituals, sometimes leading to charges by Sunni Muslims that Alevis are immoral and *kafir* (infidels). For a variety of sociocultural, spiritual, and economic reasons, however, a woman may feel the need for a more pragmatic faith that addresses her daily needs, rather than a more abstract faith that wrestles with more philosophic issues.

Nothing is more terrifying to a traditional Muslim woman than not being able to bear a son to present to her husband. Many of the women who flock to Christian or Muslim shrines to request the help of dead holy people or who seek the help of living holy people are unable to conceive children. It does not matter whether the holy person is male or female; living or dead; Christian, Muslim, or Jew. What does matter is the level of *baraka* that is present and whether people's petitions are answered.

In addition to fearing barrenness, women fear their husbands will forsake them for another woman, leaving them destitute and shamed. While women are generally tolerant of a husband who visits a brothel occasionally, especially when she is pregnant or ill, the risk of losing her husband to another lover is far more serious. In Turkey, some wives may put a few drops of their urine in their husband's tea, which is supposed to tie the husband to his wife in a magical way, preventing him from leaving her for another woman.

To understand the worldview of folk Muslims, including Kurds, one must realize that there is a sense of predestination (*qadir, kismet*), leading to resignation about life; at the same time, everything possible to change a person's *kismet* may be tried. High Islam is about submission to the will of Allah, but folk Islam is about manipulating *kismet* to change what has been "written in advance" (*maktūb*)—predestined. *Maktūb* can give people a calmness in adversity and patience to go through whatever life throws at them. On the other hand, it can lead to passivity and unwillingness to take steps to improve their life or work toward the betterment of society in general, which is a complaint that educated and successful people often make against those stuck in cycles of poverty and squalor.

It is debated whether urbanization is as strong a secularizing force as it may initially appear. Without the social pressure of the village, people who live in urban areas may not conduct the required Islamic ritual practices faithfully. However, the folk practices I have described are still preformed in the city. It is social pressure, not religious conviction, that most commonly compels people to attend mosque and appear to keep the Ramadan fast even if they break it in secret. A smaller percentage will totally break with organized religion, as did the earlier PKK members or those who joined other radical leftist organizations. Others may attend the mosque only on special holy days and are otherwise secular in their outlook.

The evolving effects of urbanization on religious practice—whether some people become more devout in order to find solace in a rapidly changing world, or others become less so—have not seemed to diminish folk practices, which continue as if little has changed. What has been "written," for many Kurds, is perceived as not desirable. The struggle to unwrite the written—to alter what has been predestined—continues.

Questions for Discussion

- Compare and contrast the three syndromes of traditional Middle Eastern values with the primary values in your own culture. Are values such as honor, hospitality, and courage deemed as important in your culture as they are among the Kurds?

- Besides the three major value syndromes, the author discusses other values, including friendship, truthfulness, social stratification, respect, and industriousness. Can you illustrate how values like these play out in your culture?

- Explain the differences between guilt-focused cultures and shame-focused cultures.

- The author discusses high and low religious rituals and practices as found among the Kurds. What aspects of low (folk) religion have you observed in your own culture or a culture with which you are familiar? Are these practices considered deviant from high religious aspects?

Notes

[1] Most of the international NGO personnel whom I knew during our years in Iraqi Kurdistan became so emotionally involved with their Kurdish employees, because the Kurds were so personable and outgoing, that they often lost their objectivity. I remember long, protracted arguments that broke out over promotions and layoffs of local staff. Expatriates were so attached to their Kurdish employees that fierce arguments over who should be promoted or demoted would break out, with each international arguing over the merits of his or her staff members.

[2] Women are allowed in mosques, and there is generally a room set aside at the back of a mosque for women. The idea is that if men see women while performing their ritual prayers, they will be distracted from their worship of Allah. Women are not required to go to a mosque for prayer whereas men are supposed to go to a mosque if possible. Therefore, men greatly outnumber women at mosques, most clearly demonstrated on Friday at the noon hour, the holiest time of the week in Islam.

Chapter 7

Rapid Urbanization and Culture Change

In Britain first, and then elsewhere, industrialization meant a shift of people from overwhelmingly agrarian activities to industrial activities, giving rise to urbanization, social mobility, new gender and family roles, a demographic transition, and specialization in labor.

—Jeffrey Sachs, *The End of Poverty*

German sociologist Ferdinand Tönnies (2002) used two German words—*gemeinschaft* and *gesellschaft*—to describe two types of society. *Gemeinschaft* (community) is found primarily in preindustrial societies and is characterized as face to face, connected by close kin or tribal ties, homogenous in culture, informal, intimate, carrying a strong sense of cooperative responsibility, deep attachment to place, and a tendency toward ascribed social status (social status inherited at birth). *Gesellschaft* (society) is urban, formal, heterogeneous, self-focused, competitive, and orientated toward achieved status (social status based on performance). Traditional Kurdish rural culture as it existed for centuries in Turkey and Iraqi Kurdistan can be classified as *gemeinschaft*. As the Kurds experience massive levels of urbanization, however, their society reflects the characteristics of *gesellschaft*.

There can be a degree of overlap between the two types of societies, as people transition from preindustrial lifestyles that are generally found in rural environments to industrialized urban contexts. Joseph Gusfield lists seven fallacies about traditional and modern societies: (1) traditional societies are static, (2) traditional culture is made up of a consistent cannon of core values and unchanging beliefs, (3) traditional societies are built on a homogenous

125

social structure, (4) when society changes, the traditional is replaced by the modern, (5) the traditional and the modern are always in conflict, (6) they are mutually exclusive, and (7) modernization always weakens the traditional (cited in Fagerline and Saha, 1989, p. 112).

According to Gusfield traditional and modern societies are not that different from each other. For example, Kurdish rural society is not static by any means. Even in the smallest villages, one meets Kurds who have been to the cities outside of Kurdistan or even abroad. They have brought modern technologies to the village and discuss the world outside with those who have remained in the village. Shepherds and farmers who cannot read use cell phones and CD players. Those who have migrated to the cities have not automatically become urbanized or modernized. The first generation who moves from the village to live in the city are basically *urban villagers*—physically in the city, but mentally in the village.

There are *push and pull* aspects of urban attraction. The push of poverty and joblessness, coupled with the social restrictions placed on freedom of expression and lifestyle by conservative social forces, have pushed millions around the world to move to major cities. Job possibilities, coupled with increasing exposure to television and its imagery of prosperity and an exciting lifestyle that can be found in cities, have been major factors in pulling hundreds of thousands of Kurds to cities like Istanbul.

Displaced Kurds

Although there are similarities between traditional and modern societies, without question, forces of urbanization and modernization have led to massive changes in the lives of hundreds of millions of people in recent years, including the Kurds. An example of the magnitude of the demographic shift from rural to urban can be seen in Istanbul, which is far away from the traditional homelands of the Kurds, but contains more Kurds within its city limits than any one city in Kurdistan itself.

Villages in both Iraqi Kurdistan and in Turkey are breathtakingly beautiful, high in the mountains with fertile farmland below and cool mountain streams flowing through the village. Yet few people continue to live there, and those who remain are mostly the elderly and children. The men have moved to cities or migrated out of the country altogether. In one mountain village, I met a man who has 10 children. All but one has left the village. The remaining son is managing the family plot of land and a few animals, while the rest of his brothers and sisters work in Istanbul. Another family said that out of their nine children, only one has remained. I saw this pattern over and over throughout my travels.

In Iraq, many Kurds are moving to cities that are primarily under Kurdish administration and have a connectedness to the villages. These Kurds have ready access to their ancestral village. Although there are an estimated one million Kurds in Baghdad and thousands more in other cities not under Kurdish administration, I was unable to make firsthand observations in those places and focused on the phenomena as it exists in Turkey.

In many mountainous regions affected by the conflict between Turkish security forces and the PKK in the 1980s and 1990s, the Turkish government has forbidden grazing animals. Animal husbandry, which had been a source of rural income for centuries, has virtually disappeared in some regions, forcing thousands of people to leave their villages. In addition, 3,000 villages were destroyed during the government operations against the PKK, and most of the displaced people have had to relocate in urban areas. According to a 2006 Human Rights Watch World Report, most of the 378,335 Kurdish villagers who were displaced during the conflict between Turkish security forces and PKK rebels have not been able to return to their villages in southeastern Turkey. Many are unwilling to return to villages that do not have electricity, telephone service, or a school, or they have found work in the city and are reluctant to give up the income they receive. A male informant originally

Displaced Iraqi Kurds living in public buildings, 1991.

from a beautiful mountain village, who found a job selling small cups of tea along the seacoast in Istanbul said: "Do you think I want to be here? I love my village; my family is there. But, what choice have I got?"

Although the government is supposed to provide compensation to the displaced Kurdish villagers, it has been unevenly applied, with some receiving and others not receiving government help to resettle. For many Kurds in Turkey, adjustment to urban contexts far removed from their beloved mountains and the natural environment of their homeland has been difficult. Turkish cities are filled with people living in marginalized squatter settlements (*gecekondu*s) or in hastily built apartment blocks. Teahouses overflow with unemployed men playing backgammon or cards while smoking, and drinking countless cups of tea. Other men wait on street corners hoping for day-to-day construction work, or they push handcarts up and down the streets trying to sell whatever they can lay their hands on.

In large Turkish cities where every job is precious, people are on a regular hunt for ways to survive. Salesmen board the trains or ferry boats and attempt to sell every type of trinket or device that they possibly can. People make tea and offer it to those sitting on benches. Others push heavy four-wheeled carts and sell everything from vegetables and fruits to discarded antiques. Children are sent out to work at an early age. The streets are full of Kurdish children shining shoes. Factories secretly hire underage workers, and people of all ages, including children, sell whatever they can.

Many displaced villagers have relocated in Istanbul. I was with displaced Kurds while they tried to sell carpets to tourists, worked as cooks, cut hair, drove taxis, and sold tea and sunflower seeds along the seacoasts. I drank tea with unemployed laborers who were not chosen for a day's construction work. These observations and conversations form the basis of this chapter in the cultural journey of the Kurdish experience.

I spent considerable time observing and talking with residents at the *meydan* in Bağcılar, a densely populated section of Istanbul with a high percentage of Kurdish residents. Mango (2004) cites a leading Turkish newspaper's coverage of life in Bağcılar. About 50 percent of the people in Bağcılar are from the predominately Kurdish eastern and southeastern part of Turkey, with another 33 percent from the Black Sea coast—which, although not a Kurdish region, is also very impoverished and underdeveloped. Mango cites statistical surveys showing that in 66 percent of the households, the chief wage earner had only a primary school education, and that 18 percent of the households' children did not attend school. Furthermore, 25 percent of the

Different styles of dress
seen on women in the
Bağcılar area of Istanbul.

households had a child who died in infancy, and 20 percent of the children
suffer from a physical handicap. Mango states that not a single female university graduate could be found.

Despite the residents' lack of education and impoverished life, Bağcılar
has a *meydan* complete with Internet cafes, outdoor restaurants, and a movie
theater that shows current movies made in the United States. Bağcılar has a
way of hiding its poverty quite well. For example, the most recent *Star Wars*
movie (at the time) was showing at the same time it was being played in the
United States. An uninformed person could easily walk around Bağcılar without being aware of the problematic social conditions that Mango describes. I
saw thousands of people, from young lovers arm-in-arm, to entire families,
strolling up and down the crowded streets. The women wore a wide range of
apparel—from *abbiya*s to sleeveless tops and tight-fitting slacks. As one informant pointed out, when women first come to the area they are conservatively
dressed in full Islamic clothing. By the following year, they are wearing a head
scarf and a dress. By the third year, they are not wearing a veil and are dressed
in T-shirts and blue jeans. The sheer number of people walking along the
meydan gave me the initial impression that people have made connections
with their families and others from their home villages. Life may be hard, but
at least people had the support systems in place to help them cope with the
complexities and alienation of urban life.

When I spent time with a young couple called Abdullah and Nurcan (not
their real names), I began to wonder about how connected people really were.

Perhaps there is alienation and loneliness that is underneath the surface. Abdullah and Nurcan are from a mountain village in eastern Turkey, surrounded by beautiful forests and clear mountain streams. At one time, animal husbandry, particularly raising sheep, had been the major source of income in Abdullah's village, but the government made that illegal in order to better control the mountains so the PKK could not use the high places to launch attacks against the Turkish military. The battles with the PKK also made it difficult to keep teachers in the village, and while growing up, Abdullah would go to school for a year or two only to experience the school being closed the next year due to a lack of teachers. After several years of on-and-off education, he finally finished primary school but did not go on to middle school in a distant town.

Jobs in the village were scarce. And to complicate things further, Nurcan became ill and needed intensive health care. The closest hospital was hours away, and the doctor said that Nurcan needed to go to the hospital at least twice a week for treatment. The expense of the travel back and forth to the hospital along with the lack of work possibilities in the village led Abdullah to move his young wife and their young children to Istanbul.

Abdullah and Nurcan rented a small flat in Bağcılar. Somehow Abdullah taught himself enough English to get a job selling souvenirs to tourists at a small shop in the Sultan Ahmet area, the center of tourism in Istanbul. He works seven days a week, leaving home at 8:30 in the morning and returning after 10:30 at night, all for a small paycheck. Working long hours with little pay is normal in the private sector. What struck me about the couple, however, was their culture shock and isolation. One usually thinks of culture shock when moving across international borders, but in their case, it was moving from a rural to an urban area that has left them disorientated, resulting in their feeling that many of the familiar social mores are no longer valid. They must learn to cope with the prevalence of looser relations between the sexes, the fast pace of life, and the sense of alienation and loneliness as they move from a face-to-face to an impersonal social environment.

Even more surprising is the isolation they have experienced. I was expecting them to have a steady stream of family members and other visitors from their *memleket*[1] (the district where a person is born and spends his or her formative years) visit them. Usually, the women go from house to house and help each other with their housework and socialize while the men are at work or at the *kahve*. Abdullah and Nurcan told me, however, that even their own relatives do not visit them due to the long hours spent at work and the hassle of moving about in the traffic of such a large city. In discussing changing family ties, George Foster (1973) cites Norbeck and Befu's observations almost 60 years ago in rapidly industrializing Japan, stating that, "The nuclear family is displacing the extended family and has come to be the dominant form in the cities of Japan. Where the extended family exists, it has everywhere diminished in size and functional importance" (p. 59). Although there are many from their *memleket* in Bağcılar, they have little social contact with them. Nurcan especially complains about the long hours alone with two small children and no one to talk to. When I suggested that she might find some female friends at the voluntary association (a group of people who have interests in common and who get together socially; the group serves many of the same needs as family and kinship ties did in the villages) established for people from their *memleket,* it was quickly pointed out that these associations are run by men and that women would not be comfortable there.

I wondered how many others are also cutoff, isolated, and feel terribly alienated. Has the move from rural to urban areas led thousands more like Abdullah and Nurcan to not walk arm-in-arm in the *meydan*? How many are invisibly hidden away in urban flats, dreaming of their old life in the village but unable to return?

Imagined Communities in Urban Regions

In areas like Istanbul's Bağcılar neighborhood, I have witnessed what Anderson (2006) calls "imagined communities." By this he means that people have a subjective sense of national consciousness that binds them together based on perceived aspects of commonality. This commonality births nationalism by inventing nations where they previously were none. As Anderson states, "Communities are to be distinguished, not by their falsity/genuineness, but by the style in which they are imagined" (2006, p. 6). So what types of imagined communities are now springing up in the urban areas far away from the mountainous habitat of the Kurdish homeland?

While I was doing fieldwork in Bağcılar, I was invited into people's homes and had a chance to observe their everyday life. I wanted to learn what types of imagined communities existed and how migrating Kurds were coping in the overcrowded neighborhood and the change from the slow pace of the village and from the social networks that have been in place for generations.

Kurds, upon moving to Istanbul, generally try to live near relatives and acquaintances from their home *memleket,* although it is not always possible due to a shortage of low-income housing. Ayşe Güneş-Ayata, a Turkish anthropologist, cites a study of the Turkish State Planning Organization showing that 76 percent of Kurdish-speaking migrants claimed to have relatives living in the same quarter. Two-thirds of all migrants claimed they socialize with their relatives more than once a week in their new urban environment (1996, p. 103). These data suggest that Abdullah and Nurcan's alienation is somewhat untypical.

In the city it is virtually impossible to avoid interacting with strangers, but the *kahve* a man goes to, the stores he buys from, and the restaurant where he eats are generally connected with the geographical region he has left. His wife's *çevre* (surroundings) usually includes people from the home region, who are often relatives. Work frequently forces Kurds out of this protected environment, but after work, men seem to find others from their *memleket* with whom they visit and carry on discussions.

In one sense then, these recent arrivals from the village bring their culture with them—good and bad—and live as much as possible like they did previously. Yet, over time, the city has the power to change people both outwardly, in dress and appearance, and inwardly, in worldview and values.

Urbanization and Traditional Values

In our village when someone did something shameful, it was if the entire village sinned. We all felt disgraced and we had to take care of the problem as a village. (An elderly village informant in eastern Turkey)

A man who had roots in the village but had raised his family in a predominately Kurdish region of Istanbul pointed out that in the old days, *namus* (honor, virtue) was preserved both within the family and in the community; and those who fell into sin were punished by the parents or brothers. Furthermore, informal types of control such as gossip and shaming are a natural part of village life and a means of informal social control. The gossip networks can be vicious, and Kurds constantly worry about falling victim to gossip whether or not the subject of gossip is true. People have to be careful about any kind of action that could possibly be misunderstood and that would bring shame to their families. In the cities, informal social control has given way to formal control. Now, formal authorities like the police often are called on to deal with flagrant violations of moral codes.

Wherever people face urbanization, family life is inevitably going to change. As Foster (1973) stated, industrialization seems to result in weaker kinship ties. The strong patriarchal system of arranged marriages between relatives, patrilocal residency patterns, and sons carrying on the traditional ways of life, particularly agriculture and animal raising, are moderated. While the father maintains his authority, the children, especially daughters, may not be as rigidly obedient as they were in the village. Greater application of official law prohibits honor killing, forced marriage, and polygyny. Divorce is more readily available to women and is considered less shameful than it is in the village. Women marry later, often after secondary school; some women pursue a university education. The number of children per family decreases.

The above characteristics apply to urbanized Kurdish families. Newspapers are full of stories about moral decay among urban families—fathers marrying their daughters off to older men in order to pay off gambling debts, and accounts of domestic violence and sex for money or career advancement constantly appear. Many of the hundreds of new, expensive condominiums in the city are being bought by transplanted rural Kurds who arrived with nothing but have found a way to become prosperous. Smuggling, especially narcotics and women, accounts for some of the monetary gain. Underage Russian girls are smuggled into Turkey and are forced to become prostitutes; they are locked up when not "working" to prevent their escaping back to Moldova, Russia, or Eastern Europe. This is different from both the legal prostitution that can be found in most large cities and the voluntary prostitution of women from the former Soviet Union, who tend to be over the age of eighteen.

If families pass through significant change upon urbanization, what about the traditional values as reflected in the three syndromes highlighted previously—hospitality-generosity, honor-dignity, and courage-bravery syndromes?

Hospitality is not practiced in the city to the degree that it traditionally has been in the countryside, because an urban man, who may work in construction or at a factory, cannot leave his job whenever a guest arrives at his home, and women in the city are much more likely to work outside of the home and cannot cater to guests as easily as their village counterparts can. While hospitality is still considered an important Kurdish value, it takes a different form in urban areas, where families often rely on carryout restaurants to feed guests. When living in the village, it would have been disgraceful to allow a guest to stay in a hotel, but in the city it no longer carries as much shame. Furthermore, people felt free in the village to visit one another's homes at any time; in the city, people tend to phone first and make more formal arrangements.

Kurds frequently say that honor no longer exists, and that the only value that remains is the pursuit of money. Kurdish society faces a time of great

social change, or to borrow a phrase that has been often used to describe conflicting values in North American society, Kurds are facing a *culture war*. The
unquestioned patriarchal authority of the father in the village cannot help but
conflict with the new morality of the city.

Asabiyya

Asabiyya is an Arabic word meaning a "group loyalty," "social cohesion,"
or "social solidarity" (Ahmed, 2003, p. 13). Pakistani anthropologist Akbar
Ahmed attributes the concept of *asabiyya* to Ibn Khaldun, the fourteenth-
century Arab sociologist. Khaldun calls these ties between family, kin, and
tribe the fundamental bond of human society. In the village, *asabiyya* was
ever present; the glue that held society together. Ahmed talks of the weakening of *asabiyya* as the major reason for the difficulties facing much of the
Muslim world today. With modernization, family and tribal cohesion have
been weakening, resulting in anomie (breakdown of social norms) and social
decay. In cities where modernization is stronger, *asabiyya* is weakening more
quickly than it is in villages—a pattern clearly evident among the Kurds. Does
this mean that all of the traditional bonds have been broken and total anomie
cannot help but occur?

Urbanization and Anomie

In the late 1930s, Louis Wirth developed the theory that urbanization
leads to impersonal, superficial relationships in which family and kinship ties
break, societal norms are in conflict, and social order is maintained by formal
organizations rather than by the informal social sanctions present in rural life
(cited in Barfield, 1997). Without the previous moral codes acting as a means
of social control, social disorganization—anomie—occurs. Anomie often
manifests itself in crime, suicide, corruption, and other types of urban decay.

On the surface, urbanization, anomie, and urban decay seem to be universal. All of the evidence of urban decay can be found in abundance in Istanbul
and other cities in Turkey. Much of this decay is blamed on villagers who have
migrated recently from the east and southeast (*Doğulular*) to western Turkey
and have not assimilated well into urban life. Yet, theories of anomie have been
criticized for overlooking the social enclaves within urban society that are
characterized by close relationships between kin, relatives, and friends. Güneş-
Ayata (1996) mentions Gan's theory that even in the most urbanized areas,

small villages still exist with families, relatives, and primary-group relations important in the transactions of daily life. Especially relevant for Turkey are the informal, voluntary associations of people from the same home province who meet at *kahves*, at community organizations, and in homes.

Foster (1973) confronts the critics of urbanization, saying:

> Because of this stereotype, as well as the poverty and suffering of slum dwellers in both industrialized and developing areas, there is a tendency to deplore the rural exodus, the flight from country to city, and to interpret it in pathological terms. Actually . . . for all of the squander of urban shantytowns in the cities of the developing countries, most rural migrants feel that they are better off than in their natal villages, most find jobs, and most have little or no desire to return permanently to the country. For in addition to the economic and other material advantages they find in cities, the faster tempo of urban life, its excitement, and the greater freedom also attract them. (p. 45)

It is important not to see urbanization only through a negative lens. Poverty and joblessness, coupled with the social restrictions placed on freedom of expression and lifestyle by conservative social forces, have pushed millions around the world to move from villages to major cities. Istanbul, with its job possibilities, its prominence in the media, and its image of prosperity and possibilities of a better life, attracts thousands of Kurds. While the first generation of migrants does struggle, often the children are successful. Stories abound of the children of parents who migrated from villages to cities—of men and women who have had the chance to get a good education, have won a place in the university system, and have gone on to lucrative careers in medicine, engineering, law, business, politics, and education. The next generation quickly acclimates to urban life, and while the parents may only outwardly conform to the culture of the city, their children are at home in it and have no intention of returning to the places their parents dream about.

Lessons from the Kurds

Societies can change rapidly from: rural to urban, oral to literate, and isolated to connected with the global community. The Kurdish experience teaches lessons that may help other groups face cultural change.

First, the home has proven stronger than the forces raging against it in transmitting a strong sense of ethnic identity and collective culture. Despite forced assimilation schemes, the lack of formal education concerning anything to do with Kurdish history or culture, and even total denial of their distinct identity, the Kurds have maintained their ethnic distinctiveness and have transmitted it to subsequent generations. High up in the mountains of Kurdistan, mothers and fathers, and grandmothers and grandfathers, most with little formal education, have been able to instill in their children with a sense of pride in being Kurds. They have kept their language alive and their culture distinct in the midst of great oppression. Language and culture death, which has happened to numerous cultures throughout history, does not have to happen if family structures remain strong.

Second, ethnic identity does not die easily. Even assimilation schemes that caused many Kurds to not know their mother tongue have not totally destroyed their sense of ethnic distinctiveness. Ethnicity is a very subjective construct and varies from person to person. Even Kurds who speak no Kurdish, and have been raised in the city far away from Kurdistan, may undergo a personal reawakening to their ethnic heritage. If the education system gives no importance to a culture's heritage, and even if it suppresses the people's language and cultural distinctiveness, people can still maintain their sense of identity and be proud of their collective experience.

Third, urbanization and modernity may pose greater threats to cultural identity than the outside forces of oppression do. Television, not oppression, has led to the weakening of family and community gatherings in which Kurdish folklore was passed down to the young. I worry more about increasing degrees of anomie than I do about outside enemies oppressing the Kurds to the degree they have in the past. Internal fighting and moral decay could be the greatest challenges ahead for the Kurds.

Fourth, new urban institutions, including cultural centers, work places, and other semiformal institutions outside of the school system (in Turkey) will have to find ways to keep *Kurdayati* alive as the old rural structures are quickly fading. Turkish Kurds especially will face a difficult battle to maintain and transmit their culture due to a weakening family structure and the struggle to survive that is so time-consuming. Music and other forms of artistic expression have grown in importance as orality has decreased. In Iraq, where the freedom to express *Kurdayati* exists as never before, we can hope that the Kurds take advantage of it, and that a great wealth of artistic expression in many genres will be created.

Fifth, societies going through much cultural change, like the Kurds, need to find ways to help subsequent generations respect and treasure the indigenous knowledge contained in their oral traditions. How tragic it would be if the wisdom of the ages that has helped preserve the Kurds through the centuries is lost. Lost—not because of oppression from outside forces, but because it is perceived to be irrelevant to modern, urban youth. When I have demonstrated interest in Kurdish informal education, and listened to their stories and quoted Kurdish proverbs, the community responds enthusiastically to the affirmation. With the rise in literacy and educational opportunities in both Iraqi and Turkish Kurdistan, stories will shift from an oral medium to a written one. Along with this positive development, there needs to be special occasions to highlight oral genres in schools, cultural centers, and at special festivals that focus on the Kurdish collective cultural heritage. As Reagan (2005) says, "Oral literature is, by its very nature, dependent on *performance*" (p. 12). Concrete forms of learning, including storytelling, need to be presented as valid education. Historically, concrete forms of teaching and learning in transmitting cultural knowledge have been the means for the majority of cultures in the world to preserve their heritage. It is a tragedy that storytelling has been so often associated only with children, depriving adults of limitless learning possibilities. Formal education can be strengthened without having to displace informal learning.

I do not want to overly idealize the traditional way of life in the villages. There were terrible blood feuds, women were often oppressed, and the poverty was stifling. Few people could read and most were ignorant of the outside world. *Agahs* and other powerful leaders carried a lot of authority and sometimes abused their power or sold their services to the highest bidder. *Sheikhs* often exploited the religious inclinations of the people for temporal gain. Most Iraqi Kurds experienced their homes and villages being destroyed several times. Countless Turkish Kurds were driven from their homes and were forced to live away from their fellow Kurds. Education, if even existent, usually never went beyond the primary level, and even that was often denied to girls.

Yet, there was much good as well. Many of my informants were teary-eyed as they recalled sitting together in the evenings, telling stories, discussing village events, singing, and reciting the poetry, epics, and legends of the ages. There were shared common values and clear standards of right and wrong. People watched out for each other. They were as close to nature, raising animals and harvesting crops, as they had been for millennia. While village life could be oppressive with its gossip networks and informal social controls, it also provided a sense of belonging that has helped the Kurds survive and outlast their oppressors.

The Kurds are no longer a totally forgotten people. Since 1991, they have been on television screens in people's homes around the world. For the present, the Kurds in Iraq are close allies of the United States and grateful for their deliverance from Saddam's forces as well as support in fighting the Islamic State. Turkey's exploding Kurdish population can no longer be ignored and passed off simply as outside forces seeking to divide Turkey. Turkey could have a majority Kurdish population within a couple of generations. How Turks will cope with that is anyone's guess.

Politics aside, Kurds need to be studied as an example of a people who have kept their identity and language alive against great odds. The scene described at the beginning of this book may not be as normative as the past, but *Kurdayati* will be maintained and transmitted in one way or the other. As a final Kurdish proverb states, *Bila Xude yar bit, hamu dinya bila neyar bit* (If God be your friend, let the whole world be your enemy). From the time of Noah's ark to the age of globalization, the Kurds have lived on the land they call Kurdistan. Somehow they have survived, multiplied, and face a brighter future than perhaps they have ever faced.

Questions for Discussion

- Massive urbanization is a global phenomenon affecting millions of people. How do the major push and pull factors that draw Kurds to the city compare and contrast with push and pull factors in your country?

- Compare and contrast urbanization among the Kurds with urbanization in your country with regard to family life and moral values.

- At the end of the book, the author lists five key lessons that can be learned from the Kurdish experience. Discuss the relevance of these lessons from the perspective of your own culture or a culture with which you are familiar.

Note

[1] *Memleket* is a place of great importance in Turkey. Almost as soon as two people meet, they ask about each other's *memleket*, which serves as a way to build rapport. People who have migrated away from their *memleket* will generally look for those from his or her home area to make contact with. For both business and social interaction, the importance of *memleket* can hardly be overstated. Even after living in Istanbul for many years, people will still say they are from the region of their birth. Yet, people who are born in Istanbul are proud to say that they are true *Istanbullu* (from Istanbul), signifying that they do not have village roots, but are true urbanites—a mark of distinction.

Chapter 8

Update

Mountains, Malls, and War

So much has happened in both Iraqi Kurdistan and among the Kurds in Turkey since first publishing this book in 2007 that I can only mention some of the highlights. I have focused on the problem of ISIS (or Islamic State of Iraq and al-Sham), as the Kurds play an especially important strategic role in a conflict that has contributed to more people being displaced than at any time since World War II. While millions have watched with horror the ISIS beheadings of Jim Foley, David Hines, David Henning, Peter Kassiq, and Steven Sotloff, countless thousands of unknown victims of ISIS—the Yazidis, Christians, Shi'a Muslims, and even Sunnis who have been declared as *takfir* (non-Muslim) by ISIS—have suffered from rape, kidnapping, beheading, crucifixion, death, and destruction.

The Cessation of Civil War

In chapter 2 I described how demoralizing the conflict was between warring factions among the Kurds, particularly Masoud Barzani's KDP versus Jalal Talabani's PUK. In 1996, not long after my family and I departed from Iraqi Kurdistan, Masoud Barzani, who succeeded his father, Mustafa, as president of the KDP, called on his former enemy, Saddam Hussein, to come to his defense against Talabani when the PUK seemed to be on the verge of forcing the KDP into a small area of Duhok province. Talabani, at the same time, sought military aid from Iran, also considered an enemy of the Kurds. Barzani, however, is now the president of Iraqi Kurdistan, while Talabani was president of all of Iraq in 2005–2014 until his death. No doubt bitterness remains among some of their followers, but it is remarkable that they have been able to put aside their conflict and work toward a united Kurdistan (Lawrence, 2008).

The Aftermath of the War in Iraq

The 2003 American invasion of Iraq continues to be a point of much controversy. The intense pain in the loss of life or permanent injury in a war that many perceive as unnecessary makes this a sensitive topic to many Americans. The number of Iraqis who died due to the invasion, balanced by how many people died at the hands of Saddam Hussein and would have continued to die if he had not been removed from power, can never be accurately accessed. The official numbers from the Defense Department are 1,111,610 Americans saw action in Iraq for a total of 2, 327,197 deployments; 4,488 died in action and another 235 took their own lives while deployed. Furthermore, 32,221 returned with serious, long-lasting injuries. Among the Iraqis 115,376 civilians were killed in sectarian violence, with 2.7 million people displaced by the fighting, according to the Brookings Institute. The question of "was it worth it?" will no doubt be a haunting question for a long time to come. Much has been written about what went wrong, and many U.S. politicians who had voted for the invasion have since tried to justify their previous support by claiming they only voted for it due to faulty intelligence about Saddam's regime having weapons of mass destruction (WMDs) and the potential use of them against America. (There is no doubt that Saddam did have WMDs at one time and used them against the Kurds.)

For the United States, hundreds of billions of dollars were spent in trying to get rid of Saddam Hussein and help establish a democratic state in a troubled region. In the Iraq Study Group Report, put together by a ten-member team co-chaired by James Baker III and Lee H. Hamilton in 2006, a survey of the Iraqi people stated that 79 percent of Iraqis have a "mostly negative" view of the influence of the U.S. in their country; 61 percent approve of attacks on U.S. forces. The committee expressed the following, "If Iraqis continue to perceive Americans as representing an occupying force, the United States could become its own worst enemy in a land it liberated from tyranny" (Baker & Hamilton, n.d., p. 29). Yet, the prime minister of Iraq met with President Obama in April 2015 pleading for more help in defeating ISIS, which had recently recaptured Ramadi in Anbar Province from the GOI (government of

Iraq), not long after a GOI victory in retaking Tikrit, the hometown of Saddam Hussein, from ISIS. It does not appear that the U.S. can totally wash its hands of Iraq anytime soon.

What Went Wrong?

Without question most of the U.S. military personnel who were deployed in Iraq saw themselves initially as liberators, and many were involved in humanitarian efforts to make life better for the Iraqis. Unfortunately some of the good will was overshadowed by one of the biggest blunders the U.S. made. (I am only focusing on one major mistake because of its relevance to the current situation.) That blunder was laying off most of the Iraqi military and much of the police force in order to rid Iraq of those who had any connection to the former Baath Party regime of Saddam Hussein. This *debaathification* policy resulted in tens of thousands of embittered men left unemployed. For most of these men, the military and the police force provided their only way of making a living, and most were not avid supporters of Saddam Hussein's tactics. Colonel Derek Harvey, a military intelligence officer, estimated that 65,000–95,000 members of Saddam's various praetorian divisions, including the Iraqi Special Republican Guard, the *Mukhābarāt* (Iraqi intelligence), and other branches were made unemployed by one stroke of the pen after the U.S. invasion (Weiss & Hassan, 2015). Higher estimates have been cited as well.

Al-Qaeda Iraq

Many of these former Baathists were susceptible to exploitation and urged to join al-Qaeda Iraq (AQI). AQI eventually evolved into the Islamic State of Iraq (ISI). The founder of AQI, Mudab al-Zarqawi, who formerly was in prison for drug running and sexual assault, discovered *Salafism,* a very puritanical type of Islam that advocates a return to the religious purity and practice of Islam as practiced in the days of the Prophet Muhammad and his early successors (Weiss & Hassan, 2015). It is chilling that al-Qaeda eventually broke off relations with AQI because its methods were too brutal for even the al-Qaeda run by Ayman al-Zawahīrī, Osama bin Laden's successor (Sekulow, 2014). Zarqawi was killed in a U.S. bombing attack in 2006, but he paved the way for ISIS to become the worldwide threat it is today.

Other former Baathists, and gradually more and more men associated with various Sunni tribes, were radicalized and urged toward a more Salafist (sometimes called fundamentalist) understanding of Islam. The number of mosques promoting jihadism increased, spewing out hatred against the

American invaders and Shi'ites. In addition to being radicalized in mosques, many people were radicalized in U.S.-administered detention centers, such as the one named Camp Bucca with 24,000 detainees (Hall, 2015), sometimes satirically called "Jihadi universities." AQI also recruited outside jihadists, and resistance to the U.S. invasion became more and more intense.

Restoration of the Caliphate

Syria is not for Syrians and Iraq is not for Iraqis, The land is for Muslims all Muslims. If you hold to it you will conquer Rome and own the world. If Allah wills.

—Caliph Ibrahim

One of the prisoners under American control at one time was a young scholar by the name of Abū Bakr al-Baghdādi who went on to get a PhD in Islamic Studies. Baghdādi is the self-anointed Caliph Ibrahim, who desires to see an end to the nation-states artificially created by the colonial powers in the Middle East after World War I. Baghdādi declared on June 14, 2014, that the name for this movement would be the Islamic State (IS) and no longer ISIS or ISIL. (Many commentators continue to use ISIS or ISIL, understandably not wanting to classify Baghdādi's group of jihadists as a "state.") Rather than nation-states, Baghdādi preaches that beginning with Iraq and Syria, the Muslim *ummah* (worldwide community) would work together to bring about one Islamic caliphate that would encompass the entire Muslim world with himself as the Caliph.

IS and the Shi'ites

Two of history's great enemies, Saudi Arabia and Iran (Sunni and Shi'a), simply will not stop until they have burnt each other out, and millions will die in the ensuing battle.

—War Correspondent Benjamin Hall

Besides despising the American invaders and non-Muslims, IS jihadists have a deep hatred of Shi'ite Muslims. Zarqawi had an almost pathological contempt of Shi'ites, and this hatred of Shi'ites is still evident in the IS movement. IS has exploited fears that the 60 percent Shi'a majority of Iraq's population, in conjunction with its neighbor Iran, which is also predominantly Shi'a, would totally dominate the 20 percent Sunni Arab Muslim minority (see notes at the end of chapter 2 for a very brief definition of Shi'a [Shi'ite]

Islam). Of course it was this 20 percent Sunni Arab minority who lost the most due to the U.S. invasion. In addition, there was a common perception that the U.S. was behind turning Iraq into a virtual Shi'ite state. Weiss and Hassan (2015) cite Emma Sky, former advisor to the U.S. military, who argues that throughout the Sunni Arab world, it is widely perceived that the U.S. and Iran made secret deals in which the U.S. basically gave Iraq to Iran.

Being brutally oppressed under Saddam's regime, coupled with being such a strong majority, it is understandable that the Shi'ites expected to be the primary power brokers in a new Iraqi government after the U.S. invasion. Now for the first time in 1,300 years, the Shi'ites are in control of today's Iraq. However, when the governing council in July of 2003 was formed with 13 Shi'ite members and only a few Sunnis, sectarian fighting became increasingly violent and bloody because the Sunnis felt powerless in the land they had dominated for so long.

As Hall mentions above, one can see this conflict played out in places in the Middle East besides Iraq and Syria. These areas include Lebanon, Yemen, Bahrain, Kuwait, and even Pakistan and Afghanistan; all have had many episodes of sectarian violence. Hall explains that Saudi Arabia originally helped Salafist groups like IS, both to struggle against Iran and to be perceived as the defenders of Islam. IS, however, grew bigger than what the Saudis expected and proved uncontrollable. Meanwhile, Iran has tried to keep Syria's President Bashar al-Assad in power, while coercing Nouri al-Malaki (when he was prime minister of Iraq) to push more Shi'ites into power in Iraq. These actions caused much Sunni unrest, which led to the rising of ISIS.

The Kurds (who make up close to 20 percent of Iraq's population) would have preferred to have been excluded from all of this. Iraqi Kurdistan has been functioning much like a de facto state since the establishment of the no-fly zone (see chapter 2). While a large majority of Kurds are Sunnis, except for a very small percentage who have radicalized into Salafist-type movements, the Kurds have tried to avoid being drawn into religious conflicts. Furthermore, they are not Arabs and have no real desire to be under either Sunni or Shi'ite Arab control. However, the U.S. discouraged Kurdish independence, and the Kurds deferred to U.S. wishes. By the end of the summer of 2012 more than 700 Iraqis were being killed each month. Due to terrible sectarian fighting, Vice President Joe Bidden initially proposed dividing Iraq into three regions: Arab Sunni, Arab Shi'a, and Kurdish. However, the general U.S. policy has been to work toward a more shared-power agreement. Time will tell whether Iraq will remain as one state or will ultimately be divided into three.

With so many Iraqis being killed each month in sectarian fighting, Sunni rejection of the predominately Shi'a government became increasingly violent. Former Iraqi Prime Minister al-Maliki pushed the Sunnis so far that it is not too surprising they rebelled and became more anti-regime. The current Prime Minister Haider al-Abadi in general is perceived by Sunnis as better than al-Maliki, but time will tell whether he can build trust and bring down the sectarian cycles of hatred and violence. In one of his first press conferences, al-Abadi said he advocated a strategic partnership between the U.S. and Iran to combat IS (Weiss & Hassan, 2015). The Sunnis under IS control, such as those in Mosul, are in a very difficult place. Most do not approve of the harsh interpretation of Shari'a Law that IS implements in areas under their control, but they also do not want to live under a Shi'ite-dominated regime. This makes for a complex scenario: the Iraqi government troops and the Kurds seek to recapture a city from IS, while unsure of the people's support, and not knowing whether the populace of the city is on the side of IS.

Establishing the Islamic State

President Obama initially dismissed IS as the junior varsity squad of terrorists, as compared to al-Qaeda. Obviously that perception has changed, and IS has become the largest, richest, and most in control of more land than any other jihadist group. As Hall (2015) points out, what al-Qaeda could not do in 20 years as it was hidden away in mountain camps, IS has done in two years: holding large areas of land in Iraq and Syria, mobilizing idealistic young people through social media, and amassing funds through the sale of oil, extortion, and kidnapping. Evening news broadcasters had great difficulty explaining how 1,000 IS jihadists put 30,000 U.S.-trained Iraqi soldiers to flight and proceeded to capture tens of millions of dollars worth of American-made tanks and other weapons when the jihadists captured Mosul in 2014. This event was a major turning point and played a key role alerting the world to the seriousness of the problem that IS presents. It also enabled IS to recruit more jihadists. A similar misfortune took place in 2015 when Iraqi troops abandoned their equipment in Ramadi.

The Appeal of IS

The Islamic State not only appeals to embittered Sunni Arab Iraqis who have been marginalized since the fall of Saddam and to Syrian Sunnis who have been under the domination of the minority Alawite regime of Bashir al-Assad, but it also draws in thousands of young Muslims who have grown up in Western societies or who are from among the more prosperous families in Muslim societies. The CIA estimated that there were 20,000–31,000 IS fighters as of December 2014 (Hall, 2015). This includes young women who have offered to fight beside and/or marry jihadists.

Journalist Lee Smith discusses the appeal of IS to a generation of young Muslims growing up in a world where their basic material needs are met but who have no defining sense of purpose. Many have found the materialism of the West to be devoid of moral and spiritual values. Pop culture may be perceived by somewhat alienated Muslim young women from European society as quite empty compared with the brave, heroic IS jihadists who appear to have a purpose that gives them not only a reason to live but a cause worth dying for. Anthropologist Scott Atran expresses very well the need of many young people to have a cause that demands a full-hearted commitment, "We keep hearing that the antidote (to jihadism) is preaching moderate Islam. I tell people on the National Security Council, 'Don't you have kids? Does anything moderate appeal to them?'" (cited in Weiss & Hassan, 2015, p. 178).

How Islamic Is the Islamic State?

Whenever the topic of IS comes up, it almost always leads to a discussion of whether the type of Islam practiced by IS jihadists is the true Islam, or is it a total deviation and sabotage of a religion that is primarily a religion of peace. Graeme Wood (2015) states that every academic he has discussed IS ideology with sends him to Lebanese Princeton scholar Bernard Haykal. Haykal totally disagrees with those who state that the texts of Islam have been distorted by radicals like IS. Rather they are faithfully practicing the type of Islam practiced by the early Muslims. He states, "Slavery, crucifixion and beheadings are not something that freakish (jihadists) are cherry-picking from the medieval tradition. . . ." Islamic State fighters, "are smack in the middle of the medieval tradition and are bringing it wholesale into the present day." Several times Wood refers to *takfir,* the declaration that Muslims can be "excommunicated" or declared apostate for not practicing Islam in the way IS does. *Takfir* has given license for jihadists not only to pillage, rape, and kill non-Muslims but to justify the killing of professing Muslims. Anjem Choudary, a well-known defender of IS tactics to British audiences, told Wood that the state has an obligation to terrorize its enemies, "a holy order to scare the shit out of them with beheadings and crucifixions and enslavement of women and children, because doing so hastens victory and avoids prolonged conflict" (Wood, 2015).

Fueling the jihadists' actions and ability to garner a steady stream of recruits is the fervent promise of reestablishing an Islamic Empire by conquering all nonbelievers, thereby ending the world as it currently exists. Only true Muslims will survive the apocalypse, and they will dominate the world.

The Eschatology of the Islamic State

ISIS is trying deliberately to instigate a war between Sunnis and Shi'a in the belief that a sectarian war would be a sign that the final times have arrived. In the eschatological literature, there is a reference to crisis in Syria and massacre of Kurds—that is why Kobane is so important. ISIS is exploiting these apocalyptic expectations to the fullest.

—Hassan Abbas, an expert on jihadist movements

If you think all these mujahideen (Islamic warriors) came from across the world to fight Assad, you're mistaken. They are all here as promised by the Prophet. This is the war he promised—it is the Grand Battle.

—A Sunni Muslim jihadi

Eschatology (doctrine of the last things) is an intriguing area of study, especially in comparing and contrasting apocalyptic end-time scenarios in Judaism, Christianity, and Islam. Eschatology includes topics such as life after death, heaven and hell, judgment, and the end of the world. It is beyond the scope of this book to examine Jewish and Christian eschatological doctrines or historical events that led to many people thinking that the end of the world was near at various times throughout history. While religious Jews pray for the Messiah to appear for the first time, and devout Christians long for the return of Jesus the Messiah to usher in an eternal kingdom, Islamic State jihadists appear to be motivated by an eschatological vision in which they play an important role in ushering in last day events as prophesized primarily in the Hadith.[1] Muslims who hope for martyrdom as a guarantee of paradise and envision it as a place filled with luscious fruit and wine, rivers of pure water, and 72 beautiful *houris* (virgins) as a reward for being a *shahid* (martyr) have often been mocked in cartoon caricatures. However, in the case of the Islamic State warriors, beautiful virgins are not just a reward for those who are killed in battle, but for those who fight now for the caliphate, as demonstrated by the practice of sexual slavery with Yazidi and Christian girls. Weiss and Hassan (2015) argue that IS relies on Islamic eschatology for both recruitment and legitimacy. It needs to be remembered that Damascus, Syria, was the center of the Umayyad Caliphate (661–750), which was later replaced by the Abbasid Caliphate (749–1258) centered in Baghdad, and these time periods represent the Golden Era of Islam. When the U.S. invaded Iraq in 2003, many saw this as an event predicted in Islamic eschatology, fueling the idea that the forces of the Antichrist have come to war against the Muslims. William McCants, in an excellent book about the apocalyptic vision of IS, cites a well-known Hadith:

> "The Hour will not come until the Romans land at al-Amaq or in Dabiq. . . . They will then fight (Muslims against Romans) and a third part of the army will run away, whom God will never forgive. A third part of the army which will be constituted of excellent martyrs in the eye of God, will be killed, and the third who will never be put to trial will win and they will be conquerors of Constantinople." (From the Hadith of Sahah Muslim, cited in McCants, 2015, p. 159).

One popular Hadith concerns the end-time battle between Muslims and Christians in Dabiq, near Aleppo, Syria. It is no coincidence that an IS propaganda magazine is named *Dabiq* after this famous battle. Some IS propaganda suggests that the hated Shi'a Muslims will join forces with the Jewish and Christian forces under the command of Dajjall (usually translated in apocalyptic literature as Antichrist, or the Deceiver) to war against the Muslims. It is interesting that the United States has been accused of handing Iraq over to the Shi'ites and now the Russians (also regarded as "Christians") are fighting to preserve Assad's basically Shi'ite regime. Furthermore, the recent agreement between the U.S. and other Western nations with Shi'a Iran to lift sanctions if Iran agrees not to develop weapons of mass destruction, has no doubt fueled the apocalyptic fervor of many jihadists as they see a perceived alliance of Christians, Jews, and Shi'ites warring against Allah's faithful warriors.

One of the best known Hadiths is that the Dajjall will be a one-eyed Jew that has *Kafir* written on his forehead, who will perform counterfeit miracles to deceive the people and will engage in war against Muslims. One IS leader in discussing this with Graeme Wood (2015) says that Dajjall and the Christian armies will kill all but 5,000 of the caliph's fighters and they will be cornered in Jerusalem. As the Dajjall's forces are on the verge of destroying the last remnant of Muslim soldiers, Jesus rescues them and leads them to victory.[2] At this time Jesus will deny his deification by his followers (Qur'an 5:116) and then go on to kill all pigs and destroy all crosses. Other Hadiths promise that Rome (probably representing Christians or the Christian world) will be conquered and its women enslaved by the permission of Allah. Shrines will be destroyed and homosexuals throne off rooftops (both of which IS is already doing).

Anytime IS warriors appear in the media, they seem to be waving black flags. These black flags that IS jihadists wave so proudly pack much historical and eschatological significance, as its predicted in the Hadith that warriors flying the black flag, like Islamic warriors did in the time of the Prophet Muhammad, will come from Khorasan (an area that now would be contained in eastern Iran and Afghanistan) and war against the Dajjall and his forces. McCants (2015) claims that half of all Muslims in North Africa, the Middle East, and South Asia expected the imminent appearance of the Mahdi in 2012. This type of anticipation will no doubt increase with the Muslim world in chaos, and the presence of infidel troops in some of Islam's holiest places.

In regard to eschatology and the prediction of coming apocalyptic events, the three great Monotheistic faiths all believe the culmination of these events will take place in Jerusalem. There the long awaited Messiah will rule and reign and establish his headquarters and establish peace and justice. Some Hadith seem to prophecy that Jerusalem will be the location of the final battle between the forces of Dajjall and the Mahdi. Of course Jerusalem is also the location of Muhammad's night journey in which he was taken up into the heavens to meet and pray with the previous prophets, including Moses and Jesus. So Jerusalem carries great significance in each of the three Abrahamic faiths. Fortunately very few Jews or Christians have tried to usher in apocalyptic events and are content to let God bring them about in due time. This is quite unlike IS jihadists who take an active role in seeking to bring about these events in our day.

The good news in all of this is that already IS has experienced enough defeats that its aura of invincibility no longer holds true. It has been reported that some former fervent jihadists have defected and tell of increasing discontent among its ranks. We can hope that the atrocities that IS has carried out against its victims will soon be only recorded in historical texts rather than in the daily news. We can also hope that Iraq and Syria will stabilize and hundreds of thousands of Yazidis, Christians, and Muslims can return to their ancient, beloved homelands.

The War and the Kurds

The survey cited earlier showing such strong negativity toward the U.S. invasion of Iraq is probably not reflective of the Kurds. In fact, while the majority of the world's Muslims tend to see George W. Bush in a negative light, most Kurds see him as the one who finally got rid of Saddam Hussein, thus freeing them from an oppressive tyrant. While no doubt there are many differing opinions among Kurds about the U.S. invasion, in general the Kurds have greatly benefited, despite U.S. mistakes. I vividly remember talking to one prominent Kurdish leader who had lived in the United States for many years but came back to help govern his beloved Kurdistan. He is both grateful and sorrowful, because he feels that the U.S. could have forged a better relationship with Iraqis if they had listened to the right people who were in touch with Kurdish/Iraqi society. For example, he pointed out how humiliating it was for the Iraqi people, who are so proud of their heritage that traces back to ancient Mesopotamia, the cradle of civilization, to be patrolled by United Nations guards from "third-world countries." He also mentioned how ridiculous it was to many people in Iraq to see Americans and other foreigners, mostly employed by American companies to do construction work and drive supply trucks, get paid exorbitant salaries, while Iraqis would have done the work for a fraction of the cost. Such work would have enabled Iraqis to feed their families, hence alleviating the bitterness that caused many to join in the resistance to American military troops and to view them as "occupiers" rather than "liberators."

The Kurds seem eager to maximize the opportunity they have been given to rebuild their region even as the rest of Iraq seems to be in chaos. Kurds claim that not one American soldier was killed in any region under their control, and today Kurdistan is truly "the other Iraq" and is as different from the rest of Iraq as night is from day. As Lawrence (2008) points out, "for Kurdistan it meant that their 60,000 irregulars including the Peshmerga now ranked as the second largest military force in the country" (p. 5). This is the force that has been the main resistance, thus keeping IS from taking over all of Iraq. Furthermore, the Peshmerga have served as the main protectors of non-Muslims and of those Muslims who will not submit to IS control. It has been especially moving to see young female Peshmerga fighters boldly fighting IS jihadists. Historically, Kurdish women have fought against the enemies of their people, but now this has been demonstrated for all to see on the nightly news.

IS Are Not the Only Bad Guys

While this book focuses on the Kurds of Turkey and Iraq, Syria cannot be overlooked. Although the Kurds are a smaller percentage of Syria's population than they are in Iraq, they are very involved in the conflict against IS as evidenced by the recent battle for Kobani (or Kobane), a medium-sized city near the Syrian–Turkish border. The Assad regime in Syria has also been guilty of mass crimes against humanity, which have fueled opposition to his reign, ranging from moderate groups that the U.S. initially supported to extremist jihadist networks like IS. A military police photographer who defected from the regime claims that 200,000 Syrians have been killed and another 150,000 detained in the regime's prisons (Weiss & Hassan, 2015). Girls as young as eleven have been systematically raped and used as weapons against opposition forces who want to see Assad removed from power. Even so-called moderate rebels fighting against the Assad regime have been as brutal as IS toward those not in their faction. In short, it is very difficult to discern who the "good guys" are in the quagmire that has resulted in so much suffering for the Syrian people, of which the majority simply want to live in peace.

From Victims to Protectors of the Oppressed

In fact the Kurds possess the numbers and the will to drive ISIS back and inflict severe losses on the jihadists.

—Jay Sekulow, Chief Counsel for the
American Center for Law and Justice

In chapter 2 I discussed how the Kurds were declared as non-Muslims (*takfir*) during Saddam's Anfal operation, which was used to justify the slaughter of 180,000 Kurds, the rape of countless girls and women, and the destruction of at least 4,000 villages. The Kurds know from bitter experience what it means to be the victims of religious-inspired violence. Now IS seems to be applying similar tactics to exploit non-Muslims like Christians and Yazidis, as well as Shi'ite Muslims, and even Sunni Muslims who stand against them, especially the Kurds. The transformation of the Kurds as victims of Saddam's oppression, when they first came to the world's attention in 1991, to being the "heroes" of the war against Islamic State jihadists as the protectors of persecuted minorities, is truly remarkable. Many think that the Obama administration has failed to provide our most faithful allies, the Kurds, with the weapons they need, especially in the light of the much better weapons that IS took from the Iraqi government troops while invading Mosul. It is estimated that 200 million dollars' worth of weapons designated for the Kurds were left in Baghdad when the U.S. departed from Iraq. Rather than giving them to the Kurds, the GOI forces, in their flight from IS, left the weapons for the jihadists. The Obama administration continues to send weapons to Baghdad rather than to the Kurdish Regional Government, which leaves the Kurds baffled. They can't help but wonder why the U.S. continually ignores the pleas of the only force that has been consistently brave enough to stand against IS.

Nevertheless, the Kurds bravely continue to battle against IS, and veteran Peshmerga in their 50s and 60s are volunteering to fight alongside the younger troops who lack the experience in fighting due to the peaceful conditions Kurdistan has experienced since the 1990s when it achieved self-rule.

Not All Kurds Are against IS

Our war with the Kurds is a religious war. It is not a nationalistic war. We do not fight Kurds because they are Kurds. They are the toughest fighters against the disbelievers amongst their people.

—Islamic State spokesman Abu Muhammad al-Adnani

A point of concern is that among Kurds in both Turkey and Iraq there has been a minority who has been attracted to the IS jihadists. In Iraq often this means Kurds fighting against their own kinfolk. Why some join IS in Turkey seems to be a mixture of religious zeal, money, access to narcotics, and sex. Different people join for different reasons and with a mixture of motivations. This seems to be true of many of the jihadists from countries not directly involved in the fighting.

Kurdistan and Turkey: Places of Refuge

It's an exodus of people unlike any we've seen since the Second World War, and the numbers are growing.

—War Correspondent Benjamin Hall

Hundreds of thousands of people have fled to Iraqi Kurdistan, making the Kurds the primary protectors of Yazidis, Christians, and non-jihadist Sunnis. IDPs (internationally displaced Iraqis) are Iraqis who have sought refuge within Iraq, including Kurdistan. The numbers of refugees (those who have crossed a national boundary to seek asylum) according to UNHCR (United Nations High Commissioner for Refugees) and the KRG (Kurdistan Regional Government), are continuing to increase. When I was in Kurdistan recently I heard the figure of 2.2 million IDPs from within Iraq and refugees from Syria estimated for the region. Two million more Iraqis may be found in neighboring countries, including Jordan, Lebanon, and Turkey, with smaller numbers in many other locations. Five hundred thousand Yazidis and Christians have fled from IS, particularly from the Sinjar region and Mosul. (It needs to be remembered that exact numbers are uncertain as conditions are still in flux). By January 2015, 12 million Syrians had been forced out of their homes, with the numbers growing daily since then. This means that at least one-half of Syria's population has been displaced. The number of refugees and asylum-seekers in Turkey in 2015 is expected to rise to nearly 1.9 million, including 1.7 million Syrian refugees (http://www.unhcr.org/pages/49e48e0fa7f.html). In addition to Iraqi Kurdistan, however, Turkey has become home to thousands from Iraq, and significant numbers from Iran, Afghanistan, and African and Middle Eastern nations. Turkey should be commended for taking in so many desperate people; without question, this huge influx of people is not only difficult to manage, but local residents complain of rising prices, job loss, and increased crime attributed to the surging refugee population.

The Decimation of Iraqi Christians

Iraqi Christians were estimated at about 5 percent of the population before the U.S. invasion of Iraq, but since 2003, their number has dwindled to less than 1 percent. Over one million Christians have fled Iraq as of summer of 2014 (Stakelbeck, 2015). The shrinking number is especially apparent in Sunni Muslim areas where Christians were assumed to share a similar religion with the American invaders. This scenario resulted in many embittered Sunnis taking revenge on their neighbors, many of whom could trace their lineage for 2,000 years in this locale. When IS took Mosul (biblical Ninevah), Iraq's second largest city, 3,000 Christians were given three options: (1) convert to Islam; (2) pay the exorbitant *jizya* tax; or (3) die. Although many of Mosul's Christians could not afford the *jizya* tax that IS demanded, they weren't killed but they were forced to flee to areas under Kurdish control. I heard from some Christians that they were given one day to vacate their homes and leave everything behind. There are cases where IS fighters snatched a baby from a fleeing family. The family continued to flee, fearing that their other children would be taken, only to receive a large ransom demand of thousands of dollars to get their baby back.

Of the thousands of Christians who fled from Mosul and the surrounding areas, one church leader told me that 7,000 sought shelter in Ankawa, a predominately Christian enclave near Erbil proper. He said that in his own small church they had housed 170 refugees for a period of time. Fortunately, many of the Christians found a degree of safety in Kurdistan, having moved in with relatives or other Christian families. The situation facing the Iraqi Christians has been documented in a very well-done film narrated by actor Jim Caviezel called *Facing Extinction: Christians in Iraq.* Some Christians have fled to other countries to apply for refugee status, while others remain internally displaced in Kurdistan and hope that they will someday be accepted by Western countries. They seem to have little hope that they will be able to return to their homes. The oppression of Iraq's Assyrian Christians continues with several hundred more having been taken by IS after Caviezel's documentary was made.

The Plight of Yazidi Girls

I kept telling him it hurts—please stop. He told me that according to Islam he is allowed to rape an unbeliever. He said that by raping me, he is drawing closer to God. (12-year-old Yazidi virgin)

Yazidi women and children are to be divided according to the Sharia amongst the fighters of the Islamic State who participated in the Sinjar operations. Enslaving the families of the Kafir and taking their women as concubines is a firmly established aspect of the Sharia that if one were to deny or mock, he would be denying or mocking the verses of the Koran and the narrations of the Prophet—and thereby apostatizing from Islam. (*Dafiq* Magazine)

When the plight of the Yazidis stranded on the mountains of the Sinjar region filled the nightly news broadcasts last year, it was reported that a number of Yazidi girls/women were taken by IS and were forced to serve as virtual sex slaves to IS jihadists; 5,270 Yazidis were abducted in 2014, and at least 3,144 are still being held, according to community leaders (Callimachi, 2015). Matthew Barber, a University of Chicago expert on the Yazidis, says the offensive on Sinjar Mountain was as much about sexual conquest as it was about territorial gain.

It is frightening to think about the recruiting potential this type of event could hold for tens of thousands of sexually repressed young men in conservative Muslim societies. According to IS thinking, not only does Allah allow IS warriors to take sexual slaves, but it is an act of worship. In other words, jihadists do not have to wait until arriving in Paradise or be killed in a jihad to have access to beautiful virgins. They can have their reward in this life as well.

Well-known journalists David Brooks (*The New York Times*) and Trudy Rubin (*The Philadelphia Inquirer*) have discussed the pitiful U.S. response to IS in general and the apathy toward the rape and exploitation of Yazidi girls, many of whom have not reached puberty. Perhaps, as Rubin points out, the lack of outrage is due to war fatigue and the relative obscurity of the Yazidis. Yet, even the sexual slavery of an American, Kayla Mueller, who was chained and raped for months by the leader of the Islamic State, Abū Bakr al-Baghdādī, and chose not to escape lest she endanger Yazidi girls who looked to her as an older sister, has caused little reaction (Rubin, 2015). Brooks says that five hundred million dollars has been pledged by the U.S. to train and equip 15,000 Syrian moderates. After three years, this training produced 60 warriors against IS with a third of them being immediately captured by IS forces (Brooks, 2015).

Newspaper accounts confirmed what Yazidi leaders told me. Most men were shot, younger boys and older women were forced to convert to Islam or face death, and young, unmarried Yazidi girls were chosen by jihadists as sexual slaves. Stakelbeck (2015) claims that busloads of girls were taken by IS. Those who converted to Islam were married off to IS jihadists or to tribal leaders who aligned with IS. Those who refused conversion were simply raped repeatedly. Married women who agreed to convert to Islam were told their previous marriages did not count according to *Shari'a* law, and they were given to IS fighters. This practice was justified by claiming that IS warriors cannot afford to marry, and to avoid sexual frustration while they are fighting they are allowed to marry Yazidi women (Stern & Berger, 2015). Hall verifies this practice and states that Yazidi women are often "married" three times a day for two hours for each warrior in a practice called "sexual jihad."

Eventually President Obama intervened, and, with the help of Kurdish forces, 20,000 Yazidis were rescued off Mount Sinjar. Seven thousand remained trapped for four more months until rescued by Kurdish forces in December 2014 (Stakelbeck, 2015). Fortunately, according to the *Times* article, more than 2,000 girls have escaped from the grip of IS, and Matthew Barber has helped create a foundation that provides psychological counseling to these victims (Callimachi, 2015). Some wealthy Yazidis, in an act of compassion, ransomed girls in order to allow them to return and reintegrate with the community. It remains to be seen whether the community will receive them with open arms.

Whether Christian, Yazidi, or Muslim, Kurdish society puts a high premium on a girl's virginity. The loss of it, even due to rape and victimization, often regulates these girls to a life of rejection as they are perceived disqualified for marriage. There have been documented cases of suicide among the Yazidi girls who have been liberated from IS. It will require a good deal of cross-cultural sensitivity and psychological insight by Yazidi leaders and camp administrators to deal productively and humanely with this issue. IS justifies dealing with Yazidis even more brutally than with Christians due to the perception that the Yazidis are "devil worshippers," an accusation that the long-suffering Yazidis claim has led to over 70 incidents of genocide against them under various Islamic regimes over the years. The 800,000 Yazidis in the area near Mosul have nearly disappeared, as have the Christians. Both communities can trace their origins to the region long before Islam arrived on the scene.

IDP and Refugee Camps

I visited some predominately Yazidi refugee camps in Iraqi Kurdistan in February. In fact I arrived a few weeks after actress and UNHCR spokesperson Angelina Jolie had visited the same camps. While no one wants to remain in a refugee camp forever, conditions seemed to be at least bearable. One of the camps had about 6,000 tents with each tent containing an average family of five to six people. The camp was about 70 percent Yazidi and 30 percent Muslim, mostly from the city of Mosul and the Sinjar region. Each tent had a small kitchen and there were public toilets for every three to four tents. Water was drawn from common faucets, but at least from a material perspective the camp was not bad off. There were shops selling groceries, clothing, household goods, and other essentials. There were even shops that sold televisions and satellite dishes. IDPs and refugees who were well-off before fleeing their homes were able to purchase what they chose, whereas poorer families were forced to survive on the rations they received from the WFP (World Food Program) and other aid programs. Electricity was frequently cut, but the camps at least had some electricity every day. The camps were well organized, and more schools and other social services were in the process of being established.

In the camps that I visited, the main complaint of IDPs was the shortage of water and a need for more supplies. Work-for-food programs have been established, offering residents a chance to work, especially in the construction sector, and receive more money for food. While relations did not appear to be overly tense, sometimes there were conflicts between Yazidis and Muslim Kurds, and the *re spis* were called to reconcile the parties.

Not all Kurds or other Iraqis who fled from Mosul, however, are staying in refugee or IDP camps. I stayed several days with a well-off, educated Kurdish family who had recently fled from Mosul to Duhok, leaving all of their possessions behind, They were able to rent a very nice fully furnished home. The matriarch of the family was 87 years old. She had lived in Mosul her entire life. A very devout Muslim, she had to flee her home and take refuge in Duhok because she was Kurdish and perceived by IS warriors in Mosul as a *kafir*.

Many of the Iraqi Kurds were optimistic that if the United States continues to launch air strikes against IS targets, they could drive the jihadists out of Iraq in two to three years. The Kurds I discussed this with said they do not want American troops to fight, because they feared it would be perceived in the Muslim world as a religious war between Christians and Muslims. However, they all expressed gratitude for air strikes and expressed a need for better weapons. Now that Russian troops have entered into the fighting, no doubt IS and other jihadist forces will have renewed motivation to fight the army of the infidels. One only has to recall the 1979 Russian invasion of Afghanistan, which led to thousands of jihadists from around the world coming to Afghanistan to do battle against the infidels. There is little reason to believe that American troops would be perceived in better light than the Russians have been if American troops enter the battle.

Camps in Southeast Turkey

More recently (June 2015) I visited a camp in southeast Turkey that was predominately filled with well over 3,000 Yazidi Kurds. There were four other Yazidi camps ranging from 160 to 900 "residents" (*Turkish Daily News*, July 9, 2015). I also visited three small camps that were predominately populated by Kurds with a Muslim background. The people in these camps did not seem to share in the relative optimism that those in the Iraqi camp shared. There appear to be two types of camps for Kurdish refugees in Turkey: Turkish government camps (AFAD), which are very orderly and have multiple resources available, and camps controlled by the Kurdish municipality (*Belediye* camps), which are inferior to the AFAD camps but the choice of many Yazidi and Muslim Kurds. I visited the municipal camps, as it was harder to gain access to the AFAD camps.

I asked a long-time Kurdish friend who has delivered relief supplies and consequently gotten to know many of the camps' residents why many of the Yazidis prefer to stay in *Belediye* camps despite having less material benefits as compared to the AFAD camps. He cited three major reasons: (1) In the AFAD camps, Arab and Yazidi refugees are mixed, and many Yazidis no longer want anything to do with Arabs, having been so persecuted over the centuries by Arab Muslims; (2) The AFAD camps allow for less movement of refugees, whereas the *Belediye* camps allow the refugees to come and go more easily; (3) There appears to be a degree of Islamic indoctrination carried out in the AFAD camps that is contrary to Yazidi beliefs and practices.

Chris McQueen, a research assistant at Nevsehir University in Turkey, concurs with this and adds that a political motivation is also present. The AKP (the Justice and Development party), which has been the dominant party in Turkey for many years, is more overtly Islamic in its practices than previous parties in power. The Yazidis often claim that their faith is the true

Market activity in a refugee camp.

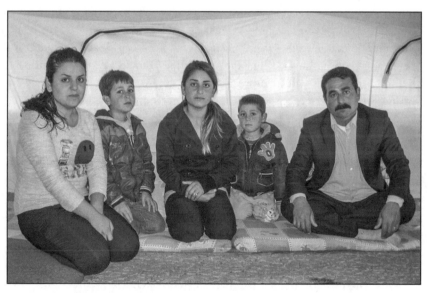

Yazidi refugee family.

indigenous religion of the Kurdish people and that they are the "true Kurds." They see Islam as an alien religion that has been forced on the Kurds by the Arabs. One can also find PKK representatives in the *Belediye* camps, who, due to their liberal ideology, would not be allowed to reside in AFAD camps.

It appeared to me and to others with whom I discussed this topic, that the Yazidis living in the *Belediye* camps did not share in the general optimism that the Yazidis sheltered in camps among the Iraqi Kurds did. Part of the reason is that the Iraqi Yazidis are among Kurds from their own country. Yazidis who have fled to Turkey have crossed an international border and are in a country that often has not been favorably disposed toward Kurdish people, let alone those who do not even share in a common religion.

Recently about 3,000 Yazidis, predominately from the *Belediye* camps, made their way toward the Bulgarian–Turkish border to seek asylum. They stated emphatically that they no longer will live in a Muslim-majority country. Two thousand were turned back before reaching Istanbul, and the thousand that did get to Istanbul were rounded up and sent back to the camp. Perhaps 250 made it to Edirne on the border before being taken back to the Diyarbakir camp (one of the municipality-run camps in southeastern Turkey). According to Radio Free Europe, 3,000–5,000 Yazidis continue to arrive in Turkey each month. As of July 2015, at least 30,000 Yazidis had fled to Turkey. A number of those have returned to Iraq, and some have paid smugglers large sums to take them illegally into Europe (*Turkish Daily News*, July 9, 2015). The sad news for the Yazidis who had hoped that they would be granted asylum in Europe is that most likely they will spend years in refugee camps before, if ever, they are finally granted the right to start life over in new locations.

UNHCR (2011) lists three options for refugees with a fourth one highly discouraged:

1. The best solution is for the refugees to return to their home countries. However, out of a worldwide displaced people count of 59.5 million (including 19.5 million refugees who have crossed national borders), less than 200,000 were able to return to their homes last year (UNHCR). Some Kurds, both among those displaced within Syria or those who crossed into Turkey, have returned to Kobani, a city not yet totally free from fighting between Kurdish forces and IS warriors, but where most of the IS forces have been driven out.

2. Integrate into a country of refuge. Eighty-six percent of refugees can be found in developing countries, which are already severely impoverished, with high unemployment and underemployment rates. Refu-

gees add to already challenging conditions in most of the countries to which they have fled.

3. Resettlement. Out of 19 million refugees, only about 105,000 or less than 1 percent were resettled in a third country. This is generally the hope that most displaced people and refugees share, but in reality, very few will ever experience resettlement in a third country.

4. An option that is discouraged but frequently occurs consists of thousands of refugees that have paid large sums of money to smugglers to take them illegally to Western countries. This option works for some, but in many other cases ends tragically. Nightly news continues to broadcast tragic stories of desperate refugees feeling to Europe, especially the Greek islands, and Italy, on small fishing boats, with many drowning. *Time* magazine in a recent cover story (October 19, 2015), claims that nearly 400,000 migrants have crossed from Turkey to Greece, mostly through paying large sums to migrant smugglers. Thousands of others have made Germany their goal, but in efforts to pass through Hungary, they have encountered a high fence with razor wire stretched across the entire length of over 100 miles, a hostile Hungarian police force, and an equally unwelcoming local populace. In an August 31, 2015, article in *The Washington Post*, Hungary has only granted asylum to 278 of 148,000 seekers. Of course Hungary is not the goal of these migrants, but people have paid thousands of dollars to smugglers to get them as far as the fence. However, the fence has proven incapable of holding back the refugees and they continue to come. According to UNHCR, 10.8 million Syrians need humanitarian assistance, including 6.5 million IDPs. Hundreds of thousands more Syrians are temporarily placed in camps throughout Turkey, Jordan, and Lebanon. The following sober statistics are cited by *Time*:

- 1 in 122 people in the world is a refugee, internally displaced (IDP) or an asylum seeker
- There are 1.9 million Syrian refugees alone in Turkey
- 42,500 people are displaced each day
- More than 600,000 have entered Europe so far this year
- Europe's population has grown by less than 1% because of the refugees, whereas Lebanon's population is now 25% Syrian refugees
- The United States has agreed to take about 100,000 refugees in 2017 whereas Germany is taking 800,000 in 2015 alone (October 19, 2015).

Can IS Be Defeated?

Weiss and Hassan finish their excellent book by saying, IS "has promised both death and a return to the ancient glories of Islam. Thousands have lined up to join it, and even more have already fallen victim to it. The army of terror will be with us indefinitely" (2015, p. 242).

Thus, arming the Kurds and other Muslim allies also threatened by IS will hopefully contribute to the defeat of IS. It must be remembered that neither the Kurds nor the Shi'ites, without help, will be able to control the heartland of Syria or Iraq's Sunni heartland. They are hated there, the Kurds for ethnic and Shi'ites for religious reasons. But as Wood (2015) points out, every month that IS fails to expand, it resembles less the victorious armies of the Prophet Muhammad with Allah on their side, and appears to be a human endeavor, another in a long line of failed attempts to bring the Middle East to general prosperity for its long-suffering populace. With time IS's apocalyptic fervor will decrease. How much destruction and loss of life will occur before its downfall, however, is yet to be determined.

I also want to make clear that most Muslims do not support the IS tactics in the killing of Yazidis and Christians and the taking of sex slaves. Elias Mallon (2015) reports that Grand Ayatollah al-Husseini al-Sistani, a leading Shi'ite authority, issued a *fatwa* (religious declaration) condemning the persecution of Christians and Yazidis and has invited them to seek refuge in southern Iraq, which is under Shi'ite control. On the Sunni side, Muhammad Haniff Hassan, a Fellow at the S. Rajaratnam School of International Studies (RSIS), and Mustaza Bahari, an Associate Research Fellow RSIS, published a list of 86 organizations and prominent individuals that have spoken out against the Islamic State. In September 2014, 126 Muslim leaders from Detroit signed a rebuttal based on the Qur'an, the Hadith, history, and analogous reasoning and sent it to al-Baghdādi. The *fatwa* refutes point by point IS's justification for their actions and exposes their tactics as contrary to Islam (*America*, March 16, 2015).

Globalization and Urbanization among Iraqi Kurds

The changes in Iraqi Kurdistan since 2007 were mind boggling for me. I knew the Kurds were entrepreneurs (see chapter 6). On my most recent trip to Iraqi Kurdistan (February 2015), I was shocked at how much things have changed. The Kurds told me that especially since 2010 the change has been most rapid. I never thought I would live to see the day when there was an international airport in Kurdistan with flights connecting to major European cities, multistory parking garages, and malls as large and modern as any American mall. There are also fast-food restaurants, luxury five-star hotels, and the latest model of every type of automobile. Even the most recent international films appear about the same time they do in the U.S. Many of the fast-food and service-sector jobs are performed by outsiders, particularly from South Asian and African countries, as well as the Philippines, because most Kurds don't "need" to do those types of jobs anymore.

It was very hard for me to wrap my mind around this as I remember the days when there was no electricity, when every public building was full of displaced people, widows lined up by the hundreds to ask for any type of aid, and destruction was everywhere.

The Infamous Nazarki Prison

Nazarki Prison encapsulates the changes in a dramatic fashion. Nazarki Prison is a notorious fortress-like building that imprisoned thousands of Kurds until the safety zone was implemented in 1991. Kurdish women and children were separated from their husbands and fathers by Saddam's soldiers, and often the men disappeared and were never heard from again. Tens of thousands allegedly were killed within the walls of this notorious prison.

The infamous Nazarki Prison.

Our NGO did a water and toilet project there in 1993 and provided plastic sheeting to keep out the cold and provide some privacy. We were told by the regional government, however, not to make Nazarki too comfortable, as the goal was to relocate the residents back to their ancestral villages. Conditions in Kurdistan, especially for the Anfal widows who no longer had a husband to claim and work their land in their ancestral village, appeared so hopeless that many widows thought Nazarki was the best they could ever hope for. Most of these Anfal widows are now being looked after by the KRG (Kurdish Regional Government) and some NGOs. The plans for Nazarki is to turn this infamous prison into a museum of remembrance, as a constant reminder of the suffering of the Kurds under Saddam, especially during the Anfal Operation.

Education Given a High Priority

Several universities, colleges, and private high schools have been opened or reopened, and foreign professors have been hired in various fields as well as Kurdish professors with graduate degrees. Private English schools offer a decent salary to native speakers of English with a college degree.

Kurdish students at Duhok University.

I visited a university in Duhok, which has about 12,000 students, including many from Sinjar, the center of the Yazidi homeland, and Mosul, the largest city under Islamic State control. In addition to the majority Muslim Kurdish students, there are Christians and Yazidis, and some international students. Students seem to get along well, and the anti-Yazidism of the past does not seem to be prevalent on the campus. There is a mixture of covered and uncovered female students. Some students have withdrawn to fight against IS, however, and some have been killed in the fight.

As in many other places where rapid urbanization is occurring, the Kurds told me that people are marrying at a later age and having fewer children per family. Honor killing still occurs in certain situations, although it is difficult to know how frequently. Love marriages rather than arranged ones are becoming more common. Strong parental involvement in the selection of a son's or a daughter's spouse is still the norm, and extended family ties are still maintained by most newlyweds. I was not able to ascertain the degree to which first-cousin marriage is still taking place, but generally with urbanization and increased education, the percentage of marriages among blood relations decreases.

Some Kurds Explore Their Pre-Islamic Roots

As I mentioned in the history chapter (see chapter 2) the Jews were exiled in the 8th century BC to the land of the Medes, the alleged ancestors of the Kurds along the Khabur River, which runs through Iraqi Kurdistan. Over the centuries, Jews no doubt were assimilated into the local Median/Kurdish culture, while at the same time it seems that many Medes embraced Judaism. Mustafa Barzani, whose importance to the Kurds can hardly be overstated, and his son, Masoud, the president of Iraqi Kurdistan, bear the same surname as Moshe Barzani (1926–1947), a well-known Jewish freedom fighter during Israel's battle for independence from Great Britain. Estimates of up to 200,000 Jewish Kurds live in the current state of Israel. An interesting autobiography on this topic is Ariel Sabar's *My Father's Paradise: A Son's Search for His Jewish Past in Kurdish Iraq* (2008). It is not unusual for even devoutly Muslim Kurds to acknowledge that they have Jewish ancestry in their not so distant past.

There are an uncertain number of Kurds that have chosen to follow *Isa al Masih* (Jesus the Messiah). Most of these new followers are well-educated adults who have a strong sense of Kurdish identity. They are distinct from Iraq's birth Christians as discussed earlier. Kurds now have the freedom in

Northern Iraq to research their history to a degree that was impossible in the past. The Kurds generally tend to be tolerant toward people of other religions. However, there have been examples of Kurds who have chosen a different path besides Islam and have paid a great price in terms of social ostracism, persecution, and in a few cases, death.

Recently, I was impressed by the respectful and warm friendship between the Kurdish Muslim NGO personnel and the Yazidi IDPs and refugees in the camps I visited. I did not sense that type of camaraderie when I was in Kurdistan in the 1990s when most of our engineers were obviously uncomfortable around the Yazidis who were widely perceived as being "devil worshippers." In my most recent encounters, I often heard the Muslim aid workers encourage the Yazidis in the IDP camps by saying, "We are all Kurds. When you suffer we suffer." This is quite a change from the attitudes of the past. The pain of past disdain by Muslim Kurds will not be erased overnight, as demonstrated by many Yazidis that no longer want to live in any Muslim majority region even if it is administrated by Kurds.

Kurdistan: Transformed but Not Paradise Yet

2014 was an incredibly difficult year for the Kurdish Regional Government in Iraq. Baghdad had refused to give the Kurds their 17 percent of its share of the revenue from oil. The KRG needs 750 million dollars to pay for its vast public sector and so debt increased each month. Then ISIS attacked in June forcing Kurds to deploy and pay for troops, and 1.3 million refugees sought shelter in Kurdistan. Now as the main warriors against ISIS they need to bargain for a permanent deal with Turkey for oil and natural gas, and a long time security arrangement with the US.

—War Correspondent Benjamin Hall

In the midst of incredible transformation, the reality is that Kurdistan is not Paradise yet. First, due to the ongoing battle against Islamic State forces, a lot of tourists and foreign investors that were expected to continue to invest and spend money in Kurdistan are no longer doing so. Second, in addition to the issues that Hall raises above, one hears consistent complaints that corruption is rampant and those with *wastah* (influential connections similar to *torpil* in Turkish) get the breaks, and those who do not find it difficult to advance. While corruption occurs in every country, it is enough of a concern among the Kurds with whom I spoke that many of the positive changes I have discussed may not be benefitting as many people as they could be. Third, there are still hundreds of thousands of displaced people that may not get to return their own homes for a long time. Because the Iraqi Kurds have often been made refugees themselves and know how difficult it is, we have to hope that they will continue to be compassionate toward those who have fled to their region.

Changes in Turkey's Attitude toward Iraqi Kurdistan

The de facto state in Northern Iraq had previously put Turkey in an uncomfortable position. The Iraqi Kurds were very emphatic that under no conditions would they allow Turkey to intervene in their affairs. Turkish troops have fought against the PKK (see chapter 2) on both sides of the Turkish–Iraqi border. The U.S., who had previously classified the Iraqi Kurds as "good Kurds" and the Turkish Kurds as "bad Kurds," was put in a difficult position. In diplomatic meetings between Turkey and Iraqi Kurds, the Kurds came away believing that America had sold out again to the Turks, while the Turks believed that the U.S. had an agenda of helping the Kurds create an independent state in Northern Iraq (Lawrence, 2008).

Although traditionally Turkey was seen as the major obstacle to any type of an independent Kurdistan in Northern Iraq, business between Turkey and Iraqi Kurdistan rapidly increased, not to mention the flow of petrol between oil-rich Kurdistan and oil-needy Turkey. Lawrence points out that since 2006, Turkish as well as Arab contractors from various countries have snapped up multi-million-dollar construction deals, and 600 hundred Turkish companies were doing 1.5 billion dollars' worth of business in Northern Iraq by 2007. The number of Turkish businesses has rapidly increased since then, and Erbil, the capital of Iraqi Kurdistan, in particular feels like a little Istanbul. Many Arabs from the rest of Iraq are also flocking to Kurdistan for work, having invested nearly four billion dollars there, and thousands more are looking to vacation in a place of comparative safety.

The Kurdish Corridor

On June 30, 2014, Islamic State jihadists captured a small Syrian city of 50,000 people named Tal Abyad, near the Turkish border at Akçakale, a major checkpoint between the Syrian and Turkish borders. Within a few weeks, IS announced that all Kurdish inhabitants had to leave Tal Abyad or be killed. Not only Kurds but also Turkmen and Sunni Arab families fled, leaving everything behind with displaced Arab refugees from other regions having taken over the abandoned homes. The city was retaken a year later primarily by Kurdish People's Defense Units (YPG, a Syrian off-shoot of the PKK), in cooperation with Free Syrian Army forces, with the assistance of U.S. and coalition partners supplying the air power. U.S. officials praised the YPG fighters as the best of the ground forces working with the U.S. against IS. In the process of freeing the city and surrounding areas, a 250-mile-long corridor from Iraqi Kurdistan all the way to the city of Kobani (or Kobane) was established. This region was declared autonomous from Syria, and some Kurdish groups have named it *Rojava* (Micallef, 2015).

In June 2015, I visited this border region and saw firsthand the chaos of hundreds of Syrians fleeing their homeland and crossing the border at Akçakale. It is not surprising that a so-called Kurdish corridor has caused much controversy in Turkey, as the Turkish government fears it could lead to a push for Kurdish independence. The population of the corridor is around 50 percent Kurdish, and while Arabs and Turkmens are cooperating with the Kurds in the battle against IS, there are both ethnic and religious differences between the primarily secular YPG Kurdish warriors, and the Islamic Turkmen and Arab fighters. Both IS and the Turkish government are spreading fear among the non-Kurdish residents of the corridor by saying that the Kurds are planning an ethnic cleansing of non-Kurds. Citing Joseph Micallef (2015):

> For now, the United States finds itself in a position where a key ally, Turkey, is effectively at war with the one ground force, the Kurds, that, when supported by American air power, have been the most effective in rolling back the Islamic State. The Turkish government has made it clear that given a choice between defeating Islamic State and forestalling any possibility of an independent Kurdish state along its southern border, it will opt to go to war against the Kurdish YPG and to tolerate the continued existence of the Islamic State. Under these circumstances is it any wonder that the Islamic State continues to thrive?

Turkey has allowed the U.S. to fly sorties out of Incirlik, a major military base in southern Turkey, in part as a reaction to the death of over 30 Turkish Kurds by a suicide bomber at a rally focusing on rebuilding Kobani. However, nothing concerning the Kurds is ever simple, as Turkey has also insisted that its allies look the other way as the Turks battle against alleged Kurdish separatist forces. So, on the one hand, the Kurds are heroes for their bravery fighting against the Islamic State jihadists. On the other hand, they are villains, warring against the best model of a democratic state in the Muslim world, Turkey.

More recently, the Kurds have managed to recapture Sinjar town, one of the traditional homelands of the Yazidi people. IS has not been able to advance to the main Shi'ite areas of Iraq or the Alawite heartland of Syria, and it has been unsuccessful in its attempts to hold Kurdish, Shi'ite, or Yazidi areas. Furthermore, U.S.-backed forces have retaken significant amounts of land in Iraq and Syria, and Kurdish and Arab opponents have made it more difficult for IS to benefit from the spoils of war, including oil fields and repossessed properties.

Turkey: Optimism and Concern

Outwardly at least, Turkey is continuing to modernize rapidly. I used to hear over and over Turks describe their country as an *az gelişmiş ülke* (an underdeveloped or little developed country). While not perceived as a third world country by its people, it was seen as far behind the West in many ways. It would be difficult to say that now, at least in terms of technology. The public transportation system is among the best in the world, with easily accessible metro (subway) trains taking hundreds of thousands of passengers to all corners of Istanbul relatively quickly and inexpensively. One can even take a metro underground between the Asian and European sides of Istanbul. The first time I rode the metro, called the *Marmaray*, I was struck by the fact that I was going by train between two continents underwater. Furthermore, construction on the world's largest airport has begun in Istanbul, which will replace the large airport on the European side. There is also a new, much used airport on the Asian side. Other plans are for a major highway system to be built under the Bosporus so that one can cross from Asia to Europe above or underground, as well as by a beautiful boat ride.

There is so much about Turkey that could be said as it continues to grow in influence in every realm: economically, religiously, socioculturally, and politically. After serving the maximum of two terms as prime minister, Recep Tayyip Erdoğan won the election for the presidency and turned the office from primarily a ceremonial one to one with great power. Erdoğan also has his critics, however. He is said to be pursuing increasingly dictatorial powers and is satirically called "Sultan" like in the Ottoman days, and some say he is trying to bring back a modern version of the Ottoman Empire. He has decreased the power of the military, which seemed impossible before his reign.

Among the Kurds, Erdoğan and his party (AKP) had been quite popular for easing up on restrictions on Kurdish cultural expression, and the Kurds seemed to prefer his and his party's deep commitment to Islam rather than the official secularism of several other Turkish parties. However, when Syrian Kurds were battling for Kobani against IS, the Turkish Kurds, in particular the PKK, wanted to assist their fellow Kurds in Syria. Erdoğan refused to let Turkish Kurds, in particular the PKK, come to their aid. While relations have improved, President Erdoğan obviously felt that the PKK cannot be totally trusted. He did, nevertheless, allow some Peshmerga from Iraqi Kurdistan to fight against IS, and now Kobani is in Kurdish hands, although there has been great destruction.

In March 2015 I was going to the Kadiköy boat docks to take a ferry from the Asian to the European side of Istanbul. I heard familiar music being played. As I got closer, I saw Kurdish *dawet* with about 25 men joined by a few women enthusiastically moving to the tune of an amplified *saz* (a stringed instrument with a long neck). The musicians were singing in Kurdish while others passed out HDP brochures. I could not imagine this happening a few years ago.

Later in 2015, I was in southeast Turkey during the long anticipated June 7th elections. While President Erdoğan was not up for reelection, his AKP party and its Prime Minister Ahmet Davutoğlu along with several other parties, including the HDP, a predominately Kurdish party, was. In past elections, Kurdish parties did not thrive very well. But in this election, the HDP won almost 13 percent of the popular vote. Perhaps most exciting for many Kurds is that over 80 representatives will be sent to parliament, giving the Kurds and non-Kurdish supporters of the party a much stronger voice in government.

Dawet in support of the HDP party.

Most of the predominately Kurdish regions voted in support of the HDP, and in places that the more Islamic parties have won in the past, a greater number voted for HDP as well. There was much celebration for several days with parades, fireworks, and an exuberance among the people. It would take too long to go into all the details, but the lack of the AKP support for the battle against Kobani no doubt influenced many Kurds to change their party alliance. Along with the festive atmosphere, however, there was a somber side.

As in Iraq, however, there is still room for concern. The towns and cities in southeastern Turkey still are very impoverished and there seems to be little investment, meaning that millions of more Kurds will probably continue to migrate to western Turkey. Istanbul is probably home to at least 17 million people (unofficially). Other western Turkish cities are also continuing to grow rapidly with a high percentage of recent arrivals being from Kurdish regions.

Turkey, which I visit every year, was not as much of a shock as Iraqi Kurdistan, in terms of globalization or urbanization. Even Bağcılar (see chapter 7), full of recent Kurdish migrants from southeastern and eastern Turkey, is continuing to rapidly modernize. One encounters Burger King and McDonald's side by side, the latest films in world cinema are shown, and evidences of globalization are everywhere present.

Every year when I go to Turkey I find that I am always amazed by the level of people's energy. It is a country on the rise. Although people may complain about corruption or the hard work with low pay and other issues, there is an optimism in the air that is refreshing. While serious problems remain, it seems that most Kurds are happy to be playing their part in contributing toward making this incredibly beautiful and bountiful country better for all. Turkey is now the world's sixth leading country in the number of tourists it attracts. Yet, despite its technological advances and surface prosperity, all is not well.

Urbanization and globalization in Bağcılar.

In discussing my love for Turkey with local citizens, I have repeatedly had Turks tell me that Turkey is wonderful if you have enough money to visit its historical sites, beaches, and natural wonders. So few have the means to do this, however, so only the rich and tourists can really enjoy Turkey. In addition to economic woes, discrimination still raises its ugly head. A Kurdish friend whom I met a few years ago in Bağcılar shared with me how when he was growing up he was regularly asked to show his *kimlik* (identity card) to policemen. Upon seeing that his place of birth was in predominately Kurdish southeast Turkey, the police would often strike him or verbally abuse him. As an amateur photographer he was taking pictures of Kurdish refugees in southeast Turkey not long ago, and the military smashed his long-lens camera, his most prized possession. He also works in a clothing factory 12 hours a day and half days on Saturday, but he is paid according to a 40-hour week. No doubt countless thousands of poor Turks and Kurds are in similar conditions, a situation that is not readily observable to the millions of tourists who arrive each year and marvel at its natural beauty and historic sites.

From Mountains to Malls

I have been following the Kurdish situation for well over 30 years. My wife and I raised our children in Istanbul and Northern Cyprus with its mix of ethnicities, and also in southeastern Turkey and Iraqi Kurdistan where Kurds are the vast majority. I have also seen the Kurds in their diaspora contexts, including Central Asia, Western Europe, and the United States. Their importance in the future of the Middle East can hardly be overstated. From being on the nightly news as victims of Saddam Hussein's brutality in 1991, to playing the role of brave heroes who are battling against Islamic State jihadists more recently, more people than ever are becoming aware of the Kurds. Can young Kurds growing up in cities with shopping malls and exposed to pop culture still identify with the most famous of all Kurdish expressions, "The Kurds have no friends but the mountains"? Will a strong sense of Kurdish identity be evident to the generations that are growing up in the shadow of malls rather than the mountains? Will the maps of the future contain an official region called "Kurdistan," and if so, what locations will be included in it? Will the primary values of hospitality generosity, family, and courage continue? Can they unite and avoid further demoralizing civil conflict pitting Kurd against Kurd? How will the four major countries in which the Kurds dwell respond to an increasingly stronger Kurdish population? Will the Kurds

From mountains to malls.

continue to open their homeland to be a place of refuge and a model of positive change in the Islamic world? These are just some of the questions that may be answered in the days ahead.

Questions for Discussion

- The chapter points out that the world is facing the largest scale refugee and displaced people crisis since World War II. Put yourself in the place of someone who has left everything familiar behind to migrate to a new place and very different way of life. What do you think life would be like in a refugee camp? What do you think would be the greatest challenges facing the thousands of refugees fleeing from Iraq and Syria to a Western country?

- Thousands of European and American youth have joined the Islamic State. Some have likened the challenge that IS offers young people to the challenge that Hitler posed to German youth. In both cases, youth were challenged to give of themselves totally to something bigger than themselves. History records what happened to the Third Reich in Germany. What do you think the future holds for the Islamic State and its supporters as well as its victims?

Notes

[1] Hadith are the alleged sayings and actions of the Prophet Muhammad, and the early Muslims, passed down orally for about two hundred years and then compiled into collections. Second only to the Qur'an in authority to guide the Muslim community, they have been the source of quite a bit of controversy. Most Sunni Muslim commentators state that there exists six authoritative collections of Hadith, with the collections of Sahih al- Buhkari and Sahih Muslim as the best preserved. The Shi'a also have some collections of their own Hadith and reject some that Sunnis hold to. McCants (2015) has probably done the most intensive research on IS's use of Hadith to portray their actions as preparing the way for last-day events as predicted by Muhammad and the early Muslim community.

[2] The idea of coming of the Mahdi is widespread in Islam despite there being no reference to this in the Qur'an or in the most authoritative Hadith. Traditionally, Shi'ite Muslims have anticipated the 12th Imam who is now in occultation to come back to life when the Islamic world is in a state of great crisis. However, many Sunni Muslims now also await the Mahdi (literally means the guided one) as an apocalyptic figure who will lead the Muslims to victory over Dajjall and his forces. Some prophecy that Jesus and the Mahdi will work together to bring about a better world after the defeat and judgment of the wicked and enemies of Islam. Others say that the Mahdi and Jesus are one and the same. There have been several people claiming to be the Mahdi throughout history, as there have been false Messiahs in Jewish and Christian history. After the anticipated return of the Mahdi did not occur as predicted in some IS literature, IS has seemed to de-emphasize this aspect of their eschatology but has continued to proclaim the restoration of the caliphate.

Bibliography

Abadan-Unat, N. (1995). Turkish migration to Europe. In R. Cohen (Ed.), *The Cambridge survey of world migration* (pp. 279–285). Cambridge, UK: Cambridge University.

Ahmed, A. S. (2003). *Islam under siege.* Oxford, UK: Polity.

Allison, C. (1996). Old and new oral traditions in Badinan. In P. Kreyenbrock & C. Allison (Eds.), *Kurdish culture and identity* (pp. 29–47). London: Zed.

Anderson, B. (2006). *Imagined communities.* Rev. ed. London: Verso.

Atkinson, P., & Hammersley, M. (1994). Ethnography and participant observation. In N. K. Denzin & Y. S. Lincoln (Eds.), *Handbook of qualitative research* (pp. 248–261). Thousand Oaks, CA: Sage.

Baker, J. A. III, Hamilton, L. H., et al. (2006) *The Iraq Study Group Report.* (n.d.) http://bakerinstitute.org/files/1044/ (Accessed October 12, 2015).

Barfield, T. (1997). *The dictionary of anthropology.* Malden, MA: Blackwell.

Barkey, H. J., & Fuller, G. E. (1997). Turkey's Kurdish question: Critical turning points and missed opportunities. *Middle East Journal,* 51, 59–78.

Barkey, H. J. (2000). Hemmed in by circumstances: Turkey and Iraq since the Gulf War. *Middle East Policy,* 7, 110–125.

Bell-Fialkoff, A. (1996). *Ethnic cleansing.* New York: St. Martin's.

Ben Amos, D. (1997). Transmission. In T. A. Green (Ed.), *Folklore: An encyclopedia of beliefs, customs, tales, music, and art.* Vol. 2 (pp. 807–811). Santa Barbara, CA: ABC-CLIO.

Bender, C. (2000). *Kürt tarihi ve ugarligi* (Kurdish history and civilization). Istanbul, Turkey: Kaynak.

Bengio, O. (2005). Autonomy in Kurdistan in historical perspective. In B. O'Leary, J. McGarry, & K. Salih (Eds.), *The future of Kurdistan in Iraq.* Philadelphia: University of Pennsylvania.

Beşikçi, İ. (2004). *International colony Kurdistan.* Reading, England: Garod.

Bianquis, T. (1996). The family in Arab Islam. In A. Burguiere, C. Klapisch-Zuber, M. Segalen, F. Zonabend (Eds.), *A history of the family: Distant worlds, ancient worlds.* Vol. 1. Cambridge, MA: Harvard University Press.

Bird, C. (2005). *A thousand sighs, a thousand revolts.* New York: Random House.

Blincoe, R. (1998). *Ethnic realities and the church: Lessons from Kurdistan*. Pasadena, CA: Presbyterian Center for Mission Studies.

Bozarslan, H. (2004). *Violence in the Middle East*. Princeton, NJ: Markus Wiener.

Brentjes, B. (1997). *The Armenians, Assyrians & Kurds*. Campbell, CA: Rishi.

Brooks, D. (2015, August 31). When Islamic State rapists win. *St. Paul Pioneer Press*. http://www.twincities.com/opinion/columnists/ci_28740731/david-brooks:-when-islamic-state-rapists-win.

Bullock, J., & Morris, H. (1992). *No friends but the mountains*. New York: Oxford University.

Burkay, K. (1997). *Gecmisten bugune Kurtler ve Kurdistan* (Kurds and Kurdistan, past and present). Istanbul, Turkey: Deng.

Callimachi, R. (2015, August 13). ISIS enshrines a theology of rape. *New York Times*. http://www.nytimes.com/2015/08/14/world/middleeast/isis-enshrines-a-theology-of-rape.html?ref=topics&_r=0 (Accessed October 13, 2015).

Chaliand, G. (Ed.). (1993). *A people without a country. The Kurds and Kurdistan*. New York: Olive Branch.

Champagne, D. (2003). Indigenous strategies for engaging globalism. In D. Champagne & I. Abu-Saad (Eds.), *The future of indigenous peoples*. Los Angeles: UCLA American Indian Studies.

Chapin, W. D. (1996). The Turkish diaspora in Germany. *Diaspora, 5*, 275–300.

Ciment, J. (1996). *The Kurds: State and minority in Turkey, Iraq, and Iran*. New York: Facts on File.

Clifford, J., & Marcus, G. E. (Eds.). (1986). *Writing culture: The poetics and politics of culture*. Berkeley: University of California.

Critchfield, R. (1981). *Villages*. New York: Anchor.

Cutts, M. (Ed.). (2000). *The state of the world's refugees 2000*. UNHCR: Oxford University.

Dagi, I. (2000). Human rights, democratization and the European community in Turkish politics: The Özal years, 1983–87. *Middle Eastern Studies, 37*, 17–37.

Denzin, N. K., & Lincoln, Y. S. (Eds.). (1994). *Handbook of qualitative research*. Thousand Oaks, CA: Sage.

Dunn, M. C. (1995). The Kurdish "question": Is there an answer? A historical overview. *Middle East Policy, 4*, 72–80.

Eickelman, D. F. (1998). *The Middle East and central Asia: An anthropological approach*. Upper Saddle River, NJ: Prentice-Hall.

Elabor-Idemudia, P. (2000). The retention of knowledge of folkways as a basis for resistance. In G. J. Dei, B. L. Hall, & D. G. Rosenberg (Eds.), *Indigenous knowledges in global contexts*. Toronto: Toronto University.

Emerson, R. M. (2001). *Contemporary field research*. Long Grove, IL: Waveland Press.

Entessar, N. (1992). *Kurdish ethnonationalism*. Boulder, CO: Lynne Rienner.

Fagerlind, I., & Saha, L. J. (1989). *Education and national development*. 2nd ed. Oxford, UK: Pergamon.

Fargues, P. (1996). The Arab world. The family as fortress. In A. Burguiere, C. Klapisch-Zuber, M. Segalen, F. Zonabend (Eds.), *A History of the family: The impact of modernity*. Vol. 2. Cambridge, MA: Belknap Press of Harvard University.

Fetterman, D. M. (1998). *Ethnography*. Thousand Oaks, CA: Sage.

Finkel, C. (2007). *Osman's dream*. New York: Basic Books.

Finnegan, R. (1992). *Oral traditions and the verbal arts*. London: Routledge.

Foster, G. M. (1973). *Traditional societies and technological change*. New York: Harper and Row.

Freire P., & Faundez, H. (1989). *Learning to question: A pedagogy of liberation*. New York: Continuum.

Galbraith, P. W. (2005). Kurdistan in federal Iraq. In B. O'Leary, J. McGarry, & K. Salih (Eds.), *The future of Iraqi Kurdistan*. Philadelphia: University of Pennsylvania.

Geertz, C. (1973). *The interpretation of cultures*. New York: Basic Books.

Geertz, C. (1983). *Local knowledge*. New York: Basic Books.

Gilbert, P. (2000). *Peoples, cultures and nations in political philosophy*. Washington, DC: Georgetown University.

Goldstein, D. M. (2003). *Laughter out of place*. Berkeley: University of California.

Günes-Ayata, A. (1996). Solidarity in urban Turkish family. In G. Rasuly-Paleczek (Ed.), *Turkish families in transition* (pp. 98–113). Frankfurt, Germany: Peter Lang.

Gunter, M. M. (1994). *The changing Kurdish problem in Turkey*. London: RISCT.

Gunter, M. M. (2005). Turkey's new neighbor, Kurdistan. In B. O'Leary, J. McGarry, & K. Salih (Eds.), *The future of Kurdistan in Iraq*. Philadelphia: University of Pennsylvania.

Gunter, M. M. (2010). *Historical dictionary of the Kurds*. 2nd ed. Lanham, MD: Scarecrow.

Gunter, M. M., & Yavuz, M. H. (2005). The continuing crisis in Iraqi Kurdistan. *Middle East Policy*, 12, 122–133.

Gürbey, G. (1996). The development of the Kurdish national movement in Turkey since the 1980s. In R. Olson (Ed.), *The Kurdish national movement in the 1990s*. Lexington: The University Press of Kentucky.

Hall, B. (2015). *Inside ISIS: The brutal rise of a terrorist army*. New York: Center Street.

Hirschler, K. (2001). Defining the nation: Kurdish historiography in Turkey in the 1990s. *Middle Eastern Studies*, 37, 145–163.

Hofstede, G., & Hofstede, G. (2005). *Cultures and organizations*. Rev. ed. New York: McGraw-Hill.

Houston, C. (2001). *Islam, Kurds and the Turkish nation-state*. Oxford, UK: Berg.

Human Rights Watch. (1995). *Iraq's crime of genocide: Human Rights Watch/Middle East*. New Haven, CT: Yale University.

Human Rights Watch. (2006). *World Report: U.S.A.* New York: Human Rights Watch.

Huntington, S. P. (1996). *The clash of civilizations and the remaking of world order*. New York: Simon & Schuster.

Ibrahim, F., & Gürbey, G. (Eds.) (2000). *The Kurdish conflict in Turkey*. New York: St. Martin's.

Izady, M. R. (1992). *The Kurds: A concise handbook*. Washington: CR.

Izoli, D. (1992). *Ferheng: Kurdi-Tırki Tırki-Kurdi* (Dictionary, Kurdish–Turkish, Turkish–Kurdish). Istanbul, Turkey: Deng.

Jwaideh, W. (2006). *The Kurdish national movement: Its origin and development*. Syracuse, NY: Syracuse University Press.

Johnson, A. G. (2000). *The Blackwell dictionary of sociology.* Oxford, UK: Blackwell.

Kendal, N. (1993a). Kurdistan in Turkey. In G. Chaliand (Ed.), *A people without a country: The Kurds and Kurdistan* (pp. 38–94). New York: Olive Branch.

Kendal, N. (1993b) The Kurds under the Ottoman Empire. In G. Chaliand (Ed.), *A people without a country: The Kurds and Kurdistan* (pp. 11–37). New York: Olive Branch.

Kendal, N. (1996). The Kurds: Current position and historical background. In P. Kreyenbrock & C. Allison (Eds.), *Kurdish culture and identity* (pp. 7–19). London: Zed.

King, D. (2000). *When worlds collide: The Kurdish diaspora from the inside out.* Unpublished doctoral dissertation, Washington State University.

Kirişci, K., & Winrow, G. M. (1997). *The Kurdish question and Turkey.* London: Frank Cass.

Klem, H. V. (1982). *Oral communication of the scripture: Insights from African oral art.* Pasadena, CA: William Carey Library.

Kvale, S. (1996). *InterViews.* Thousand Oaks, CA: Sage.

Kreyenbroek, P., & Sperl, S. (Eds.). (1992). *The Kurds: A contemporary overview.* London: Routledge.

Laizer, S. (1991). *Into Kurdistan.* London: Zed.

Laizer, S. (1996). *Martyrs, traitors, and patriots.* London: Zed.

Lawrence, Q. (2008). *Invisible nation: How the Kurds' quest for statehood is shaping Iraq and the Middle East.* New York: Walker & Company.

LeCompte, M., & Schensul, J. J. (1999). *Designing and conducting ethnographic research.* Walnut Creek, CA: AltaMira.

Lewis, B. (1998). *Multiple identities of the Middle East.* New York: Schocken.

Lewis, B. (2003). *The crisis of Islam.* New York: Random House.

Mallon, E. D. (2015, March 16). Who speaks for Islam? *America.* http://americamagazine.org/issue/who-speaks-islam (Accessed November 6, 2015).

Mango, A. (2004). *The Turks today.* London: John Murray.

Maybury-Lewis, D. (2002). *Indigenous peoples, ethnic groups, and the state.* 2nd ed. New York: Pearson.

McCants, W. (2015). *The ISIS apocalypse: The history, strategy, and vision of the Islamic State.* New York: St. Martin's.

McDowell, D. (2000). *A modern history of the Kurds.* London: I. B. Tauris.

McIsaac, E. (2000). Oral narratives as a site of resistance: Indigenous knowledge, colonialism, and Western discourse. In J. S. Dei, B. L. Hall, & D. G. Rosenberg (Eds.), *Indigenous knowledges in global context.* Toronto: University of Toronto.

McKiernan, K. (2006) *The Kurds: A people in search of their homeland.* New York: St. Martin's Press.

McKinney, C. (2000). *Globe-trotting in sandals: A field guide to cultural research.* Dallas: SIL International.

Merry, S. E. (1997). Urbanism. In T. Barfield (Ed.), *The dictionary of anthropology* (pp. 480–481). Oxford, UK: Blackwell.

Micallef, J. V. (2015, August 16). Turkey and the Kurdish corridor: Why the Islamic State survives. *TheWorldPost.* http://www.huffingtonpost.com/joseph-v-micallef/

turkey-and-the-kurdish-co_b_7994540.html?utm_hp_ref=world (Accessed October 15, 2015).

Musk, B. A. (1995). *Touching the soul of Islam*. Crowborough, UK: Marc.

Nezan, K. (1996). *The Kurds: Current position and historical background*. In P. Kreyenbroek & C. Allison (Eds.), *Kurdish culture and identity*. London: Zed Books Ltd. in association with The Centre of Near and Middle Eastern Studies, School of Oriental and African Studies, University of London.

Öke, M. K. (2005). *Dervish and commander*. New York: Nova Science.

O'Leary, B., McGarry, J., & Salih, K. (2005) (Eds.). *The future of Iraqi Kurdistan*. Philadelphia: University of Pennsylvania.

Olson, R. (1995). Turkey–Syria relations since the Gulf War: Kurds and water. *Journal of South Asian and Middle Eastern Studies, 19*, 168–191.

Olson, R. (Ed.). (1996). *The Kurdish nationalist movement in the 1990s*. Lexington: University of Kentucky.

Ong, W. (with Hartley, J.). (2012). *Orality and literacy: The technologizing of the word*. 3rd ed. New York: Routledge.

Peacock, J. L. (2001). *The anthropological lens*. 2nd ed. Cambridge, UK: Cambridge.

Pew Research Center. (2009, October). Mapping the global Muslim population. http://www.pewforum.org/2009/10/07/mapping-the-global-muslim-population/ (Accessed October 16, 2015).

Pipher, M. (2002). *The middle of everywhere*. New York: Harcourt.

Pope, N., & Pope, H. (2000). *Turkey unveiled*. Woodstock, NY: Overland Press.

Rasuly-Paleczek, G. (Ed.). (1996). *Turkish families in transition*. Frankfurt, Germany: Peter Lange.

Reagan, T. (2005). *Non-Western educational traditions*. 3rd ed. Mahwah, NJ: Lawrence Erlbaum.

Redhouse Elsozlugu (Redhouse Dictionary). (2000). *Turkish–English, English–Turkish*. Istanbul, Turkey: Sev Matbaacilik.

Rosaldo, R. (1989). *Culture and truth*. Boston, MN: Beacon Press.

Rubin, T. (2015, September 4). Trudy Rubin: A shocking silence on the Islamic State sex slavery. *St. Paul Pioneer Press*. http://www.twincities.com/opinion/columnists/ci_28759003/trudy-rubin:-a-shocking-silence-on-the-islamic-state-sex-slavery.

Ruhn, M. (1997). Enculturation. In T. Barfield (Ed.), *The dictionary of anthropology* (pp. 149–150). Oxford, UK: Blackwell.

Russell, G. (2014). *Heirs to Forgotten kingdoms: Journeys into the disappearing religions of the Middle East*. New York: Basic Books.

Sabar, Ariel. (2008). *My father's paradise: A son's search for his Jewish past in Kurdish Iraq*. Chapel Hill, NC: Algonquin Books.

Sachs, J. D. (2005). *The end of poverty*. New York: Penguin Books.

Safran, W. (1991). Diasporas in modern societies: Myths of homeland and return. *Diaspora, 2*, 83–99.

Sanjek, R. (1990). *Fieldnotes: The making of anthropology*. Ithaca, NY: Cornell.

Scott, J., & Marshall, G. (2005). *Oxford dictionary of sociology*. Oxford, UK: Oxford Press.

Sekulow, J. (2014). *Rise of ISIS: A threat we cannot ignore*. New York: Howard Books.

Semali, L. M. (1999). Community as classroom: (Re)valuing indigenous literacy. In L. M. Semali & J. L. Kincheloe (Eds.), *What is indigenous knowledge?* New York: Falmer Press.

Shuval, J. T. (2000). Diaspora migration: Definitional ambiguities and a theoretical paradigm. *International Migration*, 38, 41–55.

Sicker, M. (2000). *The pre-Islamic Middle East*. Westport, CT: Praeger.

Soguk, N. (2011). *Globalization & Islamism: Beyond fundamentalism*. Lanham, MD: Roman & Littlefield.

Somer, M. (2004). Turkey's Kurdish conflict: Changing context, and domestic and regional implications. *The Middle East Journal*, 58, 235–254.

Spradley, J. P. (1979). *The ethnographic interview*. Fort Worth, TX: Harcourt College. (Reissued by Waveland Press, Inc., 2016.)

Spradley, J. P. (1980). *Participant observation*. Fort Worth, TX: Harcourt College. (Reissued by Waveland Press, Inc., 2016.)

Stakelbeck, E. (2015). *ISIS exposed: Beheadings, slavery, and the hellish reality of radical Islam*. Washington, DC: Regnery.

Sterling, P., & Incirlioğlu, E. O. (1996). Villagers, migrants, kinship and time. In G. Rasuly-Paleczek (Ed.), *Turkish families in transition*. Frankfurt, Germany: Peter Lang.

Stern, J., & Berger, J. M. (2015). *ISIS: The state of terror*. New York: HarperCollins.

Svanberg, I. (1989). *Kazak refugees in Turkey*. Uppsala, Sweden: Almqvist & Wiksell International.

Sweetnam, D. L. (2004). *Kurdish culture*. 2nd ed. Bonn, Germany: Verlag fur Kultur und Wissenschaft.

Taspinar, O. (2005). *Kurdish nationalism and political Islam in Turkey*. New York: Routledge.

Thornhill, T. (1997). *Sweet tea with cardamom*. London: HarperCollins.

Tololyan, K. (1996). Rethinking diaspora(s): Stateless power in the transnational movement. *Diaspora*, 5, 3–35.

Tönnies, F. (2002). *Community and society*. Trans. & Ed. C. P. Loomis. Mineola, NY: Dover.

Tucker, M. (2004). *Hell is over*. Guilford, CT: Lyons Press.

UNHCR. (2000). *The state of the world's refugees 2000*. Oxford: Oxford University.

UNHCR. (2011). *Refugee protection and mixed migration. The 10-point plan in action*. Geneva: UN High Commissioner for Refugees. http://www.unhcr.org/50a4c2b09.pdf.

Uzun, M. (2003). *Bir dil yaratmak* (To create a language). Istanbul, Turkey: Gendas Kultur.

Van Bruinessen, M. V. (1992). *Agah, shaikh, and state: The social and political structures of Kurdistan*. London: Zed.

Van Bruinessen, M. V. (1998). Shifting national and ethnic identities: The Kurds in Turkey and the European diaspora. *Journal of Muslim Minority Affairs*, 18, 39–52.

van der Elst, D. (2003). *Culture as given, culture as choice.* Long Grove, IL: Waveland Press.

Vanly, I. S. (1993). Kurdistan in Iraq. In G. Chaliand (Ed.), *A people without a country: The Kurds and Kurdistan* (pp. 139–193). New York: Olive Branch.

Van Maanen, J. (2011). *Tales of the field.* 2nd ed. Chicago: University of Chicago.

Vansina, J. (1985). *Oral tradition as history.* Madison: University of Wisconsin.

Van Wolde, E. (1997). *Stories of the beginning.* Ridgefield, CT: Morehouse.

Wahlbeck, O. (1999). *Kurdish diasporas.* London: MacMillan.

Weiss, M. W., & Hassan, H. (2015). *ISIS: Inside the army of terror.* New York: Regan Arts.

White, P. J. (1998). Economic marginalization of Turkey's Kurds: The failed promise of modernization and reform. *Journal of Muslim Minority Affairs,* 18, 139–153.

White, P. (2000). *Primitive rebels or revolutionary modernizers? The Kurdish national movement in Turkey.* London: Zed.

Wolcott, H. F. (1999). *Ethnography: A way of seeing.* Walnut Creek, CA: AltaMira.

Wood, G., (2015, March). What ISIS really wants. *The Atlantic.* http://picpimp.net/BestPosts/ISIS.pdf (Accessed October 26, 2015).

Yalcin-Hecmann, L. (1991). *Tribe and kinship among the Kurds.* Frankfurt, Germany: Peter Lang.

Yavuz, M. H. (1998). A preamble to the Kurdish question: The politics of Kurdish identity. *Journal of Muslim Minority Affairs,* 18(1), 9–18.

Yegen, M. (1996). The Turkish state discourse and the exclusion of Kurdish identity. *Middle Eastern Studies,* 17, 216–226.

Yildiz, K. (2007). *The Kurds in Iraq: The past, present and future.* Revised Edition. London: Pluto.

Worldwide Population of the Kurdish People

Estimating the number of Kurds in the world is a complicated task. The governments of Turkey, Iran, Iraq, and Syria tend to underestimate their Kurdish populations. Sometimes only the Kurds who list their mother tongue as Kurdish, or who do not claim to know the official languages of their respected nation-states, are counted as Kurds. In all four countries, however, hundreds of thousands of Kurds have been assimilated into the majority populations and may not speak Kurdish as the mother language, but they still have some sense of Kurdish identity. Kurdish nationalists include this group of people in their population counts. Some Kurds claim that Turkey is over one-half Kurdish, whereas Turkish government figures show the Kurdish population to be a much smaller fraction. The truth is somewhere between the extremes.

Izady (1992) listed the total number of Kurds as being 26.3 million in 1990 and estimated a population of 36.2 million by 2000. He projected 18.7 million Kurds in Turkey (28.4% of the country's population); 9.0 million in Iran (12.6%); 6.4 million in Iraq, (24%); and 1.6 million (9.2%) of Syria's population would be Kurdish. He estimated 0.5 million Kurds in the CIS (Commonwealth of Independent States). His estimates are on the high side, however.

The Kurds of the diaspora are estimated by Blincoe (1998) to be one million in Europe, 125,000 in Israel, 75,000 in Lebanon, 20,000 in the United States, and 10,000 in Australia.

For this book I have used the figure of 35 million Kurds. It is a little lower than Izady's estimate, but it is higher than many other estimates, reflecting the reality that many Kurds are not counted in official government demographic statistics.

Appendix B

Glossary of Foreign Words

T = Turkish
K = Kurdish
A = Arabic

The origin of many words used throughout the Middle East can be difficult to state with certainty. Many of the words that appear in this text have Arabic or Farsi origins but have been diffused into Kurdish and Turkish. I classified the words as accurately as I could without being overly concerned with origins. For this research, the important point is how the words are used. It needs to be emphasized that there is seldom a standard spelling of Kurdish words. If the Turks and Kurds use the same word, I have listed it under the standard Turkish spelling in most cases.

Below is a short pronunciation guide to better enable the reader to pronounce words written with Turkish letters that are different from English letters. In the Turkish alphabet, there are a few extra letters that I have described below. The other letters are close to how they are pronounced in English.

C as in *J*anuary
Ç as in *ch*urch
Ğ (ğ) is silent, but lengthens the proceeding letter as in *neighbor*
I (ı) as in do*zen* or *girl*
Ö as in *ur*ge
Ü as in an over-articulated *cool*
Ş as in *sh*ame

Abbiya	(A) the long black tent-like covering that many Kurdish women wear
Ağah or Agah	(A, T, K) the leader of a tribe or village (In Turkey, the second letter is pronounced as a silent g, whereas among the Kurds in Iraq, the g is pronounced.)

Akraba evliliği	(T) marriage between relatives, generally referred to as first-cousin marriage
Anfal	(A) an Arabic word taken from the Qur'an meaning to plunder
Asabiyya	(A) social cohesion
Askerlik	(T) required military service
Avruplaşmış	(T) to Europeanize
Baraka	(A) blessing, positive spiritual energy
Be namus	(K) dishonorable
Burka	(T, K) a garment that fully covers the body and the face
Canı Yakın	(T) literally means close to soul, or likeable and outgoing
Çevre	(T) a person's surroundings or circle of influence
Dawet	(K) Kurdish circle dancing
Dişdaşa	(A, K) normal daily attire of Kurdish women
Diwan	(A, K) (T-divan) a room set aside for villagers to meet in
Doğu, doğulu, doğulular	(T) east, one from the east, those from the east, respectively
Esmer	(T) dark brown, used to characterize people with a more Arab-like coloring
Eşiret	(K, A) tribe, clan, or subclan
Gecekondu	(T) houses that are constructed overnight, mostly by recent arrivals to the city
Giriv, giriviyati	(K) the person and the institution, respectively, in which Kurds swear undying, unconditional friendship upon the circumcision of a child on the *giriv*'s lap
Günah	(K, T) sin, transgression
Gund	(K) village
Hajj	(A) pilgrimage to Mecca, one of the five pillars of Islam
Halk	(T) people
Hijab	(A, T, K) a woman's scarf like head covering
Hoca	(T, K) a practitioner of folk Islam and thought to have spiritual power
Injil	(A, T, K) the New Testament

Inkarcı	(T) one who denies his or her own ethnic identity
Intifada	(A) uprising; (T) *ayaklanma*; (K) *seri rakirin* or *serhaldan*
Jahil	(A, T, K) ignorant
Jash	(K) a Kurd who supported the Iraqi regime
Jileki Kurdi	(K) traditional Kurdish costume
Jinn	(A, T, K) spirit beings who may be good or evil; important in folk Islam
Kafir	(A, T, K) infidel
Kahin	(T, K) traitor
Kahve	(K, T) a place where men gather to drink tea and coffee, socialize, or play games
Kalache	(K) a Kurdish sweet
Karama(t)	(A) dignity
Kısmet	(T, K) fate, fatalism
Köy	(T) village
Köy heyeti	(T) village committee
Kumral	(T) a lighter shade of skin coloring than *esmer*, but darker than *sarışın*
Küzey Kurdistan	(T) northern Kurdistan or Turkish Kurdistan. The other three regions are, respectively, southern Kurdistan (Iraqi Kurdistan); western Kurdistan (Syrian Kurdistan), and eastern Kurdistan (Iranian Kurdistan). Kurdish nationalists use these phrases to show that the four nation-states are occupying Kurdish territory
Mal	(K) home, but usually designates the family or kin relatives as well
Maktūb	(A) an Arabic word meaning "written" and carries the idea of fate or predestination
Maşallah	(A, T, K) "May God protect"
Medeniyetli	(T) civilized
Medrese	(A, T, K) a school, increasingly being used to signify schools where fundamentalist Islam is taught
Memleket	(T) a person's home province
Meydan	(T) public square
Millet	(T) nation or people. In the Ottoman days, millet signified the religious community that one was born into—Muslim, Christian, or Jew

Milliyetçi	(T) nationalist
Milliyetçiliği	(T) nationalism
Muhtar	(A, T, K) government-appointed head of village
Mujama'at	(A, K) collective villages where the Kurds were placed after their villages were destroyed
Namus	(A, T, K) honor, virtue; (K) *be namus*—without honor
Nan	(K) bread
Nargile	(A, T, K) Turkish water pipe
Nazar boncuğu	(T) a blue bead that functions like an amulet to ward off evil
Nu	(K) new
Nuroj	(K) means new day, the beginning of spring, most important Kurdish holiday
Pir	(T) wise, elderly person
Pis	(T) dirty, obscene
Partiye Karker e Kurdistan	(K) Kurdish workers party (PKK)
Qadir	(A) fate, destiny, chance
Qenci u xirabi	(K) good and evil
Ravandin	(K) bride-napping
Re spi (ryspi)	(K) literally white beards, the elders of a village
Sakat	(T) physically challenged
Sanjaq	(T, K) administrative unit in the Ottoman Empire
Sarışın	(T) light coloring, blond
Satılmıs	(T) one who has sold out
Şehit	(A, T, K) martyr
Shari'a	(A) Qur'anic law
Sheikh	(A, T, K) the head of a Sufi, mystical order
Sherim	(K) shame, shameful
Serok	(K) an important leader
Sözü geçen adam	(T) a man whose word can be trusted
Stranbezh	(K) traveling Kurdish musician
Tahini	(K) a paste made from sesame seeds
Tarikat	(K, T) religious order, an order of dervishes
Türk halkı	(T) Turkish people
Üç ükağıtçı	(T) trickster, con artist
Ummah	(A) the community of Muslims
Vahşi	(T) wild, untamed
Vilayets	(T) provinces

Xude	(K) God
Xwin dari	(K) blood feud; (T) *kan davas*
Yalan	(T) a lie; (K) *direw*
Zakat	(A) almsgiving, one of the pillars of Islam
Zenci	(T) a dark-skinned person, a person of African ancestry
Zina	(A, T, K) adultery
Zirek	(K) hard working, industrious, intelligent